THE EUCHARISTIC COMMUNION AND THE WORLD

THE EUCHARISTIC COMMUNION AND THE WORLD

JOHN D. ZIZIOULAS

Edited by

LUKE BEN TALLON

t&t clark

Published by T&T Clark International
A Continuum Imprint
The Tower Building, 11 York Road, London SE1 7NX
80 Maiden Lane, Suite 704, New York, NY 10038

www.continuumbooks.com

British Library Cataloguing–in–Publication Data
A catalogue record for this book is available from the British Library

ISBN: 978-0-567-01520-4 (hardback)
978-0-567-32660-7 (paperback)

Typeset by Fakenham Prepress Solutions, Fakenham, Norfolk NR21 8NN
Printed and bound in Great Britain

CONTENTS

INTRODUCTION

John Zizioulas presents a beautiful theological vision. That is what initially attracted me to his theology and what has kept me coming back again and again. At one level this collection serves simply to allow more readers to encounter more of this theological vision. Zizioulas's theology has certainly attracted the attention of many theologians over the past generation and the breadth and depth of his theological influence is even more remarkable when one considers that it is due principally to *one* collection of essays, published in English in 1985: *Being as Communion*. Not surprisingly, this dense and difficult work has been interpreted in a variety of ways by both admirers and detractors from across the ecumenical spectrum, with Zizioulas emerging variously as a true teacher of the orthodox Church, an existentialist in theologian's garb, or a despiser of the material world. Given the small sample of work upon which many of these judgements depend and their often mutually contradictory character, the recent publications of Zizioulas's *Communion & Otherness* (2006) and *Lectures in Christian Dogmatics* (2008) were welcome events (with special thanks due to the editorial work of Paul McPartlan and Douglas Knight, respectively). The latter work, in particular, shows the overall shape and content of Zizioulas's theology with lucidity and brevity.

The present collection of essays aims to reveal a further dimension of depth in Zizioulas's theological vision by bringing together writings that deal specifically with the Eucharist and its relation to the world. Interpreters of Zizioulas often note that the Eucharist is the heart, basis and goal of his theology, but less often do they provide a description of the concrete Eucharist that Zizioulas assumes as the context for his more well-known teaching regarding personhood, communion and otherness. The following essays provide this context as Zizioulas approaches the Eucharist from several different angles. In accomplishing this positive task, I hope that this collection will also accomplish the negative task of demonstrating the problems involved in a few of the common interpretations of Zizioulas — interpretations shown to be rather implausible in light of the understanding of the Eucharist and its relation to the world evident in the following essays. For instance, the many discussions in these essays of a) the place of creation in the concrete celebrations of the Eucharist and b) the Church's affirmation of the material world in the Eucharist militate against reading Zizioulas as denigrating creation. Likewise, the discussions of the Eucharist as an *active* communion that forms an *ethos* in its participants that has radical implications for daily life make problematic (to say the least) interpretations of Zizioulas as unconcerned with human action.

Most important, however, is the opportunity to see how Zizioulas goes about the work of theology and the form and content of his 'eucharistic' (and therefore 'worldly') theology. Several aspects of this work merit special comment.

Zizioulas's engagement with scripture. Although scripture certainly is woven into Zizioulas's other work, these essays (particularly the first chapter) manifest a deeper engagement and more patient exposition. Unsurprisingly, Zizioulas reads scripture canonically, allowing the canon to form the context for interpretation. Historical critics would no doubt be disappointed, but Zizioulas's eucharistic-liturgical herme-neutic and attention to the Christological-ecclesial *scope* of the canon opens up some fruitful juxtapositions of the Johannine and Pauline texts. Particularly interesting, if rather undeveloped, are the implications that Zizioulas's navigation of the difference-in-continuity between the historical events and the Church's *remembrance* might have for biblical interpretation beyond the accounts of the Last Supper. Even more interesting (and unremarked) are the implications of Zizioulas's account of *eschatological causality* for the study of scripture (and church history), given that such study generally assumes *protological causality*.

The relationship between ecclesiology and Christology. Nearly every argument in this collection depends in some way upon Zizioulas's understanding of Christ as the *totus Christus* — Christ as the 'one' who unites the 'many', Christ the head *with* his ecclesial body. The argumentation is not laid out as it is in *Being as Communion* and *Communion & Otherness*, but here we see more of the practical implications of this recurring motif. The *totus Christus* provides the theological muscle for Zizioulas's claim that the local Church of a particular place gathered together to celebrate the Eucharist *is* the catholic Church, for the presence of Christ in a eucharistic gathering means the presence of the *whole* Christ. This is to say that Zizioulas's *catholic* Christology is a *pneumatological* Christology. Just as Jesus Christ only *is* by the Holy Spirit and is inconceivable apart from the Spirit, so too Jesus Christ, the 'one', cannot be separated from the 'many' he incorporates in the Spirit. As the *totus Christus*, Jesus Christ is *the sacrament*. This *person* is the *mystery* of God's reconciliation of the world to himself, the *way* the 'many' become 'one' while remaining themselves. The other 'sacraments' are not objective signs or channels of God's grace, each distinct from the other, but ways in which the Holy Spirit realizes the eschatological and catholic Christ in history and therefore *every* 'sacrament' depends upon the outpouring of the Holy Spirit.

Eschatological memory and eschatological being. An *eschatological* account of the eucharistic 'remembrance' stands at the heart of Zizioulas' doctrine of the Eucharist. First, Zizioulas argues that it is crucial to recognize that this remembrance is *personal*. Jesus did not ask his followers to remember merely 'my words' or 'my actions' but to remember 'me'. Second, the resurrection means that the Church's remembrance of Christ will be different from other remembering. Other remembrance is oriented to the past, who someone *was*. In the Eucharist, however, the Church remembers the risen one who *is to come*. As this coming one, Jesus Christ, is the recapitulation of creation, his significance for the rest of creation is *ontological*. Creation does not exist in and of itself; it came from nothing and would return from nothing apart from the grace of God. Yet, in Jesus Christ we see the future of creation, for in him God's will to share his life with creation is revealed and *realized*. As creation ultimately will receive her being from Jesus Christ, who comes to us from the *eschaton* (as *ho eschatos*), our very being is eschatological. This leads Zizioulas to develop an *eschatological* account of created *being*. Things *are* not by virtue of what they were but by virtue of what they will be in the age to come. The *future*, not the *past*, causes things to be. This emphasis on the *personal* and *ontological* are much needed, given the temptation of merely *psychological* remembrance.

Liturgy as icon: symbol of the eschaton. Zizioulas argues that the eucharistic liturgy is an *icon* of the Kingdom, which is to claim that it bears the image of the eschatological Kingdom of God through participation in it. The persons, things and act of the Eucharist are symbolic, bridges between the uncreated and created. Unlike other religious symbols, however, the eucharistic symbols *participate* in the unique union of created and uncreated in the *person* of Jesus Christ — an historical event that occurred in freedom and did not depend upon any correspondence between the divine and human natures. In other words, liturgical symbols are *icons* that 1) depend only upon the free decision of God (freedom as love) and not any correspondence between created and uncreated; 2) are drawn from events in *history* and cannot be based on *natural* properties; and 3) have their source in the eschatological event of the Kingdom of God. Thus, the water of baptism is not a symbol of the cleansing power of water, but of Israel's exodus from Egypt through the sea, even as the exodus is a type of baptism and not *vice versa*. In this way liturgical symbols are iconic: dependent upon the historical event of the hypostatic union even as they remain distinct from it; Christ is present *personally* (not *naturally*) through them. This would seem to have implications for our understanding of the presence of Christ in the bread and wine of the Eucharist, but Zizioulas leaves them undeveloped. As persons, too, may serve as liturgical symbols, Zizioulas also views the eucharistic *orders* as iconic symbols that image the structure of the eschatological Kingdom (indeed, the discussion of *persons* in chapter three provides the context for Zizioulas' more well-known discussions of personhood as an *ontological* category). Ultimately, the Eucharist as a whole is an image of the eschatological Kingdom of God and can only be understood as such.

The Eucharist as prayer for the Holy Spirit. As the Church receives its being *eschatologically*, its true character is revealed in the eucharistic *epiclesis*, the prayer over the bread and wine for the sending of the Holy Spirit. Just as the *person* of Christ cannot be divorced from his *work* in space and time, the taste of the *eschaton* given in the Eucharist cannot be isolated from either the fruits of *creation* (the bread and the wine) or the *history* the people of God. Yet, the Eucharist is a foretaste of the life of God only through the work of the Spirit, not because the created elements or the history of the Church objectively guarantee the inbreaking of the *eschaton*. As the community does not possess the means to make Christ present in the Eucharist, it can only pray for the Spirit to bring this transformation about and look for it in hope (that is, *epicletically*). For this reason, the foretaste of the *eschaton* given in the Eucharist does not lessen the Church's hunger for the *parousia* of Christ, but actually *intensifies* it. Far from leading to triumphalism, the Eucharist *intensifies* the Church's struggle with the evil and death present in the world. This renders impossible any armistice between the Church and death, any ontological linkage of being and death (as in some strands of existentialism). The presence of the eschatological Kingdom in the midst of the eucharistic gathering, however, reveals that the Church cannot oppose death by fleeing space and time, materiality and history; for in the Eucharist, the life of the world to come meets the Church in space and time, indicating that it must be transformed, not abandoned.

The Holy Spirit. As indicated in the previous comments, the Holy Spirit appears (or is assumed) at nearly every critical juncture in this book. Christ accomplished the reconciliation of God and the world in the Holy Spirit, and now lives in the Holy Spirit. The Holy Spirit makes Christ the *catholic* Christ, in whom the 'many' become 'one' without losing their particularity. The *eschaton* enters history by the power of the Holy Spirit. The Holy Spirit 'reminds' us of Christ and thereby transforms our eucharistic 'remembrance' into *eschatological* remembrance. At its heart, the Eucharist is the *koinonia* of the Holy Spirit — a mystery of love, as Paul explains in 1 Corinthians 13. This last observation leads Zizioulas to a eucharistic understanding of spiritual gifts: while they are by no means limited to the eucharistic *synaxis*, they do find their *telos* there. The Church, then, cannot operate with an *ordination-charism* binary. On one hand this means that ordination is a *gift* of the Spirit and cannot be understood as a sacrament in itself (an objective possession, with the accompanying dilemma as to whether it is ontological or merely functional). Rather, it must be understood as an epicletic prayer that cannot be isolated from the personal relations of the local community and the presence and activity of the living Christ therein. On the other hand this means that there are no *private* gifts, no work of the Spirit that does not have as its ultimate end the Church's eucharistic participation in Jesus Christ, the *eschatological* and *catholic* Adam.

Christ, Spirit, Eschaton and Order. The preceding comments indicate the importance of the *structure* or *order* of the Eucharist in Zizioulas's theology and his *theological* justification for it. This reflects Zizioulas's belief that ecclesiality is not merely a matter of piety, ethics or historical institution, but of *rightly ordered relationships*, or *ordinations*. The reality of the Eucharist and the Church that gathers to celebrate it depends upon the assembly of all four orders: the local 'people', or *laos*, in all its diversity, as well as the presence of the deacons, presbyters and bishop. The bishop stands in the place of God and images Christ, gathering the many gifts of the Church, offering them to God as one and receiving them back as one before distributing them to the many. The college of presbyters gathered around the bishop to discern the body of Christ image the twelve thrones around the throne of God and the eschatological judgement of all creation. The deacons' gathering of the gifts of creation and distribution of the gifts of God images the eschatological ministry of humanity as the priests of creation. In these orders we see how *differences* are preserved even as any divisions between the 'one' and the 'many' are abolished.

The concern for the practical and concrete. These essays are provocatively concrete and practical, demonstrating that Zizioulas's teaching on persons, communion and otherness has radical implications for the life of the Church and its relationship to the world. It may be that some readers will prefer the abstract thinker they imagined Zizioulas to be over Zizioulas as we encounter him here. For instance, the centrality Zizioulas assigns to the structure of the Eucharist is one of the more difficult aspects of his thought. At this point a great deal of freight rides upon his contested reconstruction of the biblical and early Christian testimonies to the structure of the Eucharist. Moreover, Zizioulas does not specify just how far the structure of a Eucharist can deviate from his formal standard before it is compromised. Zizioulas allows, however, for an imperfect coincidence of theory and practice and thus for the possibility that a Church that does not accept the theory of episcopal office or ordination in historical apostolic succession may in fact outstrip an episcopal Church claiming apostolic succession in its practice. Full communion, Zizioulas judges, will require all Churches to reform their eucharistic practice in some way. Further questions are raised by Zizioulas's emphasis on the necessity of the *whole laos* for the celebration of the Eucharist. If private masses or Eucharists restricted on the basis of age, gender, profession, race, etc. are improper, what of those churches in socio-economically and racially segregated areas of the world (for instance parts of my own United States)? Even if the whole local *laos* were gathered, the Eucharist could still be quite 'restrictive'. All in all, Zizioulas's concern is for the connection between *form* and *content*, *symbol* and *truth*, even if he does not address many of the questions it raises.

The Eucharist and love for the world. Zizioulas discusses love at several points in the following essays with an eye to its eschatological and pneumatological dimensions. Just as the unity of the 'many' in the 'one' in the Eucharist is an eschatological event, so too is the love that Christians are called to show each other and their enemies. This love is not simply a matter of *ethics* — of a different *action*. Rather, it is a matter of *eschatology*, knowing others not as they have been (past sins, etc.), but as they may be in the *eschaton* (a member and neighbour in the Kingdom). In loving each other and their enemies, Christians refuse to live according to the present evil age and live according to the age to come — something possible only by the Holy Spirit. These discussions of love reveal that Zizioulas's hesitancy to speak of the Christian life as an *ethic* by no means stems from a desire to deny the *active* character of the Christian life. Rather, Zizioulas strives against the moralism that so pervades Christianity — the tendency to turn this dynamic life in communion into a list of 'do's and 'do not's. The Eucharist entails new actions, but they are meaningless apart from the new *mode of being* we receive in it: an *ethos*, or way of life, that heals our distorted relations, moving us towards our life in the Kingdom of God.

The Eucharist and judgement of the world. As a foretaste of the *eschaton*, the Eucharist also involves a foretaste of the eschatological judgement of the world. The eucharistic gifts and the members of the eucharistic community are *holy*, and this involves an element of opposition to the world, even if it is ultimately in service to the world. At one level this opposition means that the Church and her members are on trial during the Eucharist: members must be reconciled one to another and if a member persists in offending the body, he or she must be shut out in the pastoral hope that this will result in renewed *metanoia*, and thereby renewed *koinonia*. It is instructive that Zizioulas understands the problem of intercommunion as a post-baptismal, pre-Eucharist rupture and recommends that the churches treat them as such. At another level, this Church-world opposition means that the world stands trial during the Eucharist. This is seen most clearly in the character of the Eucharist as a communion of the baptized: those who have accepted the judgement rendered when they were confronted with the Word of God and turned towards God (*metanoia*) in the death, burial and resurrection of baptism. Although the Church is set apart from the world and judges the world in a certain sense, it is ultimately *for* the world. Its relationship to the world flows from the fact that Christ recapitulated *all creation* and not only the Church. In partaking in Christ through the Eucharist, the Church receives a foretaste of not only forgiveness of sins, but also of the *new creation* in Christ. Therefore the Church lifts up creation in the *anaphora* in hope of *the whole world's* rebirth in baptism.

The human as the priest of creation. The Eucharist provides an eschatological vision of the world as a cosmic liturgy in which humans act as the priests of creation, lifting up creation to God and receiving it back, blessed with God's own life. Apart from this blessing, finite creation will perish. This is to say that apart from the gift of God, creation will return to the nothingness from which God called it forth. Humanity was created to be the mediator of this life. Humans, however, rejected this priestly vocation and idolatrously attempted to make themselves into God, condemning the cosmos to return to nothingness. The incarnation reveals God's utter unwillingness to abandon creation to this fate. Through the incarnation, Jesus Christ recapitulated creation by fulfilling humanity's priestly vocation. The eucharistic vision reveals that the priestly transformation of the world does not involve its destruction or abandonment, in whole or in part. All aspects of the Church's life are oriented to participating in Christ's priesthood: from the baptismal death that ends the human claim to be gods to the celebration of the Eucharist in which the Church offers the created world to God and then distributes the life of God to creation. This understanding of humanity and our priestly vocation has several implications for ecology: 1) the current crisis concerns our very being and not just human well-being; 2) our approach cannot be simply *negative* (the cessation of destruction) or *moralistic*, for the situation calls for the *creation* of an ecological-liturgical *culture*; 3) this culture will involve the *transformation* of nature, not in order to fuel human idolatry, but so that it might survive into the age to come.

In closing this introduction, I would like to thank Elizabeth Theokritoff, who has translated so much of Zizioulas's work from Greek, and Alan Torrance, my PhD advisor and Zizioulas's erstwhile colleague, who enthusiastically endorsed my decision to give Zizioulas's theology serious study, challenged me to go my own way in interpreting Zizioulas, and in fact encouraged me to undertake this present project.

CHAPTER ONE

BIBLICAL ASPECTS OF THE EUCHARIST

Preliminary Remarks

The testimony of the New Testament concerning the Eucharist is both extremely limited and, by its nature, difficult to interpret. It is limited because the only explicit accounts of the Lord's Supper which have reached us are found in a few verses of the Gospels (Mk. 14: 17-26; Mt. 26:20-30; Lk. 22:14-23) and the first letter of Paul to the Corinthians (11:23-26). We have even less information regarding the form that the celebration of the Eucharist took in the apostolic Church. This lack of information is surprising. Indeed, it is difficult to explain the paucity of sources unless we attribute it to the Church's desire to protect the secret discipline from non-Christian eyes,[1] or to the natural tendency not to define or discuss that which constitutes the core of our life.[2] In both cases, the relative silence of the New Testament reveals the close relationship between the Eucharist and the mystery of the Church, making it rather difficult to interpret this testimony.

In fact, everything the New Testament tells us about the Eucharist is inseparably linked to the Church's experience of this act, so it becomes very difficult to understand the Eucharist strictly in its primitive phase, because the Eucharist was instituted in order to be repeated ('Do this in remembrance of me'), and by the very obeying of this command the Church has become a living reality that we must understand in one way or another. Our understanding of the first act is not identical with the act itself. This difference exists because (and this is important) the original act occurred *before* the death and resurrection of Christ, but it was reported in the New Testament *after* these events had informed the conscience of the Church. Thus, the apostolic Church's interpretation of the act of Christ is so deeply connected to the act itself in the New Testament accounts that any attempt to study these two

---

1   For a discussion of this issue, see J.J. von Allmen, *The Lord's Supper*, 2002, p. 17ff.
2   It should be noted that in the early centuries of the Church there was no definition of the Eucharist, or even of the Church itself.

aspects separately (original act and its ecclesial interpretation) would create immediately problems as intractable as those created by the distinction between the 'historical Jesus' and the 'Christ of faith' in the Gospels.

Therefore we will not allow ourselves to be detained by the problematics raised by some modern schools of New Testament exegesis based on assumptions different or even opposite to the one just mentioned. In the following section, we intend to go back to the first Eucharist — as the apostolic Church presents it to us in the New Testament — and to search for the meaning it had for the Church of that time.

I. The Eucharist: Eschatological Meal in the History of the People of God

1. The Passover Meal and the Last Supper

We are able to make a preliminary remark on the Eucharist as the New Testament presents it to us: this *meal* is situated in the context of *the history of the people of Israel.* Exegetes do not all agree that the Last Supper was indeed a Jewish Passover,[3] but there is no doubt that it took place in the context of the Easter celebration.

The descriptions of this meal in the four major accounts of the New Testament (cited above), although different in several respects, nevertheless offer a basic sketch:

- The meal took place at night (in all accounts of the Last Supper);
- Our Lord took the cup, blessed it (or 'gave thanks') and gave it to his disciples (only in Luke);
- He 'dipped a piece' with the disciple who would betray him (in Mark, Matthew and John);
- He took bread and gave thanks (in all accounts);
- He broke the bread and distributed it to the disciples, explaining the significance of the bread (all accounts);
- At the end of the meal, he took the cup and gave thanks (in all accounts — though only certain manuscripts of Luke);
- He circulated the cup, explaining what it meant (in all accounts — though only certain manuscripts of Luke);
- After singing the final song, he and his disciples went out to the Mount of Olives (Mark, Matthew, Luke).

---

3   For an argument that the Last Supper is not a paschal meal, see D.E. Nineham, *Saint Mark*, 1963, pp. 455–458; for an argument that the Last Supper is a paschal meal, see J. Jeremias, *The Eucharistic Words of Jesus*, 1955.

All these elements are obviously part of the ritual Passover meal, which means that we cannot understand the original structure of the Eucharist if we do not recognize its essential role in salvation history — its role in the history of God's chosen people, Israel. However, this structure also has several elements that make the Last Supper a meal which, by its *eschatological nature*, transcends history. Let us study some of these elements.

First, and negatively, we should note that the New Testament ignores several elements of the Passover meal, even elements integral to the structure of the Passover meal. For example, there is no description of the main meal with the paschal lamb, or references to the four cups that the householder was to be circulating during the course of this meal. We could explain these omissions by saying that the New Testament writers did not intend to give a full account of the Last Supper, but it is precisely this willingness to *make a choice* among the various elements of the meal that is so significant. This choice cannot have been merely random, for one finds the same basic account throughout the New Testament, despite the differences on other points. How, then, could we safely claim that the Church *chose* from the original structure of the meal (at an unknown date and in an unknown way) the elements reported by the New Testament? Or would it be better to claim that the Last Supper, as celebrated by the Lord, took place according to a pattern that did not include *certain* elements of the Passover meal? If we take seriously the fact that the apostolic Church considered that the structure of the Last Supper, as described in the New Testament accounts, was (in the words of Saint Paul) a direct transmission from the Lord to the Church, the second hypothesis is much more appealing. Whatever our decision, this choice remains significant, even in its negative sense, because it indicates the importance of the history of Israel for the formation of the Eucharist, even while indicating at the same time that its formation *relativizes* this history

This all takes a positive meaning if one considers not only the omissions, but the real differences between the Passover meal and the Last Supper described in the New Testament. There are differences both with regard to the participants and with regard to the general interpretation of the Last Supper. We shall first examine the participants.

In the description of the Last Supper, there is, I believe, an important element that is usually neglected: while the Passover meal is a *family* event, the Last Supper is an event that concerns a *group of friends* with Christ presiding. This difference indicates that with the Last Supper we move away from a sort of natural community in order to move to another kind of community — formed by a *group of friends* who love their master and love each other (to use the idea so strong in and so characteristic of the Johannine farewell discourses [cf. Jn. 13-17]). Much more than a moral or sentimental notion (as is commonly thought), this fundamental difference between the participants at the Passover meal and at the Last Supper reveals clearly the *eschatological character* of the Last Supper.

In the New Testament, such transcending of natural family ties as they exist in the present is rooted deeply in the eschatological character of the Church. Indeed, as soon as the eschatological light is turned upon historical existence, marriage and family lose their original meaning: 'For in the resurrection they neither marry nor are given in marriage, but are like angels in heaven' (Mt. 22:30). According to this witness, those who hope that the Lord will acknowledge them at the critical moment before his Father on account of their faithfulness must be prepared to abandon all familial ties (Mt. 10:32-37; 19:29; Lk. 14:36, etc.) or even to have none at all, exactly as Paul preferred not to marry precisely because he saw that 'the appointed time has grown short' (1 Cor. 7:29) and the Kingdom of God is here. All this is not without connection with the Last Supper.

The New Testament presents the Eucharist through images, such as the 'wedding feast' where guests are friends of the groom, that is to say all those who have abandoned everything: their natural existence, their family and their life for him (Mt. 19:27) — just as he has done for them (Jn. 15:13). These festal images, which are found in the parables of the Kingdom (Lk. 14:16-24; Mt. 22:2-14; 25:1-13, etc.), as well as the marriage of the Lamb in Revelation (19:7), can be interpreted in the context of the Eucharist — understood against its eschatological backdrop. Inasmuch as the Last Supper is not an event of familial life but an event for 'the friends of the Lamb', the Supper marks an eschatological 'inbreaking' in the natural course of historical life.

The gathering that celebrated the Supper was a figure of the eschatological reality of the Church, indicated clearly by the fact that this gathering was composed only of the Twelve and of Christ. Even Judas, the traitor, had a part and had to participate in the banquet as well. According to the Fourth Gospel he left *after* eating a piece of dipped bread (Jn. 13:28-9). Perhaps we should see the concern of the author to preserve the purity of the Last Supper. The presence of the Twelve as a group has an important eschatological significance: they are those who 'in the last days' will sit on twelve thrones and will judge the twelve tribes of Israel (Mt. 19:18; Lk. 22:30). In this sense they appear to be the cornerstones of the Church in the description of the last days in Revelation (21:12-21).[4] By making the Twelve the sole participants

4   Referring to Ex. 28:21.

at the Last Supper, Christ made the Eucharist an eschatological reality arising in the history of the people of God.

But what new reality does this eschatological 'inbreaking' bring into history? The new *interpretation of the meal* given in the accounts of the Supper show us even more deeply yet what this new reality is. We know that the food served at the Passover meal was accompanied always by a comment made by the head of the family who celebrated it and was a fundamental part of the ritual of this meal. This element also appears in the New Testament, but the commentary is different and these differences reveal the exact meaning of the eschatological character of the Eucharist.

The following points emerge from the New Testament accounts of Christ's commentary on the meal:

- the bread that he blessed, broke and distributed to the disciples is *his body* (in all the accounts) given for 'you' (Paul and Luke in certain manuscripts); similarly, the cup that he blessed and circulated is *his blood of the covenant* (Mark and Matthew) or 'the new covenant in his blood' (Paul and Luke in certain manuscripts);
- the disciples must do this, that is to say, break the bread and drink the cup after they have been blessed, '*in memory of* him' (Paul and Luke in certain manuscripts).

Here, again, the contrast with the Passover meal is very informative and concerns the *sacrificial character* of the meal. In the Passover meal, which was a sacrifice in itself, the sacrificial character centred upon two points: 1) the slaughter of the paschal lamb, which took place before the meal and 2) the consumption of the slaughtered lamb in the meal of communion. Now it should be noted that these points are both absent from the New Testament accounts of the Last Supper, because Jesus Christ took the place of the paschal lamb. Therefore, from a Christian perspective, it would be impossible to reconstruct the Last Supper upon the basis of the Jewish Passover meal. Elements of the Passover meal as essential as the killing and eating of the lamb are able to be dropped from the Last Supper because Christ himself is the Passover lamb.

In order to understand the words 'this is my body…, this is my blood', we must always remember that Christ has taken the role of the paschal lamb. Body and blood are the very elements of a victim, elements that were separated when they slaughtered the paschal lamb.[5] Given their Jewish culture, to mention these two elements together at the Supper would automatically evoke the image of the paschal lamb among the disciples. Saint Paul is faithful to the meaning of the Eucharist when he

---

5   Cf. Gen. 9:4; Lev. 17:11; Dt. 12:23; Ezek. 39:17ff. Heb. 13:11.

writes that 'our paschal lamb, Christ, has been sacrificed' (1 Cor. 5:7), as is the author of the book of Revelation when he speaks of 'the lamb' in a eucharistic context (5:6, etc.).[6]

By comparing the Last Supper to the Passover we see the new element: Christ takes the place of the lamb. But we must say more because this new element is presented here in a very special way. When Christ spoke the words that identified the paschal lamb, he did so with reference to two elements of the meal: the bread and the cup of wine. In the Passover meal, these elements existed *alongside* the paschal lamb and were not identified with it. The head of the family pronounced the 'blessing' on those elements by recounting the mighty acts of God that had saved the people of Israel in the past (particularly the exodus from Egypt).[7] In this sense these elements were a 'memorial' (remembrance) that actualized the past experience of the Jewish people. But when these elements are identified with the lamb, as is the case in the Last Supper, the 'blessing' itself and the 'memorial' itself no longer relate to God's past action in history, but now relate to an *imminent reality* — i.e. the sacrifice that will take place the next day and also all that will follow after, including the future Kingdom where Christ will eat this meal 'new' with his disciples (Mk. 14:25; Mt. 26:29). Therefore the 'memorial' of the Last Supper has several dimensions: through it, in the present, the past becomes a new reality, but the future becomes a reality that is already. That the reality to come is already present in advance is due to the nature of the Last Supper. To make the eucharistic remembrance simply an actualization of the sacrifice of Christ on the cross is to have an incomplete and altered understanding of remembrance. In fact, this is inconsistent with the Last Supper. It would be better to understand it also to include the future[8] — to make the future, the *eschaton*, a reality here and now. To understand the remembrance in this way makes the Eucharist not only a re-presentation of the sacrifice and resurrection of Christ, but also a *foretaste of the Kingdom to come*.

2. The Last Supper and the Church's Eucharist

This is precisely the most difficult point for a correct interpretation of the Eucharist: how to understand the meeting of the past and the

---

6   Cf. Heb. 9:13-14: 'For if the blood of goats and bulls, with the sprinkling of the ashes of a heifer, sanctifies those who have been defiled so that their flesh is purified, how much more will the blood of Christ, who through the eternal Spirit offered himself without blemish to God...'.

7   Ex. 11; cf. Dt. 16.

8   In the liturgy attributed to Saint John Chrysostom, the remembrance includes 'everything that has been borne for us, the cross, the tomb, the resurrection on the third day, the ascension to heaven, the reign at the right hand of the Father and the second and glorious coming'.

eschaton in the Eucharist? This problem leads us to what is really the heart of the difficulty concerning the witness of the New Testament to the Supper. For this problem raises the question of how the Church, despite living *after* the cross and the resurrection and *before* the second coming, is able to experience this kind of history as a present reality in the Supper. The New Testament offers a possible answer to this question, that for centuries was in fact the background of many controversies concerning the Eucharist,[9] and we find it in the *pneumatology* of the primitive Church.

If we read the New Testament as a whole, we realize that it is precisely through the action of the Holy Spirit that Christ becomes an existential reality that concerns the Church in its historical dimension. Even the Incarnation as an historical reality is presented in the New Testament as the work of the Spirit (Mt. 1:20; Lk. 1:35), just as Christ's ministry begins with the assertion that Jesus is anointed by the Spirit (Lk. 4:6). In the same way, the *eschaton* penetrates historical reality always by the power of the Spirit. Pentecost, the day *par excellence* of the outpouring of the Spirit, is described precisely as '*the last days*' (Acts 2:17), in reference to the eschatological expectation of Joel (2:28–32): 'In the last days, God declares, I will pour out my Spirit upon all flesh'. The Church in general and the Eucharist in particular follows immediately upon the event of Pentecost (Acts 2:46). Pentecost is the natural atmosphere of the Eucharist.

The accounts of the Last Supper in the synoptic Gospels make no mention of the Holy Spirit. They tell of the Supper without trying to bring out the relationship between this event and the Church. Their witness as to the role of the Holy Spirit is only negative. It is clear from these accounts, the disciples present at the Supper could understand neither its meaning, nor its importance, as demonstrated by their subsequent conduct. But in the Fourth Gospel, which takes advantage of the experience of the Church and gives an account of the Supper more properly described as 'eucharistic', the role of the Church is described so that it becomes clear that the understanding of this role depends on our understanding of the eucharistic *anamnesis*.

In the sixth chapter of the Fourth Gospel, in the discourse on the Eucharist, it is established as clearly as possible that it is the Spirit that quickens the flesh and that it is nothing without the Spirit: 'It is the spirit that gives life; the flesh is useless' (6:63). It is interesting to note that this statement comes in response to a 'scandal' caused by the absolute incomprehensibility of what had been said: to partake in the

9   We think here, for example of problems such as 'renewal' in the Eucharist of the once and for all sacrifice of Calvary, etc.

Eucharist is to 'eat the flesh of the Son of Man' (6:53). This case is no different from the eucharistic remembrance (*anamnesis*). In both cases, the underlying question is how it is possible that the Eucharist represents realities that transcend the historical dimension within historical life. That is why Christ's response to the 'scandal' concerning the vivification of the flesh implicitly appealed to his resurrection and ascension — a move that might appear strange at first glance: 'Does this offend you? Then what if you were to see the Son of Man ascending to where he was before?' (6:61-2).

It is even more instructive to look at the long speech of Christ to his disciples the night before his passion. In the Fourth Gospel this discourse takes the place of what might be called the 'commentary on the meal' in the synoptic accounts. This is the Eucharistic experience lived by the Church that sprang from this speech and it is therefore even more important for the question that occupies us at present. If we read this passage carefully with respect to the Holy Spirit, we can make three observations. First, the Holy Spirit is the Comforter (*Paraclete*) after the departure of Christ *precisely for the time that will span until his second coming*, that is to say (recalling Saint Paul's reference to the Eucharist), for the time 'until he comes' (1 Cor. 11:26). Then, during this time, the Holy Spirit will not only teach, but will also '*remind*' the Church of all that Christ said and did (Jn. 14:26). Finally, the Holy Spirit is the one who will 'announce' or 'proclaim' the 'things to come' (Jn. 16:13).

We need not engage here in an exegetical discussion of these passages, but we cannot overlook the importance of the term 'remind' which suggests the same idea as that of remembrance. If the Church is able 'remember' Christ in the sense in which he asked at the Last Supper, it is only thanks to the action of the Holy Spirit which 'reminds' it of Christ in the fullest sense of remembrance (that is, *making Christ present in its life*). And this is not only to 'remember' what Christ has already done. Rather, it is also to proclaim the things to come in a sense comparable to the 'announcement' of the death of Christ in the Eucharist, which is to speak of an anticipation of the *eschata* here and now. This is the meaning of the eucharistic anamnesis that can only be realized through the invocation of the Holy Spirit. The eucharistic remembrance is inconceivable apart from the eucharistic epiclesis.

All this makes the Eucharist a '*spiritual* food' and '*spiritual* drink' (1 Cor. 10:3-4), expressions that may provide a taste of a pre-Pauline Eucharist. Then, too, the hymns that accompany the Eucharist of the Church become the 'spiritual songs' (Eph. 5:19-20) and the Church herself is a 'spiritual house' where one offers 'spiritual sacrifices (1 Pet. 2:5). The Eucharist becomes, then, the *gift of the Father* (Jn. 6:32), as the Holy Spirit, in 'reminding' and 'proclaiming' the work of Christ and the Kingdom present in the Church, ultimately 'takes and proclaims' on behalf of the Father (Jn. 16:14-15). Through its spiritual reality, the Eucharist receives its *trinitarian significance.*[10]

Considering the Eucharist as a remembrance in the context of epiclesis, as described above, leads to a conception of history which eliminates any question of 'renewing' the Supper and the sacrifice of Christ — accomplished 'once for all'. In reality, there is good reason to believe that these questions appeared precisely in a vision of history that did not have enough room for pneumatology. For in fact there are two ways of envisaging history. In one view, history (including the history of salvation and of the Church) *develops* progressively towards the end of time. In this case, the mystery of the Eucharist is viewed from a more or less Christo-monist perspective that tends to see everything that happens in the Eucharist in light of Christ's work — as if it developed from this work. In this vision, it is not surprising that a particular moment of the Supper would be considered as the source from which it developed, for example, the words of institution, to the point of giving rise to suspicions of 'magic' and to questions of the 'renewing' of a past act.

The other view does not understand history to be outside the realm of pneumatological action. This does not mean that the history of salvation and the past work of Christ are not given their true value, but that the value is *always conditioned* by the *coming of the Spirit.* Therefore everything that happens in the Eucharist can never be explained completely by evolution and historical progress, but also, and at the same time, the mystery of Christ's presence in everything that he has done and will do for us *depends totally and absolutely* on the coming of the Holy Spirit. Here the 'words' cannot produce the reality of the Eucharist and the 'Word of God' in general cannot be placed alongside the Spirit,[11] but when it becomes an existential reality for the Church it is 'subject' to the action of the Holy Spirit. In approaching things in this way, we free ourselves from an historicist interpretation of the eucharistic body of Christ, but at the same time, we lose any objective security given by historicism. By becoming a *'spiritual* offering', the Eucharist takes refuge in *prayer* — even more, it is enveloped and totally permeated by prayer. This prayer is not part of the eucharistic canon, but is the very essence of the Eucharist, prayed as if the Church could not rely on an objective reality (neither 'words of institution' nor 'the

10   It is in fidelity to the New Testament that the Church, from the beginning, has addressed its eucharistic prayer to the Father. See, for example, 1 Clem. 59:2-4; or *Did.* 9:2 and 10:2. The eucharistic prayer is a call to the Father to send the Holy Spirit.

11   As for example in M. Thurian, *L'Eucharistie, memorial du seigneur,* 1959, pp. 219, 226, etc.

Word of God'), and as though the one to whom the Church calls so insistently in the Eucharist was not the very one who has already come and 'who was and is and is to come' (Rev. 4:8).

It is precisely this vision of history as always dependent upon the Spirit that is behind the first liturgical acclamation, 'Maranatha', and that still sets the tone for the eucharistic experience of the Apocalypse. The phrase 'Maranatha' (1 Cor. 16:22; Rev. 22:20; cf. *Didache* 10:6), with its two possible meanings, has posed a problem for exegetes, either *maran atha* (the Lord comes) or *marana tha* (Lord, come). But the ambiguity itself is very instructive because it reveals that history and objectivity are based upon epiclesis and that it is not in any way explicable by the other New Testament witnesses. The book of Revelation situates the Eucharist precisely in this same spirit. There, the Church sees clearly 'The Lord God the Almighty and the Lamb' (21:22), those who accompany the Lamb — the Twelve participants from the Last Supper in their eschatological role as representatives of the people of God (21:12-4) — and the new reality of the Kingdom, 'Behold, I make all things new' (21:5). The latter indicates what Christ was thinking when he said that he would eat the 'new' meal in the Kingdom of God (Mt. 26:29). Yet, as if this foretaste of the eschatological Kingdom and the blood of the Lamb were not already there, the prayer addressed to the Lord ('Come... Come... Come' [22:17-20]) sets the tone for the celebration. Moreover, the response ('Surely I am coming soon' [22:20]) comes from the one who has already come and is present — who was and is to come all at the same time: 'the Alpha and the Omega, the first and the last, the beginning and the end' (22:13). This is the meaning of the eucharistic epiclesis by which the historical and eschatological dimensions are joined together, not in an objective reality, but in *prayer*,[12] where we need not fear magic or 'renewal'. In the last analysis, this prayer is nothing other than the prayer of the Holy Spirit himself who 'intercedes with sighs too deep for words', because we ourselves 'do not know how to pray as we ought' (Rom. 8:26).

After all that has been said so far, it seems natural that the Apostolic Church experienced the eucharistic meal 'with glad and generous

---

12   It is in this sense that the sacrifice of Christ is literally permeated by the idea of intercession in the Epistle to the Hebrews. It is the eternal intercession of Christ before his Father that constitutes the eucharistic vision of this text (cf. 4:14-5:10; 6:20; 7:3; etc.) United in this intercession are a) the entry of the eternal high priest into the heavenly 'tabernacle' in the historical sense, a sanctuary where he does not cease his ever-actual intercession and 2) the arrival of 'the one who is coming' (10:37). We can see this unity only in faith, for faith gives assurance of the things hoped for (11:1). And the eucharistic 'tabernacle' of the Church (13:10) — identified with Christ himself — is precisely the point at which the Eucharist appears as intercession, that is to say as prayer, the very intercession of Christ, the high priest *par excellence*.

hearts' (Acts 2:46). The problem that has so preoccupied historians studying the Eucharist[13] (that is, if there were not really two different Eucharistic traditions in the primitive Church — one based on the commemoration of the cross and another based on the resurrection of Christ) involves the assumption that the proclamation of Christ's death (Paul) and the joy of the resurrection (Acts) cannot exist together at the same time in the Eucharist. This assumption rests upon an understanding that does not depend upon the history of the Holy Spirit, and as such is incompatible with the very essence of the *remembrance* we have described above. The 'proclamation of the death' of Christ, spoken of by Saint Paul in connection with the Eucharist, is not at all incompatible with the 'joy' that pervades the description of the eucharistic life of the early Church in Jerusalem (Acts 2:46), just as the persistent vision of the 'sacrificial lamb' does not remove the light, the colour and the songs that surround the experience of the Eucharist in the Book of Revelation. In the Eucharist, proclamation of the death of Christ is placed in the light of the resurrection, the ascension,[14] and his second coming.

After the resurrection, we cannot read the accounts of the Last Supper without thinking about the meal that Christ took with his disciples during the 'appearances'. On the road to Emmaus, the vision of the cross that saddened the disciples (Lk. 24:17) took on its full meaning in the eucharistic act that followed (24:30): 'their eyes were opened' (24:31), exactly as happened to the eleven disciples 'gathered' (24:33-52),[15] and afterwards they regarded the death on the cross and even the whole of Scripture (24:45) in a new light and 'with great joy' (24:52). In the Fourth Gospel, all this happens during the two Sunday reunions of the disciples, (20:19-25 and 26-9), undoubtedly referring to the Eucharist (but there is a very instructive reference to the Holy Spirit as well [20:22]). The proclamation of the Lord's death in 'joy' and 'until he comes' is in tension with a history always dependent upon the Spirit in 'these last days' — seen by the Church since Pentecost as it undertakes the remembrance of the whole of salvation history through its eucharistic epiclesis.

---

13   This appears quite clearly in the well-known theory of H. Lietzmann (*Messe und Herrenmahl*, 1926) regarding the existence of two types of eucharistic celebrations in the early Church: those of Jerusalem based on the resurrection, and those of Paul and the Synoptics, based on the memorial of the death of Christ.

14   On the importance of the ascension for understanding the Eucharist, see B. Bobrinsky, 'Worship and the Ascension of Christ' in *Worship and the Acts of God* (ed. W. Vos), 1963, pp. 73–88.

15   This should include a eucharistic implication. Cf. *anakeimenois* in Mk. 16:14 in relation to the place of the participants at the Supper (Mt. 26:20; Mk. 14:18).

II. The Eucharist, Communion and Community

Thus far, we have seen that the Eucharist in the New Testament is the moment in the life of the Church where — by the Holy Spirit — the 'eschaton' enters into history. We have also seen that the Church, even in its historical existence, saw the presence of Christ together with the whole history of salvation — inclusive of his death and resurrection — and was already experiencing the coming Kingdom. In this way, while the Church is still God's people walking in history towards the Kingdom, in the Eucharist she becomes what he was looking forward to. But what characterizes this 'new era' of the Church, this 'new' eschatological status of the people of God that is realized in the Eucharist? In order to answer this question, we return again to the accounts of the Supper and then to the experience of the Eucharist in the apostolic Church.

1. The 'One' and the 'Many' in the Lord's Supper

Despite their differences on many issues, all accounts of the Last Supper agree on one point. When our Lord explains the significance of the meal, he not only identifies the bread and wine with his body and his blood, but he links this identification with another concept: it is 'for you' or 'for many' that he offers himself (Mt. 26:28; Mk. 14:24; Lk. 22:20; 1 Cor. 11:25). These words of our Lord connect the Supper to the biblical tradition of the 'Servant of God' (*ebed YHWH*) and we should read these words in this context in order to best understand them.[16] But the main characteristic of the 'Servant of God' figure lies in the fact that it is he who takes upon himself the sins of the 'multitude' (Isa. 40-55) to the extent that he identifies fully with the 'many' — to the point that several exegetes have seen in this figure the 'corporate personality'[17] of the People of God.[18]

This idea that 'one' represents the 'many' is so deeply rooted in the eucharistic tradition of the New Testament that Saint Paul refers to it as the correct interpretation of the Lord's Supper when he writes: 'The cup of blessing that we bless, is it not a *sharing* (*koinonia*) in the blood of Christ? The bread that we break, is it not a *sharing* in the body of

---

16   O. Cullmann, *Christology of the New Testament*, 1958, pp. 59–82.

17   The concept of 'corporate personality' is applicable to the whole history of Israel. For more details concerning this theory (fundamental for understanding the biblical ecclesiology), see J. de Fraine, *Adam and the Family of Man* (trans. D. Raible), 1959.

18   Even when the Lord speaks of 'the blood of the new covenant', this allusion cannot be understood outside the context of the covenant at Sinai (Ex. 24:1-11) which includes all of the people of God (*Qahal*). Cf. J.M.R. Tillard, *L'Eucharistie, Pâque de l'Église*, 1964, pp. 108ff.

Christ? Because there is one bread, we who are many are one body, for we all partake of the one bread' (1 Cor. 10:16-7). And it is precisely because of this tradition that both the primitive liturgical hymns (e.g., Phil. 2:6-11) and the oldest eucharistic prayers that we possess are addressed to the Servant of God and are based upon this idea.[19]

However, the connection between the Supper and the Christological idea of a 'one' who unites in himself the 'many' is found also in another tradition of the New Testament, that of the 'Son of Man'. This is particularly true for the original Johannine Churches which, although aware of the relationship between the Eucharist and the 'Servant of God' tradition,[20] seem to prefer (at least according to the witness of the Fourth Gospel) the relationship between the Eucharist and the tradition of the 'Son of Man'. Again, it is interesting to note that the figure of the 'Son of Man' not only represents an eschatological concept of the glorious appearance of Christ to come, but is also at the same time (even from the first reference in the book of Daniel [7:13]) the 'corporate personality' of the 'holy nation', that is, the people of God.

In the Fourth Gospel, the relationship between the 'Son of Man' and the Eucharist appears precisely in the light of the 'one' who sums up in himself the 'many'. If chapter six of this Gospel refers to the Eucharist — as the main stream of tradition and exegesis accepts — it is significant that the figure that dominates is that of the 'Son of Man'. It is the 'Son of Man' who gives 'the food that endures for eternal life' (6:27). Unlike the manna that God gave Israel through Moses, this food is 'the true bread' that came down from heaven — nothing other than the 'Son of Man' who is characterized precisely by the fact that he came down from heaven (Jn. 3:13). It is for this reason that the Fourth Gospel describes the Eucharist as the eating, not simply of the flesh of Christ, but of the flesh of the *Son of Man*: 'Very truly, I tell you, unless you eat the flesh of the Son of Man and drink his blood, you have no life in you' (6:53). It is also for this reason that Christ appears specifically as the 'Son of Man' when he himself says that he incorporates the 'many': 'Those who eat my flesh and drink my blood abide in me, and I in them' (6:56). The phrase 'remain in him' is emphasized in a very significant way in chapters 13-17 of the Fourth Gospel, where the eucharistic context of the Last Supper is clear.

All this shows that, while the Synoptics and Paul's writings may prefer the 'Servant of God' tradition or the expression 'body' when they

---

19   For example, *1 Clem.* 59:2-4; *Did.* 9:2 and 10:2.

20   The use of the word 'lamb' to describe Christ in Jn. 1:29 and 36 (cf. 19:36) is certainly a reminder of Isa. 53:7 and we can say the same of the image of 'the lamb' that dominates the Book of Revelation.

refer to the Eucharist, and while the writings of John appeal more to the 'Son of Man' tradition or the expression 'flesh' instead of 'body', both traditions share the same fundamental belief: in the Eucharist the 'many' become 'one' and the 'one' incorporates the 'many' — the People of God. It is therefore mistaken to see in the Johannine writings a tendency towards individualism in the eucharistic communion and in ecclesiology in general. For although his writings speak of the communicant as an individual, they always see this person as a member of the community. Specifically regarding the notion of the 'Son of Man', which concerns us at present, the understanding of a 'many' incorporated into 'one' as a community (and not simply as the sum of individuals) is so powerful that we encounter a curious philological phenomenon: mixing the first person singular and the first person plural when one speaks of the Son of Man. 'Very truly, *I* tell you, *we* speak of what *we* know and testify to what *we* have seen; yet you do not receive our testimony. If *I* have told you about earthly things and you do not believe, how can you believe if *I* tell you about heavenly things? No one has ascended into heaven except the one who descended from heaven, *the Son of Man*' (Jn. 3:11-13; cf. 1 Jn. 1:1-4). It is clear that this syntactical anomaly may be explained by way of ecclesiology.[21]

2. The Ecclesiological Meaning of the Eucharistic Assembly

All this explains why the apostolic Church, in its eucharistic experience, did not consider the 'body of Christ' in a merely *objective* sense, as a *holy thing* for communion. Naturally, this is one aspect of the Eucharist that was not alien to the apostolic Church and to which we will return later. But the *ecclesiological* meaning of the eucharistic body of Christ appears as an inevitable and immediate consequence when we consider the Lord's Supper from the perspective (intrinsic to it) of the 'one' and the 'many'. It is therefore not surprising that Paul calls the Church the 'body of Christ' (Rom. 12:4-5; 1 Cor. 12:12-26; Eph. 1:23; 4:12-16; 5:36; Col. 1:18-24). This image of the Church, the reason for so much discussion among New Testament exegetes, cannot be understood apart from the eucharistic experience of the apostolic Church, just as this experience cannot be understood if we refuse to see Jesus Christ as the 'One' who incorporates within himself the 'many'. Similarly, the other images of the Church in the New Testament ('building' [1 Cor. 3:9; 14:5-12; 2 Cor. 12:19; Eph. 2:21; 4:12-16], 'house' [1 Tim. 3:15; Heb. 3:6; 1 Pet. 2:5], 'perfect man' [2 Cor. 11:2; Eph. 4:13], or the analogy of marriage [Eph. 5:29-32; cf. 1 Cor. 6:15-20]) become clear when we view them in light of this experience.

---

21   Cf. E. Schweizer, *Gemeinde und Gemeindeordnung im Neuen Testament*, 1959, §11a.

But it is necessary to go beyond the theological concepts in order to give the Eucharist its ecclesiological sense. The New Testament Churches, especially those planted by Paul, seem to have so identified the Eucharist with the Church herself that the terms 'Eucharist' and 'Church' are interchangeable in the existing witnesses — an exchange that is both very striking and very informative. Exemplary here is chapter 11 of 1 Corinthians, where Paul gives practical instructions for the eucharistic gatherings in Corinth. While it is clear from the context that Paul is thinking of the eucharistic gathering in this chapter, he calls this gathering 'Church': 'When you come together as a church...' (1 Cor. 11:18). If the Corinthians who read this sentence were living today, they would certainly wonder: 'What does he mean by, "you come together as a church"? Are we not the Church when we are not gathered?' But apparently this question never occurred to them because at that time the term 'Church' was not related to the theories and the idea of universalism, and actually meant this 'gathering' meeting for the purpose of celebrating the Eucharist. This is precisely why Paul, immediately after, does not hesitate to say that to injure the eucharistic gathering is to injure the 'Church of God' (1 Cor. 11:22). Moreover, he continues by identifying the Eucharist with the Church in a striking way when he connects everything that he said about the former to what he says about the latter by simply 'for', as the one sufficed as an explanation for the other: 'do you show contempt [by your conduct in the Eucharist] for the church of God...? For I received from the Lord what I also handed on to you [i.e., the Lord's Supper]' (1 Cor. 11:22-3). Therefore, according to Paul's usage in this passage, the expressions 'to gather' or 'to gather in one place', 'Lord's Supper', and 'Church' or 'Church of God' are identical. Similarly, other New Testament expressions that seem to be technical terms for designating the Church were originally used in apostolic times to speak of the eucharistic gatherings. So, for example, 'house Church' (*kat' oikon ecclesia*), an expression that does not mean a Christian family, but the house where (according to early tradition, e.g., Acts 2:46)[22] the local church usually met for the Eucharist (the family — even a very Christian family — is clearly distinguished from the Church in Paul's thought, cf. 1 Tim. 3:4-5, and even 1 Cor. 11:22). For this reason we should not consider the 'house Church' as a special type of Church, but as an indication of where the Church gathered for the Eucharist, a place that naturally received the

22   The meaning of *kat' oikon* in this passage is not 'from house to house', but 'in the house' as opposed to the Temple or other places where people could gather for activities apart from the Eucharist (prayer, preaching, etc.) in the early Church. Compare Acts 2:29; 13:14, 45; 14:1; 17:1-2, 10, 17; 18:19; and 19:8 with 2:46 and 20:7.

name of the owner of the house (Philemon 1-2; Rom. 16:5-16), just as the houses in Rome that were later known by the names of their owners (Saint Clement, etc.) because they had been used as a place for the eucharistic gatherings of the local Church.[23]

Indeed, all this found its expression in the very life of the apostolic Church. This allows us to account for the fact that the eucharistic gathering appears as a manifestation of the Church herself in the New Testament accounts. When we look closely at the structure of the eucharistic gathering, this becomes obvious. To reconstruct the eucharistic gathering according to the witness of the New Testament is an extremely difficult undertaking because, as we said at the beginning, the early Church does not provide very much information concerning its eucharistic life. Nevertheless, by relying upon the fragmentary evidence that we do possess, it is possible to make some basic observations.

Our first observation — a very significant observation — is that, unlike other assemblies in the New Testament context, there was *only one* Eucharistic gathering in each city, so that each one gathered *the whole Church* 'residing in' a certain place. It is interesting to note that Paul never uses the word 'Church' in the plural when he speaks of a city (Rom. 16:1; 1 Cor. 1:2; 2 Cor. 1:1; Col. 4:16; 1 Thes. 1:1; cf. Acts 8:1; 11:22), while he does when he speaks of a region larger than a city (Gal. 1:2-22; 1 Thes. 2:14; 2 Cor. 8:1; 1 Cor. 11:16; 14:22-34; 16:5; Rom. 16:16). It is striking that we never encounter the expression 'the Church in (or of) Macedonia' or 'the Church in (or of) Judea', etc., for while Paul speaks of 'the Church' in these regions, he does so only with the plural. This curious phenomenon of syntax cannot be explained except by the fact (as we have tried to show) that whenever the term 'Church' is used for a specific place, it has the sense of a convocation of *all* the Christians of that place in a single gathering so that each gathering is able to represent the *whole* Church. And it is precisely for this reason that Paul speaks of the Church gathered in the house of Gaius in Corinth (probably for the Eucharist) as 'the whole Church' (Rom. 16:23), exactly as he speaks of the eucharistic gathering of Corinth as a gathering of 'the whole Church' (1 Cor. 14:23). Furthermore, it is for the very same reason that the New Testament knows only of one single 'house Church' in each city.[24] Multiplication of the eucharistic gatherings within the same city is a much later phenomenon.

---

23   Cf. J.A. Jungmann, *The Early Liturgy to the Time of Gregory the Great*, 1959, p. 13.
24   We cannot discuss these arguments in favour of this point here, but see my book, *Eucharist, Bishop, Church: The Unity of the Church in the Divine Eucharist and the Bishop During the First Three Centuries*, 2001.

This fact is important for it shows the eucharistic *synaxis* to be a manifestation of the whole Church, of the Church in its catholicity. The Eucharist, therefore, is able to figure the unity of the 'many' in 'one' exactly as this unity appears in the Kingdom of God. For, as we said in the previous section of this chapter, the *eschata* are present already in the Eucharist. This is the fundamental distinction between the eucharistic gatherings and the other gatherings in the New Testament world (for example the *collegia* in the pagan world and the 'synagogues' in the Jewish world): although these other gatherings may have been based on strong bonds of love (perhaps even more profound than those uniting Christians),[25] the eucharistic gatherings did not discriminate between profession, race, etc. The Eucharist, because it is a manifestation of the 'catholic Church', transcends in itself not only the social divisions, but also the divisions in the natural order such as age (Mt. 14:21; 18:2-5; 19:13-15; Mk. 10:13; Lk. 18:16), gender (Gal. 3:28), race (Gal. 2:28), etc. Contrary to the practice of contemporary Churches — at a time when we have lost the original meaning of the Eucharist — a Eucharist celebrated especially for 'children' or 'students' etc. would have been inconceivable in the New Testament because it does not reflect the eschatological transcendence of all of these social and natural divisions. The 'many' — dispersed and divided — become 'one' in the Eucharist because it partakes of a 'single bread'.

Relying on the New Testament testimony regarding the eucharistic gatherings, we are able to make another point: these gatherings were structured to symbolize the eschatological unity of all in Christ. More than any other New Testament writing, the book of Revelation offers us an idea of the eucharistic celebration of the early church, presenting the eucharistic worship of the Church as actually occurring before the throne of God in heaven. Accordingly, everything that happens in the Eucharist should not be considered as a reality *parallel* to heaven, but as *identical* to it. Thus, the author of Revelation sees the throne of God and the Lamb surrounded by the thrones of the 'presbyters' with the 'seven spirits of God' and 'a sea of glass, like crystal' (Rev. 4-5). This corresponds roughly to the structure of the eucharistic gathering as described to us clearly by the earliest sources.[26] Actually, the 'place (or throne) of God' in the eucharistic synaxis is occupied by the 'bishop',[27] that is to say, the president of the eucharistic gathering, who is surrounded by the thrones of the 'presbyters' and assisted by the deacons, with the people facing him.

---

25   Reading, for example, Gal. 5:15; 1 Cor. 1:10-13, 18-21; etc.
26   E.g., Justin, *Apol.* I, 65 and 67; Hippolytus, *Apost. Trad.* (ed. G. Dix), pp. 6 and 40ff.
27   E.g., Ignatius, *Magn.* 6.1.

With the exception of the book of Revelation, the New Testament does not give us explicit indication of this arrangement, although some texts allude to it indirectly. In linking them to the witness of Revelation, however, they allow us to contemplate this structure in order to understand better the meaning of the Eucharist in the apostolic Church.

This structure is remarkable and unique, for it expresses both the historical and eschatological dimensions of the Eucharist, as well as the double aspect of the Church ('unity' and 'multiplicity'), all at the very same time. The theocentric character of the Eucharist ('*my Father* who gives you the true bread' [Jn. 6:32]) is marked by the central place the throne of God occupies. At the same time the sacrifice of Christ, taking place at the right hand of the throne of God (Heb. 2:9) as he makes his eternal intercession for us (Heb. 7:23-8), appears in the form of the 'Lamb slain', standing before the throne (Rev. 5:6).

Accordingly, the primitive Church's claim that the one who presides over the eucharistic assembly, that is to say the bishop, is 'the place of God' or is 'the image of Christ', was based faithfully upon the Eucharist. At the same time, the Church saw in this president the one who unites in himself the whole local Church by virtue of the fact that he offers it as the Body of Christ to God; this expressed precisely the fundamental idea of the Eucharist: the unity of the 'many' in the 'one'. Note also the significance of the thrones of the 'presbyters' in the meeting, which we have unfortunately lost sight of in the course of history: through them the Eucharist vividly appeared as the convocation of the people of God (the elders play a vital role in the history and eschatology of Israel), the gathering according to a particular order of those who were scattered in order to face the judgement of Israel and of the world in the last days (cf. Mt. 19:28-30; and Lk. 22:30). Here again the primitive Church was following closely her actual experience in the Eucharist when she saw in the college of the presbyters the bishop's 'council'[28] who were to judge and to decide all of the issues liable to divide the faithful, during the Eucharist and before communion. For the eucharistic assembly, according to the testimony of the New Testament, was itself a tribunal, the eschatological final tribunal that was to judge everything concerning the faithful (Mt. 18:18-20; and 1 Cor. 5, close to the Syriac *Didascalia* 11);[29] this tribunal was so convinced of its eschatological character that it was going to 'deliver this man over to Satan for the destruction of the flesh, so that his spirit may be saved in the day of the Lord' (1 Cor. 5:5). Finally, the 'seven spirits of God', appearing as the

---

28   Ignatius, *Phld.* 8.1; cf. *Magn.* 6.1 and *Trall.* 3.1.
29   In the Syriac *Didascalia* 11 (ed. R.H. Connolly, 1929, pp. 109–115).

'seven lamps burning' before the throne of God, indicate the place and role of the deacons in the eucharistic liturgy (the number seven and the responsibility of these spirits for service to God are both associated with the primitive tradition concerning the deacons).[30] For the eucharistic gathering takes, through them, its character of mission and of service for the people of God and for the world, which we will discuss later. Through them, as through the angels, the Servant of God is the servant of the world (Heb. 1:14) and in a double movement he offers on the one hand the gifts of the world to the bishop that they might become Eucharist and on the other hand he offers the Eucharist to the world as the communion in the life of God.

This image is completed by the presence of the people, present in the 'prayers of the saints' that ascend to the throne of God as incense (Rev. 5:8) and in the responses and acclamations that punctuate the liturgy that takes place before the throne of God. This people is precisely the one that answers 'Amen' to the thanksgiving described by Paul (1 Cor. 14:16) and the early Church was thus in full fidelity to the biblical image of the Eucharist when it reserved this 'Amen'[31] to the order of the laity. The eucharistic assembly simply is not possible without these responses. If the Eucharist is the image of the whole people of God summoned in a place, the people must be present. The laity represents the *laos* of God or the multitude (*plèthos*, Acts 2:6; 4:32; and 6:5) and like the people of Israel, must follow 'Moses' and adhere to him through its responses.[32] It is the 'multitude' that must have a sort of eschatological foretaste of its unity by becoming 'one' in the 'One' who was responsible for all as the Servant of God and the Son of Man. A Eucharist celebrated without the 'people' or without the 'orders' that we have mentioned does not reflect faithfully its fundamental significance as the eschatological gathering of the 'multitude' of God's dispersed people in the body of the 'one' who took them upon himself. The Eucharist, therefore, if it wants to be faithful to itself, must conform to a structure that includes the basic elements that we have mentioned and the 'orders' that express both the historical and the eschatological character of the Church.

---

30 In Acts 6:2 we hear of the 'seven' chosen 'to wait (*diakonein*) on tables'. It is difficult to discern from this text whether the 'tables' were eucharistic or not, but it should be noted that the deacons are related closely to the 'bishops' from the beginning (Phil. 1:1; 1 Tim. 3:1-13). In the same vein it also should be noted that very early in the liturgical tradition there developed a close relation between the number seven and the ordination of deacons and bishops.

31 Justin, *Apol.* I, 65.

32 The terms *plèthos* and *laos* are interchangeable in the earliest documents (even in specifically ecclesiological reference, for example in Ignatius, *Smyrn.* 8), which is ever instructive for understanding the term 'multitude' as we use it here.

3. The Eucharistic Community and the Ministry of the Church

It follows from this that the Eucharist, even in the form and structure of its assembly, both expresses and transcends the contradiction between 'multiplicity' and 'unity'. This contradiction is of the same kind as that which exists, as we saw in the previous section, between history and eschatology. This raises the following question: how can the Church, which is the people of God scattered and dispersed, experience its 'unity' in the Eucharist without losing its historical character? This question gives rise, in turn, to the question of the meaning of the Eucharist as the *koinonia* (communion) of the Body of Christ.

Again, the answer will depend in large part on the importance and the value that we give to the pneumatology of the New Testament. According to Paul, the Eucharist is called '*koinonia* in the body' and '*koinonia* in the blood' of Christ' (1 Cor. 10:16). The eucharistic *koinonia*, however, remains in the context of another *koinonia* — that of the *Holy Spirit*. The well-known salutation of 2 Cor. 13:13, which from the beginning was certainly a part of the eucharistic celebration[33] and very soon found a permanent place in the ancient liturgies, applies the concept of *koinonia* especially to the Holy Spirit: 'The grace of the Lord Jesus Christ, the love of God, and the *communion of the Holy Spirit* be with all of you'. For our topic, the meaning of the phrase 'communion of the Holy Spirit should be considered principally according to two aspects of the pneumatology of the New Testament.

First, the Holy Spirit acts in the Church: it is he who actualizes the presence of Christ for each person. It is no exaggeration to say that without the Holy Spirit, the presence of Christ means nothing to the members of the ecclesial community: 'no one can say "Jesus is Lord" except by the Holy Spirit' (1 Cor. 12:3; cf. Mk. 12:36). And the communion in the body and blood of Christ is not existentially applicable to every Christian unless the Eucharist is located in 'the Spirit' (1 Cor. 14:16). The Holy Spirit is the one that transforms the objective communion in the body and blood of Christ into a personal and existential reality.

Second, this transformation of an historical and objective reality into an existential reality is precisely the one that transforms the Church into a *charismatic community* and makes the eucharistic *synaxis* the place *par excellence* where the charismatic character of the Church is revealed and realized. We are insistent at this point because it is essential.

That the Eucharist represents the special moment in the life of the apostolic Church in which the different charisms were emerging is

---

33   See the reconstruction of the early liturgy attempted upon this basis by H. Lietzmann, *op. cit.*,
      p. 237.

apparent from a careful study of the First Epistle to the Corinthians where Saint Paul refers extensively to the eucharistic assembly of Corinth. Chapters 10–14 deal in one way or another directly with the Eucharist. Against the background of Israel's history, Paul discusses spiritual food and drink, then he establishes for himself and for the Church the tradition of the Lord's Supper and explains its meaning before proceeding immediately to the eucharistic assemblies themselves as if these assemblies were nothing other than the Eucharist itself. It is precisely at this moment that he introduces his lengthy instruction on the charismatic life of the Church. This instruction — it is clear — is presented in the context of the eucharistic assembly of the Corinthians *during which* ('when you come together' [14:26] or 'If… the whole church comes together' [14:23] — meaning the Eucharist) *the charisms are manifest*.

Paul calls this instruction regarding the charisms — and this is important — 'concerning spiritual *gifts*' (12:1). For him, as the 'blessing' of the Bread and the Cup is 'with the Spirit' (14:16) — an implicit reference to what we call *epiclesis* — so all the charisms manifest themselves during the eucharistic celebration. The charismatic life, judging from Paul's description, is part of the Eucharist. Viewed outside of this context, the Eucharist loses its proper meaning, as does the charismatic life that must always remain linked to the eucharistic life of the Church[34] even if, by extension, it sometimes expresses itself outside of the eucharistic celebration. This is precisely why Paul analyses, so to speak, the concept of the 'Body of Christ' in strictly pneumatological terms: Christ has 'many members' (12:12), but membership is set out *in a charismatic perspective*. This has a very profound sense: being a member of the Body of Christ does not depend on what one is in oneself, that is to say as an individual, but on what one is charismatically — which is to say as a person[35] existentially linked to the other members. And it is this which constitutes the 'communion of the Holy Spirit'.

The mystery of this 'pneumatic'[36] life in the Church — revealed

34 Therefore, the habit of conferring ordinations during the celebration of the Eucharist is not simply a matter of tradition, but also of ecclesiology.

35 Arguably, the most important aspect of the mystery of *koinonia* — of all *koinonia* in the true sense of the term — is linked to the notion of the *person*. To be a person is to be in communion. Without this communion, one is an *individual*, but not a *person* (on this topic, see the important remarks made by N. Berdyaev, *Solitude and Society*, 1938, p. 168; and M. Buber, *I and Thou*, 1958, p. 62. This applies not only to humanity, but to God himself, at least the triune God, whose existence is characterized precisely by personal communion. And the Eucharist, as it transcends in itself the antinomy between the 'one' and the 'many', reveals and accomplishes the very meaning of the person and the community.

36 We have avoided the usual term 'spiritual' in favour of 'pneumatic' because the former term unfortunately has been used in a way foreign to the Greek New Testament — becoming the opposite of 'flesh' and 'body' in a dualist sense.

par excellence in the Eucharist — is precisely an aspect of the mystery of the one and the many. This can be seen in the same passage of Paul concerning the *pneumatics*. This instruction takes place inside the paradox: one Spirit, many charisms. The Spirit is one (1 Cor. 12:3, 9, 11, 13, 18; and Eph. 2:18; 4:4) and the one whose work is to build the one Body of Christ is at the same time the one who 'divides' (*diairoun*) and distributes the charisms to each one 'as he sees fit' (*bouletai*) (12:11). This aspect of 'distribution' is essential to New Testament pneumatology, as shown by the account of the descent of the Holy Spirit on the day of Pentecost (Acts 2:3: 'Divided tongues, as of fire, appeared among them, and a tongue rested on each of them'). This also has important consequences for a full understanding of the ministry of the Church.

We have already seen that the Eucharist, in its true form of assembly, was the moment in which the Church was revealed as a charismatic community, but that this does not exclude — but on the contrary demands — the existence of an 'order' (1 Cor. 14:40) and therefore of 'orders'. If we consider the phenomenon of 'order' in light of what has been said, we are compelled again to make the distinction already made earlier on another occasion, between a strictly historical vision of the reality of the Church and a historical-pneumatological vision. Similar to the question of the renewal of the sacrifice of Christ in the Eucharist, this question of the order of the Church has raised long and bitter controversies for centuries. Since all these controversies took place at a time when we had lost the eucharistic vision of 'order', it is perhaps necessary to emphasize certain points which emerge from studying the New Testament era when, as we have seen, the charisms and order still were seen and understood eucharistically. The following points, then, should be remembered.

It is important that the concept of 'order' and of ministry be freed from an objectifying sacramentalism that considers the gift of a charism or the ordination of a minister as 'sacraments' in themselves. If we consider the epicletic character of the sacrament — this is exactly what it means to relocate all ordination within the framework of the eucharistic service — we are led to speak of the orders and ministers of the Church neither in ontological terms nor in functional terms (a dilemma in which many of the earlier controversies have been trapped),[37] but in existential and personal terms, just as Paul speaks of the charisms in 1 Corinthians 12. By 'personal' and 'existential' (terms which, of

---

37   Even Afanasiev, despite his eucharistic ecclesiology (and there is no need to reiterate its importance here), has not managed to escape the dilemma between 'ontological' and 'functional'. Thus, he attached a 'functional' character to the diversity of ministries in the Church, for example in 'L'Eglise de Dieu dans le Christ', *La Pensée Orthodoxe* 13 (1968): p. 19.

course, are not ideal because they can have several meanings) I mean first, in a negative sense, no ministry is possible above or outside of the community as an individual and ontological possession and second, in a positive sense, that each ordination and each ministry is existentially linked to the Body of Christ. It is not defined by its 'utility' or by its 'horizontal social structure', but it is a reflection of the very ministry of Christ, the same energies of God the Father and the gifts of the Spirit (1 Cor. 12:4-5) *in* and *for* the one body of Christ (1 Cor. 12:12-30). This means that the concept of 'hierarchy' in the Church should not speak in terms of rank or merit (Paul firmly excludes this view of the charisms in 1 Cor. 12:22-31), but in terms of personal charisms and of activities that put a person into profound existential relationships with others — something like the hierarchy existing in the Holy Trinity where obedience is not absent, but is based upon the activities of each person, themselves determined precisely by the relationships they have with one another and with the world they have created and love.

Understanding the ministry and order in this way and viewing them in the eucharistic context leads inevitably to a Christocentric vision (so striking in the New Testament). The Holy Spirit is the one who distributes the ministries, and without this sharing no charism is possible in the Church. But in this distribution, the Spirit takes everything from Christ (Jn. 16:14) so that what seems to be a personal ministry in the Church is nothing other than a reflection of the ministry of Christ. It is striking to realize how many times the New Testament repeats that Christ is the 'minister' (Heb. 8:2), the 'priest' (Heb. 2:17; 5:6; 8:1; 10:21), the 'apostle' (Heb. 3:1), the 'deacon' or 'servant' (Rom. 15:8; Lk. 22:77; cf. Phil. 2:7; Mt. 12:18; Acts 3:13; 4:27), the 'bishop' (1 Pet. 2:25; 5:4; Heb. 13:20), the 'teacher' (Mt. 23:8; Jn. 13:13), the one who has 'first place in everything' (Col. 1:18). Christ remains the sole source of ministry because in the Eucharist he is the one who incorporates the many: every ministry and every order does not come from him simply to be then an individual possession, but to *reflect him*.[38] And in order to reflect him, this ministry is diversified so that it is accommodated to the many. The work of the Holy Spirit, who is the bond of the body (Eph. 4:3), assures the 'diversity of the ministries' (1 Cor. 15:5, indeed, 'Are all apostles?' [1 Cor. 12:29-31; cf. Jas. 3:1; etc.]) so that no ministry can be considered objectively in and of itself or as an individual possession, but always must be understood *in relation to the others* that form the one body of Christ. This allows Paul to do what he forbade himself to do

---

38   This highlights the well-known problem: is the Eucharist itself accomplished as *opus operantis* or as *ex opera operato*? Yet, if Christ is essentially the minister of the Eucharist, then this problem loses its significance.

(cf. 1 Cor. 12:22), that is, to speak of a hierarchy of worth in the gifts, by placing love over all others (1 Cor. 12:12-31). What does this mean?

To differentiate love, the greatest of gifts and the subject of the famous hymn of 1 Corinthians 13, it is necessary to grasp the context in which it appears. This passage should not be taken by itself — and it should not be used as it is often used in all sorts of homilies. In context, this praise of love is the *only way* Paul is able to explain *the mystery of the personal character of the charismatic life of the Church* that we have tried to highlight here. The reference to love in 1 Corinthians 13 is not self-contained, but must remain linked to the exercise of the ministries in service to the *one* body, as if this reference were the *only way* to conceive of this exercise.

To explain the concept of ministry by love is a most instructive approach, because all the ontological and functional problems disappear and there remains only the *bond of love*, not in the sentimental or moral sense, but in the sense of a relation. This relation makes personal existence dependent upon another, which can also be expressed by saying that *one affirms his or her existence only in the context of relations* ('I' has meaning only in relation to 'you'). This relation allows us to understand the 'indelible' character of ministry, for when love confers a charism it is indelible, not objectively (in itself), but in connection with the community. This is precisely where *agape* in 1 Corinthians 13 places the accent and thus clarifies our understanding of ministry[39] in its eucharistic context.[40]

III. The Eucharist, Food for the Life of the World

1. The Eucharist is Food

In the New Testament the Eucharist is associated with the idea of food. This appears from the beginning in the accounts of the Last Supper that imply a sacramental participation of the disciples in the death of Christ. The words 'take... eat... drink' followed immediately by the reference

---

39 In this connection it is interesting to note the similarity between the celebration of ordination and the celebration of marriage in the Orthodox Church.

40 We will not deal here specifically with *agape* because, despite the fact that the question remains open (and always will) at the level of research, the meal seems to the majority of theologians not to be identified with the Eucharist itself. However, it should be noted here that the fact that the term *agape* lends itself to the designation of a meal that was originally linked to the Eucharist is significant in itself. The relationship between the celebration of the Eucharist and the meal seems so intimate in the early Church that it is without a doubt a single rite in two parts (in Acts 2:46 does *koinonia* = *agape*?), which may have been described with the very same word (Jude 12). This shows both that the Eucharist is *agape* and that *agape* is eucharistic, in the thinking of the early Church.

to the sacrifice of the body and blood of the paschal lamb establish a connection between participation in the meal and participation in this death and sacrifice. These words must be read in light of what the Lord said to his disciples on another occasion: 'You will indeed drink my cup...' (Mt. 20:22-3; Mk. 10:38-40), speaking of the cup of his death and thereby identifying three realities: the Eucharist (the cup), the death on the cross, and the participation of the disciples in both. In the same way, the proclamation of the death of Christ is tied to the Eucharist in Paul's account (1 Cor. 11:26) thereby revealing that the food of the Eucharist is a communion in the sufferings of Christ by the Church and for the Church — as if his suffering had to be so borne by his body, the Church (cf. Col. 1:24). The early church was faithful to the biblical meaning of the Eucharist when she attached a eucharistic implication to martyrdom.[41]

But just as the Eucharist in its totality cannot be considered apart from the light of the resurrection in the New Testament (as we have already observed in other passages), so the resurrection also absolutely dominates this aspect of the Eucharist. After the light of the resurrection shines on the Last Supper, it becomes clear that to participate in the death of Christ is automatically to participate in his life. For those who have seen the risen Christ — seen him just as the disciples who shared the meal with him on the way to Emmaus (Lk. 24:30-35) — the cross and the tomb of the Lord become a source of life. This applies to all the aspects of the life of the Church, from the baptism that offers communion in both the death and the resurrection of Christ, even to martyrdom which, precisely because of the resurrection, and despite being a participation in the death of Christ, is an event full of joy and a participation in the life of the risen Lord. In the same way the Eucharist also appears in the New Testament as food: 'Day by day, as they spent much time together in the temple, they broke bread at home and ate their food with glad and generous hearts, praising God and having the goodwill of all the people' (Acts 2:46-7).

The Fourth Gospel speaks clearly and at length of the Eucharist as the 'bread of life', but this tradition is not absent from the Synoptics and Paul. It is by no means easy to specify the exact meaning of the expression *artos épiousios* (often translated 'daily bread') in the Lord's Prayer; for the phrase is unknown in Hebrew (or Aramaic?) and the Greek translation itself is very obscure. There are, however, several reasons to believe that this expression is a reference to the eucharistic bread.[42] In addition to the patristic tradition that sees the Eucharist

---

41 Ignatius, *Rom.* 4.1-2.

42 For a discussion of this whole matter, see von Allmen, *op. cit.*, pp. 81–82.

itself in this expression and the ancient liturgical practice of never teaching the Lord's Prayer to the catechumens (it was reserved for the baptized, who were allowed to share in the Eucharist), there is evidence in the New Testament itself of a relationship between the Lord's Prayer and the Eucharist. For instance, while the Fourth Gospel does not mention this prayer, it gives in its place the dialogue between Jesus and those who ask him to give them always the 'bread of God' (cf. Luke's version of the Lord's Prayer: 'Give us each day our daily bread', that is to say, always, forever). Christ's answer to this question provides an explanation of the term *artos* (bread) in the Lord's Prayer: '*I am* the bread of life'. And in the prayer itself, we must understand the expression '*our* Father' in association with the expression '*our* bread'. This is the bread of the community that lived this prayer, and it is no coincidence that in the first centuries there was an identity between this community and that formed by those who received communion at the Eucharist.

If this is a possible interpretation, it is interesting that this 'bread' is described as *épiousios*, a term that means either 'bread *of* or *for* or *in-excess-of* subsistence' or 'bread that comes'. Although it is difficult to choose one or the other of these interpretations, both suggest the idea of food given for life or for the very essence of life, which is to say the life of God, eternal life, or the life 'to come' (eschatological life, which amounts to the same thing). In either case or in both cases we have the real meaning of the Eucharist as food. This food is identified with the life of Christ, the life of God, given upon the cross, but victorious over death by death in the resurrection (choosing between the two is an impossible dilemma because it is the same life in both cases). This life will be given for eternity in the last days and is given now in the Eucharist — food for the life of the world presented as a 'medicine of immortality, an antidote against death'.[43] This interpretation of the Eucharist as food leads to several other remarks.

First, if this 'food' is communion in Christ's life, it cannot be separated from his historical and eschatological work. In other words, it is not an individual who communes in the divine life, for example in the sense of the pagan mysteries. The Eucharist cannot be understood outside of its context of *anamnesis*; it is only 'divine life' in so far as it is rooted in the 'remembrance of Christ' — remembrance that includes, as we have already noted, the whole history of salvation, both past and future. But in affirming this, we must be very careful *not* to imply that this food is communion *only in the work* of Christ. The tendency to isolate the *works* of God in history and to consider them as the only ground upon

43   Ignatius, *Eph.* 20.2.

which humans may meet God (by 'works' we also include the Word of God) is a dangerous tendency and leads into error when he acts in the Eucharist. The New Testament makes it clear that the life of God given in the Eucharist is not only what God *did* and *said* in Christ, but the *person* of Christ in its totality. This is why Christ requires that the Eucharist be a remembrance, not of 'my work and my teaching', but of 'me'. For, 'God gave us eternal life, and this life is in his Son. Whoever has the Son has life' (1 Jn. 5:11-12). As this is in reality nothing but the very life of God (1 Jn. 1:2), while avoiding defining it, we must not forget that it extends to include the audacious expression of Peter: we are 'participants of the divine nature' (2 Pet. 1:4).

In the second place, the Eucharist is the food of life precisely in the very form in which it appears: bread and wine. When the Lord utters the words, 'This is my body..., this is my blood', he refers to the bread and the wine, so that he leaves no doubt regarding the *realism* of his words. And when he states that, 'Those who eat my flesh and drink my blood have eternal life... for my flesh is *true* food and my blood is *true* drink.... The one who *eats* this bread will live forever' (Jn. 6:54-58), his use of these expressions is so realistic that he provokes his disciples to remark, 'This teaching is difficult; who can accept it?' (Jn. 6:60). Indeed, the biblical witness on this subject and the realism of these words have continued to cause scandals through the centuries — and yet it truly has retained its realism, without any reservation.

This realism is absolutely biblical and cannot be jettisoned in a correction interpretation of the Eucharist. Yet, in view of what has been said about the meaning of the eucharistic food, it should be noted here that this realism should not lead to an *objectification* of the eucharistic food. In fact, this danger was not averted in the course of history: the eucharistic piety that has developed from this realistic approach and the long controversies regarding the eucharistic elements demonstrate this. But this occurred precisely because the Eucharist had become an *object* considered by itself and out of the context the New Testament gives it. For if the Eucharist is really and truly the body of Christ, it should not be seen first and foremost as a miracle that manifests the power of God, for it must be placed first in the history of salvation: the body of Christ in the Eucharist is food for eternal life. And if this eternal life is, as we have already said, the life of God in Christ, given in the sacrifice of the cross and triumphantly manifested by the Resurrection, then the eucharistic elements are food, but always *in relation* to the risen Christ who is 'the firstborn from the dead' (Col. 1:18; Rev. 1:5), the head of the community he gathers. It is therefore true to say that in a biblical vision of the Eucharist one cannot separate the elements from the community that forms the eschatological body of Christ

(1 Thes. 4:14-17), and this makes all objectification of the Eucharist impossible, in terms of either theology or piety.

Finally, and in accordance with all that has come before, not only does Christ in the Eucharist feed us his body and his blood, but we are also provided with *spiritual food* and *spiritual drink* (1 Cor. 10:3-4). Although we have already done so, it is important to stress again this idea, when speaking of the 'objective' aspect of the Eucharist as food. The spiritual character of this 'food' and 'drink' again shows that the transformation (*métabolè*) of bread and wine into the body and blood of Christ is possible only by the Holy Spirit. It is in this sense that we must interpret the words of Christ pronounced precisely in relation to the eating of his flesh in the Eucharist: 'It is the Spirit that gives life; the flesh is useless' (Jn. 6:63). Whatever happened in the history of the form in which this *métabolè* was expressed in the eucharistic liturgy, the New Testament seems to indicate the *epicletic* character of this *métabolè* in a clear and definite way. In the liturgy, however, this epiclesis must be more than just an introduction to a prayer to the Holy Spirit. First of all, this epiclesis sets out with certainty the *foundation* of the Eucharist, for the Holy Spirit cannot, so to speak 'by definition', act upon an object without involving a community existentially.[44] Subsequently, the spiritual character of the *métabolè* reveals the eschatological character *and purpose of the community*. It is to this character and purpose that we now turn our attention.

2. The Eucharist is Judgement

The Holy Spirit is associated with the 'last days' (Acts 2:17) and the life of Christ triumphant over death in the resurrection. Indeed, it is the life of the last days itself when Christ appears at the head of the multitude, the 'nation of the saints'. In celebrating the Eucharist in the Holy Spirit, the Church becomes particularly aware of this; so that the last days and all that they imply are already both in the community that is the Church and in the eucharistic food. The first thing that they imply is the judgement of the world. How is this related to the Eucharist in the New Testament? On this subject we have a very informative testimony regarding both how the Church understood the Eucharist and how she lived in the course of the celebration.

We must first note that in the New Testament the eucharistic gifts are called *hagia*, that is to say 'holy things', exactly as the members of the Church are called *hagioi*. 'Sacred' or 'holy' did not have a moral sense

---

44   The *epiclesis* in the Liturgy of Saint John Chrysostom invites the Spirit to descend not only upon the gifts, but also upon *us* — the community.

at that time, but meant 'set apart', someone or something removed from the world, implying the idea of judgement. This judgement, this separation, is an essential element of eschatology, because at the dawn of the end time a tribunal for the judgement of the world will be established (Mt. 25:31-2 and parallels). And the world will be judged by its attitude towards the community of the 'least of these' (Mt. 25:40-5), which is synonymous with the very body of the 'Son of man' ('just as you did it to one of the least of these…, you did it to me'), the multitude, the 'holy people', the Church. Thus, the Eucharist considered as an object is 'holy' and considered as a community is composed of 'saints' who, therefore, form 'the holy temple of God' (1 Cor. 3:17). In this way the eucharistic communion is simultaneously *communio in sacris* and *communio sanctorum*.

In this eschatological vision, when the apostolic Church celebrated the Eucharist, she believed that the world was *really* on trial at that moment. Since 'the saints will judge the world' (1 Cor. 6:2), it was not only the privilege, but also the duty of the eucharistic community to judge its members before communion. The convergence of most of the testimony indicates that this element of judgement existed in the first eucharistic liturgies; this not only corresponds to what Paul says in 1 Corinthians 5, but also to the fact that the members of the Church were to seek reconciliation before communion (Mt. 5:23): 'So when you are offering your gift at the altar, if you remember that your brother or sister has something against you, leave your gift there before the altar and go; first be reconciled to your brother or sister, and then come and offer your gift';[45] and also in Matthew 18 when Jesus discusses the judgement of the Church. Careful study of this chapter shows that the Church (most likely, *ecclesia* here has the sense of *synaxis*) ultimately judged all that was considered as sin among its members (*hamartia*, particularly in relation to the Church and its members). That this judgement was definitive, that it was eschatological in nature and that it was concretized by the exclusion from the eucharistic communion, all this is clear from the conclusion of the admonition: 'if the offender refuses to listen even to the church, let such a one be to you as a Gentile and a tax collector. Truly I tell you, whatever you bind on earth will be bound in heaven, and whatever you loose on earth will be loosed in heaven' (Mt. 18:17b-18). In the Fourth Gospel the words, 'If you forgive the sins of any, they are forgiven them; if you retain the sins of any, they are retained,' are pronounced on 'Sunday' when the disciples were gathered and 'the doors… were closed' and they are linked to the gift of the Holy Spirit (Jn. 20:19-23). Such words express a prerogative

---

45   Very early on the Church saw the Eucharist in this text, for example Irenaeus, *Ad. Haer.* 4.18.1.

that the Church exercised in the eucharistic assemblies through the president of the assembly surrounded by the presbyters seated upon their thrones (cf. Rev. 4:4),[46] a prerogative based on two things often forgotten in the history of penance: the context of the eucharistic gathering and the eschatological reality that this gathering contains.

By recalling this we see more clearly the original meaning of excommunication in the Church: this decision normally arose in a eucharistic assembly understood as an anticipation of the eschatological judgement. In order to share in the life of God, it is necessary that God should judge us, for God is 'holy', indeed, thrice holy (*hagios, hagios, hagios*, cf. Isa. 6:2-3) and it is no coincidence that the Church has chosen to insert this hymn in the unfolding of the Eucharist (Rev. 4:8). If God is 'holy', members of the Church must be 'holy' as well (1 Pet. 1:15-16), in order that they might participate in his life in the Eucharist. It is for this end that they must undergo a judgement that will set them apart for God. This judgement first appears in a confrontation with the Word of God — which is 'sharper than any two-edged sword' (Heb. 4:12) — and that is why the Scripture reading, immediately followed by preaching, was part of the essential structure of the liturgy from very early on.[47] Hearing Scripture is part of the turning of one's whole life toward God (*métanoia*), dying to the world in the death of Christ and being born to new life in Christ's resurrection (baptism). Having undergone this judgement and having become a member of the community, the Christian, although in principle incapable of sin (1 Jn. 3:9; cf. Heb. 10:26), can sin against his brothers and sisters, especially in a lack of love (Mt. 5:21-6; 18:15-20) and in general 'against the body itself' (1 Cor. 6:18), that is to say against the community, by despising or 'without discerning the body' of Christ in the eucharistic sense (1 Cor. 11:29).[48] This case shows participation in the Eucharist itself to be a judgement whereby participants may 'eat and drink judgement against themselves' (1 Cor. 11:29). In fact, what was to be participation in the life of God may turn out to be a loss of this life (1 Cor. 11:30). But the Church must ensure that this does not happen.

Excommunication was precisely the instrument by which the Church, guided by *concern* for the eternal salvation of its members, took responsibility for preventing the eternal condemnation of one member by denying him or her access to communion. '[W]hen we are judged

46   Cf. Ignatius, *Magn.* 6.1; *Trall.* 3.1; and *Phld.* 8.1 in relation with *Didascalia* 11 (ed. R.H. Connolly, 1929, pp. 109–115).

47   Justin, *Apol.* I, 65 and 67.

48   Again, we understand 'the body of Christ' not only objectively but also ecclesiologically — designating the Church.

by the Lord, we are disciplined so that we may not be condemned along
with the world' (1 Cor. 11:32). In the last analysis, excommunication
was a *pastoral* act which was only meaningful because the Church took
seriously the eschatological character of the eucharistic gathering. This
explains the terrifying words of Paul: 'you are to hand this man over to
Satan for the destruction of the flesh, so that his spirit may be saved in
the day of the Lord' (1 Cor. 5:5). According to the criteria of the New
Testament Church, it was better that someone (or that the community)
enter into eternal life with one less member, than to retain the integrity
of the body and to be sent to the eternal fire (Mt. 18:8-9; note here
that the context is ecclesiological and not individual). This is why the
'little' member should not be despised, but that everything should be
done to save 'these little ones', even to the point of treating them as 'a
Gentile and a tax collector', that is to say excommunicating them, in
which case 'whatever you bind on earth will be bound in heaven' (Mt.
18:10, 17, 18). All this explains why the Eucharist was given 'for the
remission of sins' and perhaps also why it is Matthew who stresses this
in his account of the Last Supper (26:28). The pastoral concern in the
Church appears here in a perspective tightly focused on the Eucharist.

3. The Eucharist and the World

Everything we have said so far shows that the Eucharist is the moment
in the life of the Church in which the destiny of the world is finally
decided. It is therefore essentially linked to the world, it concerns the
world as the world concerns it. If it begins with a 'setting apart' from
the world, if it 'closes its doors' to the world, it is not because the world
has nothing to do with the Eucharist or because it is judged in the
Eucharist. The 'Eucharist-world' relationship is more positive, and we
must see what it means in the light of the New Testament.

We will not dwell on the meaning of the act of eating, or on the
meaning of the bread and the wine as indispensable elements of the
Eucharist, though the Bible has much to say regarding these things.
Christ invited his disciples to eat his body at the moment in which the
one presiding over the Passover meal usually would have pronounced
the blessing and given thanks to God, 'the king of the universe who
has brought forth the bread from the earth'.[49] Similarly, he invited
them to drink his blood at the moment when the one presiding usually
would have blessed the cup, giving thanks to the Lord 'who created
the fruit of the vine'.[50] It is for this reason that the Church established

49   *Berakoth* 61; cf. Jeremias, *op. cit.*, p. 107.
50   *Ibid.*

such a positive and meaningful relationship between the Eucharist and creation and very early on saw creation in the eucharistic elements.[51]

Here it is perhaps necessary to insist upon the eucharistic implications of the 'cosmic' Christology that appears explicitly in the epistles to the Ephesians and the Colossians and which must have influenced the interpretation of the Church in a decisive fashion. 'Blessed be the God and Father of our Lord Jesus Christ, who has blessed us in Christ with every spiritual blessing in the heavenly places' (Eph. 1:3): it is almost certain that we have here the beginning of a ritual prayer that is almost surely a eucharistic prayer. In this case it is interesting to see the extent to which the eucharistic worship in the apostolic Church was deeply imbued with the idea that in Christ not only do the members of the Church have 'redemption through his blood' but *all creation* is recapitulated (Eph. 1:7-10). This universal recapitulation in Christ makes possible a new understanding of the 'body of Christ'. For Christ is not only 'the firstborn among a large family' (Rom. 8:29), but also 'the firstborn of *all creation*' (Col. 1:15) since he is 'the firstborn from the dead' (Col. 1:18). Then the 'body of Christ' is not only the 'community of the saints', but also 'the fullness of him who fills all in all' (Eph. 1:23).

One can imagine how such perspectives would have helped the apostolic eucharistic communities to locate themselves in relation to the world. To participate in the body of Christ does not mean simply to partake of this one 'in whom we have redemption, the forgiveness of sins' (Col. 1:14), but also to partake in the order of the new world (a new world order) where all 'powers and principalities' and all created things depend on him because they have been connected to their Creator. This return of all creation to its creator is expressed in what the ancient liturgies called the eucharistic *anaphora* and this concept was not alien to the anthropological aspect of salvation or the work of Christ. For everything that happens to humanity when it departs from its Creator categorically affects 'the whole creation' which 'has been groaning in labour pains' (Rom. 8:22). And the return of all creation to God cannot be imagined apart from the sacrifice and the resurrection of Christ. Christ became 'the firstborn of all creation' and the 'first in everything' precisely because he is 'the firstborn from the dead' (Col. 1:15, 18), that is to say by his death and resurrection. As is evident from the Epistle to the Hebrews, which also presents a theology of 'the firstborn' brought 'into the world' (1:6), the idea that all creation is subject to Christ presupposes the he became the 'pioneer [*archègos*, synonymous with 'firstborn'] of our salvation' by his suffering (2:10). And all this makes him the 'merciful and faithful high priest' of God

(2:17), who goes before us (*prodromos*, another synonym for 'firstborn') in the eternal sanctuary of God (6:20).

If the sacrifice of Christ has thus restored the true relationship between the world and its creator, this means that we must consider the role of the Church in the world in light of the *priestly aspect of the Eucharist*. As this restoration came about by the priestly action of Christ — by his sacrifice and his resurrection — it is extremely important for the life and the destiny of the whole world (all material life, spiritual life, social life, etc.) that the Church acts in the Eucharist as the *priest of the world* as it applies (actually and existentially) the action of Christ. The Church cannot despise anything in the world, for everything in it must return to the Creator because everything comes from him. The Church cannot ignore or neglect any aspect of the life of the world, for all the 'powers and principalities', that is to say, the different forces that determine the life of humanity and nature have been reconciled to God by Christ and subjected to him (Col. 2:15). Everything that makes up the world must be related to God and Christ is the only one who can act as a priest because Adam (the first human) refused this role. The eucharistic synaxis accomplishes this priestly act and it is in this sense that all the faithful who participate in the Eucharist are a 'royal priesthood' (1 Pet. 2:9; cf. Rev. 5:10).

In this vision of the Eucharist the world receives sacramental significance and ceases to be a field separate from the Church. The dichotomy between sacred and profane that has so deeply troubled the life of the Church turns out to be, in light of the Bible, a false dichotomy left behind in the Eucharist. The Church lives *in* the world (Jn. 17:11) and in the Eucharist she takes the world and refers it to God as Christ's own sacrifice and resurrection. But in doing so the Church judges the world, for the hands that take the world and offer it to God are the hands of the *baptized*, that is to say the hands of those dead to the world. And the eucharistic offering of the world presupposes that it will undergo its own *baptism* at the hands of the baptized — its own death and resurrection to a new life. A Eucharist not preceded by baptism is inconceivable. That is why the Church not only does not cease to repeat God's call to the world to repentance, but also, because it is the priest of the world, the Church will maintain 'closed doors' until the return of the Lord.

Concluding Remarks

We have attempted to consider the Eucharist as seen in the light of the New Testament. This is not an easy task because, over the course of the centuries that separate us from that time, the Eucharist has been overloaded with comments and accents that have obscured the original figure. The task is also made difficult by the paucity of testimony — in the final analysis — that the New Testament provides. Finally, the limits of this short chapter made the task difficult by preventing an exhaustive study of all the problems relating to our subject. Nevertheless, a few points stand out clearly in our brief presentation. From them, we are now able to formulate some general conclusions about the meaning of the Eucharist for the Church today.

a) The Eucharist was instituted by our Lord as a meal in the context of Easter and the story of the people of God in general. That is why the Eucharist is really about *historical human existence*. In its nature as *anamnesis* it affirms the identity of humanity with the history of salvation: with all that God has done, is doing and will do for humanity and for all of creation, as well as 'with all the saints' of all the ages. The Eucharist is the most historical act of the Church; it is the sanctification of time and of memory to the point of bringing them both into the very life and love of God.

However, because of this affirmation and sanctification of time and memory, history in the Eucharist is 'conditioned' very clearly by eschatology, that is to say by the 'new age', by the 'things to come'. It is a memorial that also includes the Kingdom of God by anticipation, or rather by giving a foretaste. In the Eucharist the Church realizes in its historical (yet sacramental) existence what it is destined to become when the Lord comes. Its celebration should therefore manifest this mystery and make it profoundly felt. This eschatological 'in-breaking' in the historical dimension that takes place in the Eucharist, this foretaste of the 'new age', is only possible 'in the Spirit'. The New Testament knows of no other way that 'the last days' enter into history than in 'the outpouring of the Holy Spirit' (Acts 2:17). And the Eucharist cannot be an *anamnesis* of Christ (that is to say it cannot realize here and now not only what Christ *has done*, but also what Christ *will do* when he makes 'all things new'), except by the coming of the Spirit. The Eucharist only becomes what it ought to be by *epiclesis*, and therefore it is not based only upon historical realities, but on *prayer*.[52]

Thus, the Eucharist occupies a central place in the historical existence of humanity. The Eucharist offers humanity the opportunity to be included fully into history without becoming a slave. It enables

---

52   This means that we must not understand the Eucharist as something static, but as a *dynamic* reality, as the Church's journey towards the *Kingdom*. And yet we must not believe that this march is *progressive*, leading the Church inexorably to its goal. The 'epicletic' character of the Eucharist does not permit this sort of historical determinism, explicitly or implicitly, because in each celebration the Kingdom *in its fullness* enters into history and is realized existentially *there and then*.

humanity to look beyond what *is* determined in time and space, towards what *might be* and what must be, that is to say, towards what constitutes the *ultimate meaning* of time and history.

b) In the New Testament the Eucharist is *communion*. To eat the body of Christ and to drink his blood is to participate in the One who took upon himself the 'many' (the 'Servant of God' or the 'Son of man') in order to make *a single body, His body*. That is why the Eucharist concerns the *personal existence* of humanity. For in the Eucharist, humans affirm their personal existence in the context of communion. It offers them the possibility of being fully themselves without being slaves to themselves, and it makes each one fully capable of saying 'I', but always in relation to 'you' and 'us', which is to say, it helps humans to lose themselves as individuals and to become persons.

Again, however, this cannot be realized except 'in the Spirit', which pours out the charisms upon the members of the body (1 Cor. 12). The eucharistic *synaxis* is the place of the manifestation of the charisms par excellence (1 Cor. 14), for they find their meaning in personal existence, that is to say in the relations of communion (1 Cor. 12:12-31). That is why the greatest charism is love (1 Cor. 12:31; 13:13), which survives into the *eschaton* (1 Cor. 13:8-13) and gives the Eucharist its character as *agape*.

This means that the Eucharist, being communion, cannot be simply a *horizontal* communion, which would reduce human existence to its historical dimension. This dimension certainly must not be destroyed in the Eucharist, which is a *meal*, a *food*, and a *celebration*, terms that must be taken in the strongest sense when they express communion in terms of everyday life. It is necessary to reject (just as vigorously as the modern proponents of 'secularization') all 'disembodied' eucharistic piety that would do away with this historical dimension. Yet the New Testament also indicates that the Eucharist is more than this. The 'spiritual' and 'charismatic' character of the Eucharistic communion does not destroy the 'horizontal communion', but rather highlights the real and ultimate meaning of communion: not to be enslaved by the historical dimension in which we live. The possibilities of 'communion' are so immense that they go beyond our experience of communion in the life of God. In the eucharistic point of view, humans will not grasp themselves until they are placed in the light of the *ultimate* meaning of communion (1 Jn. 3:2) and thus are led beyond the 'horizontal' dimension without in any way abandoning it.

c) As the New Testament demonstrates, communion in the Eucharist is an 'eating of *food*' (Acts 2:46). As food, it places humanity in relation to nature, affirming and illuminating our *natural life* in two ways. First, it emphasizes the fact that nature and creation, seen as a whole, must not be rejected under the pretence of some sort of 'super-natural'. The Eucharist accepts and sanctifies *all* creation 'recapitulated' in the unique body of 'the firstborn of all creation'. Second, by that very fact the Eucharist judges the world, because it calls the world to be reconciled with God in Christ — whose death and resurrection make this reconciliation possible. This concerns humanity first and foremost, because it is our rebellion against God that has reversed the order of the world (Rom. 8:22). The Eucharist calls humanity to relate the world to God; it *is* itself this offering to God, an *anaphora*. It follows that the Eucharist is linked inseparably to the proclamation of the *Word of God* that calls humanity, and through humanity all creation, to return to God (*métanoia*) *and to baptism* which brings humanity and the world, by its renunciation, to a new life (*anagenesis*). Accordingly, in the Eucharist, humanity acts as the priest of creation in the name and because of the priesthood of Christ, the high priest *par excellence*.

Consequently, the Eucharist illuminates the relationship between humanity and nature. It offers humans the possibility of fully enjoying nature and the possibility of being kings without being enslaved and without each one claiming for his- or herself alone. For when humans claim creation for themselves, the order of the world is reversed and creation wars with God. The Eucharist reveals that humanity, rather than being the owner of creation, is the priest who offers it to God, thus freeing nature and humanity from their own limitations.

d) Finally, the New Testament presents the communion of the Eucharist as a community. It is essential to the witness of the New Testament that the Eucharist is the 'gathering in one place' of the people of God scattered, the convocation of the 'many' so that it might become 'one'; that is to say the body of the one who has taken upon himself the 'many', in order to save them by bringing them back to God. Thus, the Eucharist is the eschatological *synaxis* where the eschatological unity of the people of God, the Church, is prefigured. The structure of this *synaxis* is therefore the essential structure of the Church itself and its president occupies the place of the one through whom the 'many' became a single body. Each 'order' cannot be considered in itself, but only in relation to the community just as it appears in this context.

e) The Eucharist is thus a *closed community*; this is clear from the testimony of the New Testament that we have examined and it is supported by the fact that, in the Eucharist, the Church becomes the eschatological judge of the world. This manifests itself in *two* ways. On the one hand, the Eucharist is a closed community when we view it as a celebration with its 'doors closed' to the world, which means first that the world *hates* the Church (Jn. 15:18-25; 20:19) because its mere presence is a sign of the final judgement of the world. It is for this reason that the Church and the world are in a state of *opposition* (as the writings of John make clear), but they are not therefore in a state of *separation* (as theologians erroneously understood them to be for the last several centuries). *Baptism* expresses at the sacramental level that the Church, and the eucharistic community in particular, excludes the world. As the prerequisite for the Eucharist that is also linked inseparably to it, baptism forms the *border* between the eucharistic community and the world, again not in the sense of separation, but in the sense of a *crisis within* creation itself. This is one of the ways that the Eucharist described by the New Testament is shown to be a closed and exclusive community.

On the other hand, there is a form of exclusion *within* the community of the baptized. As we have seen, the members of this community stand trial before receiving communion, every time a problem disturbs the relations within the community (1 Cor. 5; Mt. 18:7; etc.). And while it is true that exclusion from communion has here an eschatological significance (Mt. 18:17-20), it is located on the other side of the 'renunciation' that occurs in baptism and should not be confused or identified with this decision.[53] The Churches with their divisions are themselves found in this situation of *post-baptismal* exclusion.

In the New Testament, the rupture of communion appears at the level of individual excommunication. The 'schisms' referenced in the first letter to the Corinthians do not suggest that the communion has been fractured and separated at the level of 'groups' in the Church at Corinth. The rupture of communion between communities is a post-New Testament phenomenon and the formation of 'confessional' communities with a closed communion appears very late indeed. So the problem of 'intercommunion' as it appears today is beyond the scope of the New Testament. But we are able to find, thanks to its light, information that may help to solve this problem if we liken the current situation to the case of exclusion that we discussed above. Our current eucharistic rupture corresponds to the *post*-baptismal, but *pre*-Eucharist exclusion mentioned in the New Testament. From the liturgical point of view, we can say that these exclusions occur, not at the moment of baptism that precedes the Eucharist, but at the moment of the kiss of peace (due to a lack of love) or at the moment of the 'sermon' (which is to say because of differing interpretations of the Word of God), or in some cases at both of these moments.

---

53   There has been in the history of the Church attempts to confuse or to identify these two kinds of 'exclusiveness'. But the fundamental decision not to re-baptize and the encouragement of the practice of penance demonstrates that the Church has taken a clear stand against all identification or confusion.

Our question today can be formulated as follows: to what extent can a community be eucharistic without being one in spirit and in heart? And, given the historical relativism in which the Church lives, to what extent are we able to establish the minimal unity of spirit and love before communion? These legitimate questions are raised when the problem of intercommunion is contemplated in the light of the Eucharist as we have treated it here. But keeping the liturgical image, any formulation of the question that would *reverse* the order of the Eucharist, and place the eucharistic communion *before* the kiss of peace or the reading of the Scriptures, would alter the biblical vision of the Eucharist in a fundamental way, for then receiving communion would lose its eschatological (ultimate and final) character. The problem of intercommunion is thus inextricable from the very roots of our divisions. But on the road to a solution to this problem, the Churches should remember the biblical order: 'So when you are offering your gift at the altar, if you remember that your brother or sister has something against you, leave your gift at the altar and go; *first* be reconciled to your brother or sister, and *then* come and offer your gift' (Mt. 5:23-24).

CHAPTER TWO

THE EUCHARIST AND THE KINGDOM OF GOD

For the things of the Old Testament are the shadow. Those of the New are an image. Truth is the state of things to come.

- Maximus the Confessor

Introduction

The Divine Liturgy is an image of the Kingdom of God, an image of the last times. There is nothing so clear as this in the Orthodox liturgy. Our liturgy begins with the invocation of the Kingdom, continues with the representation of it, and ends with our participation in the Supper of the Kingdom, our union and communion with the life of God in Trinity.

Strangely, our theology in recent years does not seem to have given appropriate weight to the eschatological dimension of the Eucharist. Its principal interest appears to lie in the relationship of the Eucharist less with the last things than with the past, with the Last Supper and Golgotha. Perhaps we have yet another serious influence from the 'Babylonian captivity' of Orthodox theology, to quote the ever-memorable Georges Florovsky.[1] Western theology, both Roman Catholic and Protestant, has indeed focused its attention on the relationship between the Eucharist and Golgotha, because in the West, culminating in the theology of Anselm, the quintessence of the divine Economy is to be found in Christ's sacrifice on the Cross.[2] Everything flows from this, everything leads up to it. The Kingdom is something that has to do only with the end of history, not with its present. For

---

1   In his book *The Eucharist*, 1988, Alexander Schmemann is sharply critical of academic theology in relation to other aspects of its eucharistic theology. His criticisms deserve particular attention.

2   Characteristically, the Roman Catholic theologian Maurice de la Taille is quite clear in his monumental work *Mysterium Fidei de Augustissimo Corporis et Sanguinis Christi Sacrificio atque Sacramento*, 1921, p. 581: the *res tantum*, that is, the ultimate meaning of the Eucharist and all the sacraments, is our union with the sacrifice of Christ on the Cross. Compare this with Saint Maximus the Confessor, below.

Western theology as a whole, the resurrection of Christ is nothing more than a confirmation of the saving work of the cross. The essential part has already been accomplished in the sacrifice on the cross. Besides, for Western Christians the crucial and constitutive moment of the Eucharist is the repetition of the 'words of institution' of the Mystery: 'Take, eat, this is my body...' and not the invocation of the Holy Spirit, whose presence is necessarily linked with the coming of the 'last days' (Acts 2:18).

Thus the question which has for centuries dominated the dispute between Roman Catholics and Protestants in the West is whether or not the Eucharist is a repetition of the sacrifice on Golgotha, not whether it is an image of the last times. Orthodox theology also became embroiled in the same question, particularly from the seventeenth century onwards (the Orthodox *Confessions* of Peter of Mogila, Cyril Loukaris, Dositheus of Jerusalem, etc.), with the result that the connection of the Eucharist with the last times, with the Kingdom of God, was overlooked.

This tendency to forget the eschatological significance of the Eucharist would not concern us if it had not had very grave consequences for the way the Liturgy is celebrated, the piety of the faithful and the whole life of the Church. As a result, it is necessary even today to emphasize and bring to the forefront of our consciousness the connection between the Eucharist and the Kingdom. Despite being glaringly obvious in our Liturgy, this connection tends to disappear or lose its force under the weight of other kinds of questions and other forms of piety, with the result that we are misled into notions alien to the true Orthodox tradition, often thinking that we are defending Orthodoxy, whereas in fact we are reproducing and promoting ideas foreign to its tradition.

I. Part One

1. The Biblical Evidence

Proving the eschatological character of the Divine Eucharist in the New Testament would not require much effort. The description of the Last Supper in the Gospels already orientates us towards the Kingdom of God. The Twelve partake of the Supper as a foreshadowing of the new Israel, and for this reason the Evangelist Luke places within the narrative of the Last Supper the words of Christ to the Twelve: 'As my Father appointed a *Kingdom* for me, so do I appoint for you that you may eat and drink at my table *in my Kingdom*, and sit on thrones judging the twelve tribes of Israel' (Lk. 22:29-30). As we shall see later, this passage is very important in the origin and shaping of the various functions in the Eucharist, and in the Church more generally. For the moment, we note the fact that the Last Supper was an *eschatological* event, inextricably bound up with the Kingdom of God. This is why in the course of the Supper, Christ refers to the Kingdom explicitly and with particular intensity of feeling: 'I have earnestly desired to eat this Passover with you before I suffer, for I tell I you I shall never eat it again until it is fulfilled *in the Kingdom of God...* for I tell you that from now on I shall not drink of the fruit of the vine *until the Kingdom of God comes*' (Lk. 22:15-16, 18 and parallels).

In the context of the strongly eschatological character which the Last Supper has in the Gospels, Christ's commandment to his disciples, 'Do this in memory of me', cannot be unrelated to the Kingdom of God. As has already been observed by well-known biblical theologians (Joachim Jeremias[3] and others), the 'remembrance' of which the Lord speaks is most likely to refer to the remembrance of Christ before the throne of God in the Kingdom which is to come. In other words, the eucharistic remembrance is in fact a remembrance, a foreshadowing, a foretaste and a 'fore-gift' of Christ's future Kingdom. As we shall see below, the Divine Liturgy of Saint John Chrysostom which is celebrated in our Church expresses this with a clarity which challenges our common sense. The remembrance, then, of the Last Supper, and by extension of the Eucharist, is a remembrance not only of past events, but also of future 'events', i.e. of the Kingdom of God[4] as the culmination and fulfilment of the whole history of salvation.

But the most significant point in confirmation of the eschatological character of the Eucharist is the fact that the roots of the Eucharist are to be found historically not only in the Last Supper but also in Christ's appearances during the forty days after the resurrection. During these appearances, we have the breaking of bread and the risen Christ eating with his disciples (Lk. 24; Jn. 21). The prevailing atmosphere is one of joy, since the resurrection has demonstrated God's victory over His

---

3   In his classic work *Die Abendmahlsworte Jesu*, especially the third edition, 1960.

4   The phrase 'Kingdom of heaven' should not be understood as some kind of static state above the earth (a kind of Platonic notional or ideal reality). It is quite simply a paraphrase of the expression 'Kingdom of God', since the phrase 'the heavens' paraphrases the word 'God', which the Jewish Christians voided using out of reverence (cf. Saint Matthew's Gospel, where the phrase occurs 31 times — see Jeremias, *New Testament Theology*, I, 1971, p. 97). This observation has been thought necessary because in the thinking of the faithful, the phrase 'Kingdom of heaven' is very often translated as 'heavenly Kingdom', i.e. in spatial and often Platonic contrast with whatever exists or is done on earth (see below). In the New Testament, as Jeremias observes, 'the Kingdom is always and everywhere understood in eschatological terms. It signifies the time of salvation, the consummation of the world, the restoration of broken communion between God and man' (*New Testament Theology*, p. 102).

enemies, which is the dawning of Christ's Kingdom in history. It is not accidental that in the Acts of the Apostles, Luke stresses that the early Church celebrated the Eucharist 'with glad hearts' (Acts 2:46). Only the Resurrection and the Parousia could justify, or rather necessitate, such an atmosphere of rejoicing.

This eschatological orientation of the Eucharist is evident in the first eucharistic communities. The Aramaic expression *maranatha* (1 Cor. 16:22), which is unquestionably a liturgical-eucharistic term, is eschatological in content (the Lord is near, or is coming, or will come). When the Apostle Paul repeats the eucharistic words of the Lord (1 Cor. 11:23-26), he adds a reference to the Second Coming ('until He comes').[5] The Revelation of John, which is basically a eucharistic text and seems to have had an influence on the shaping of the Orthodox Liturgy, does not only consider the Eucharist an image of the Kingdom, something that takes place before the Throne of God and the Lamb; it also ends with an emphatic reference to the expectation of the last times: 'The Spirit and the Bride say, "Come." And let him who hears say, "Come" ...Amen. Come, Lord Jesus!' (Rev. 22:17, 20).

This vivid expectation of the last times has disappeared from our eucharistic consciousness. And yet if the Book of Revelation is inaccessible for various reasons to the members of our eucharistic assemblies, there is another text which is not only at the heart of the Divine Liturgy but on the lips of all believers within the Liturgy and outside it, which ought to remind us strongly of this expectation. It is the Lord's Prayer.

This prayer has now lost both its eschatological and its eucharistic character in our minds. And yet we must not forget that this prayer was not only eschatological from the first, but also formed the centre and the core of all the ancient Liturgies: it is not impossible, indeed, that its historical roots were eucharistic. In this prayer there are two prominent references to the last times[6] which usually escape us. One is the petition 'hallowed be Thy Name, Thy Kingdom come', which reminds us of the 'Maranatha' and 'Come, Lord' of the first eucharistic liturgies. The second, and more important, is the petition 'Give us this day our daily (*epiousion*) bread'. Exegetes have been unable to agree on the meaning

---

5   The meaning of this passage is: 'we proclaim the death of the Lord looking with joy for His coming' (J. Moffat, *The First Epistle of Paul to the Corinthians*, 1954, p. 169). Cf. Acts 2:46: 'in gladness'. The earlier theory of H. Leitzmann, that the Eucharist was celebrated in the Pauline Churches in an atmosphere of sadness as a remembrance of Christ's death, but in an atmosphere of joy in the Church of Jerusalem, is shown to be wrong. In each case, the Eucharist was celebrated in an atmosphere of joy and gladness because of its connection with the Kingdom.

6   It is probable that the other petitions, such as 'forgive us our trespasses' and 'lead us not into temptation' also have an eschatological meaning.

of these words.[7] There is, however, plenty of evidence leading to the conclusion that the 'bread' we ask for in this prayer is not the ordinary bread we eat every day, which is the way we usually understand it, but the Bread of the Eucharist, which is *epiousios* in the sense that it is 'of that which is coming' or 'to come' — in other words, of the Kingdom which is to come. However much this phrase in the Lord's Prayer admits of differing interpretations, the position in the Divine liturgy which this prayer has occupied with notable consistency from earliest times, i.e. immediately before Holy Communion, is evidence that, at least in the mind of the early Church, the petition for *epiousios* bread refers not to the bread we eat every day, but to the meal and the nourishment of the Kingdom. This is 'the bread which comes down from heaven', in other words the flesh or body of the 'Son of Man' (Jn. 6:33-34) — who, it should be noted, is also an eschatological figure. In the Eucharist, we ask today for the bread of tomorrow, the future or 'coming' bread of the Kingdom.

One could add many other elements from Scripture which bear witness to the eschatological character of the Eucharist and its connection with the Kingdom of God. But where we find this connection expounded in depth and established in the consciousness of the Church is in the theology of the Greek Fathers and the eucharistic liturgies of the ancient Church, which continue to be in use in our Church.

2. The Kingdom which is to Come — The Cause and Archetype of the Church

Amidst the wealth of patristic evidence for a connection between the Eucharist and the Kingdom, we may single out one truly important passage from Saint Maximus the Confessor which, so far as we know, has not yet received the attention it deserves from our theologians. This passage indicates not only the unbreakable connection between the Eucharist and the Kingdom, but also the *radical overturning of the ancient Greek notion of causality*. Apart from anything else, this demonstrates how unjust and far from the reality is the very prevalent notion that Maximus was influenced by ancient Greek philosophy, Platonic and

---

7   The question hinges on whether the term *epiousios* comes from *epeinai* or *epousia*. If the latter, it would mean 'essential for our existence', but if it comes from *epienai*, which would mean 'coming' or 'day which is to come'. The antithesis in the text between *epiousios* and 'this day' and the evidence of the ancient sources in both East and West both point to the second of these two meanings. But even if it is talking about the bread we eat every day, as Ernst Lohmeyer points out (*The Lord's Prayer*, 1965, p. 15), all Jesus' references to bread and meals have an eschatological meaning.

Aristotelian. First we shall set out this passage in its entirety, so that we can go on to comment on it in relation to our theme. In his *Scholia* on Dionysius the Areopagite's work *On the Church Hierarchy*, Maximus writes:

> [The Areopagite] calls 'images (*eikones*) of what is true' the rites that are now performed in the synaxis… For these things are symbols, not the truth… From the effects. That is, from what is accomplished visibly to the things that are unseen and secret, which are the causes and archetypes of things perceptible. For those things are called causes which in no way owe the cause of their being to anything else. Or from the effects to the causes, that is, from the perceptible symbols to what is noetic and spiritual. Or from the imperfect to the more perfect, from the type to the image; and from the image to the truth. For the things of the Old Testament are the shadow; those of the New Testament are the image. The truth is the state of things to come.[8]

In this passage, Saint Maximus interprets in his own way the concept of the Eucharist as *image* and *symbol* in relation to the concept of *causality*. What takes place in the Divine Eucharist is an 'image' and 'symbol' of what is 'true'. Reading this passage up to a certain point, one seems to be moving in an atmosphere of Platonism. The things 'accomplished visibly' are images and symbols of the 'unseen' and 'secret': perceptible symbols are images of what is 'noetic and spiritual'. In accordance with the Platonic view, the perceptible and visible world is an image of a stable and eternal world which, being noetic and spiritual, is the truth, the true world. In consequence, one would say that what is accomplished in the Divine Liturgy is an image and reflection of the heavenly Liturgy which is accomplished eternally, and which is the 'archetype' of the earthly Eucharist. That would indeed be a typically Platonic understanding of the Eucharist.

But Maximus has a surprise in store for us at the end of this passage. The Divine Eucharist is for him an image of the true Eucharist which is nothing other than 'the state of things to come'. The 'truth of what is now accomplished in the synaxis' is to be found not in a Platonic type of ideal reality but in a 'reality of the future', in the Kingdom which is to come. The crucial element which overturns the Platonic relationship between archetype and image is *the category of time*. To get from the image to the prototype we do not have to go outside time, but we certainly have to pass through the expectation of an 'event' or state which lies in the future. This changes the whole mentality

8   PG 4:137.

from a Platonic to a biblical one. For while it is impossible in Platonic thought to pass from the image to the archetype through time, as if the archetype were to be found at the end of history, in the biblical understanding it is essential. On the biblical understanding, as in that of Saint Maximus, what is represented in the Eucharist is *what is to come*, *He who comes* and the *Kingdom* which He will establish.

But this passage is important also because it poses the problem of causality, thus overturning not only Platonic but also Aristotelian notions of 'entelechy' and causality. Causes, says Maximus, are those which do not in any way owe their cause to anything else. In ancient Greek and Western thought, as in common sense, a cause is logically but also chronologically prior to its effect. In the thought of Saint Maximus, however, the further back we go in time, the further we get away from the archetype, from the cause: the Old Testament is 'shadow', the New Testament is 'image' and the 'state of things to come' is truth. In other words the archetype, the cause of 'what is accomplished in the synaxis', lies in the future. *The Eucharist is the result of the Kingdom which is to come*. The Kingdom which is to come, a future event (the state of things to come), being the *cause* of the Eucharist, gives it its true *being*.

This is what comes out of a careful reading of Maximus. Later on we shall look at its existential significance — because this is what concerns theology in the final analysis, and not the historical or philosophical curiosity in which the theologians of our own day usually expend all their energies. For the time being, we note that the biblical connection between Eucharist and Kingdom, far from losing its force in the patristic period, was securely established on an ontological basis: the Eucharist is not simply connected with the Kingdom which is to come, it draws from it its being and its truth. Liturgical practice formed, and continues to form, the language in which the Church expresses this thesis. And we should pay attention to it.

3. Liturgical Practice

We usually think of the order of service as something secondary and unimportant. And it is indeed true that our Liturgy has come to be loaded down with a whole lot of secondary symbolisms and aesthetic decorations; but this does not mean that every rite in the Liturgy is unrelated to its essence. Liturgiologists, who are usually historians of liturgy with no theological or ecclesiological interests, do not enlighten us as to the theological content of the rites and the difference between the essential and the inessential. Thus our clergy especially, but also the laity, either consider every aspect of the order of service equally important and keep it religiously, or — and this is dangerous — they abbreviate, leave things out, change the order of these rites, etc., destroying the 'image' of the Kingdom that the Liturgy is meant to be. Thus we end up losing the representation of the last times in our Liturgy either because we have overloaded it with rites which do not express the coming of the Kingdom, or because we remove or mix up fundamental elements of the Liturgy and thus dangerously distort its eschatological character.

It would take an entire volume to describe what our Liturgy has suffered at the hands of its clergy. Instead of being guardians of the Apostolic Tradition — and let us not forget that Hippolytus gives the title of 'Apostolic Tradition' to nothing other than the description of how the Liturgy is performed — our bishops have become as a rule spectators, if not actual perpetrators, of this abuse. But many of these abuses produce such a distortion of the image of the last times that they should be noted, albeit briefly, since we are talking about the Eucharist as an icon of the Kingdom which is to come.

4. The Gathering 'In One Place'

One of the basic elements of the coming in the last days is the gathering of the scattered people of God — and by extension of all mankind — 'in one place' around the person of the Messiah, in order for the judgement of the world to take place and the Kingdom of God to prevail. In Saint Matthew's Gospel the Kingdom of God is likened to 'a net which was thrown into the sea and *gathered* fish of every kind' (Mt. 13:47), while in the description of the Parousia of the Son of Man we read yet more clearly that on that day of the last times 'before Him will be *gathered* all the nations' (Mt. 25:32). In John, again, the purpose of Christ's Passion and, by extension, of the whole work of salvation is considered to be not only the salvation of Israel, 'but to *gather into one* the children of God who are scattered abroad' (Jn. 11:52).

It is not incidental, therefore, that the Eucharist as image of the Kingdom is very early described as a 'gathering' (*synaxis*) or gathering 'in one place'. In the sixth chapter of Saint John's Gospel, in a passage which is clearly talking about the Eucharist, after the multitude has eaten its fill Jesus commands the fragments left over to be 'gathered up', which is considered a sign that He is 'He who is to come' (Jn. 6:12-14). We also know that the Eucharist is described as a gathering 'in one place' in Saint Paul (1 Cor. 11:20-23). The *Didache* gives us the most explicit description of the Eucharist as an image of the eschatological gathering of the scattered children of God, the Church: 'Even as this broken bread was scattered over the hills, and was gathered together and became one, so let Thy Church be gathered together from the ends of the earth into Thy Kingdom'.[9]

Indeed, what has become of this strong eschatological sense of the eucharistic gathering over the course of time? In Ignatius it clearly still survives,[10] and, as we have seen, in Maximus in the seventh century the Eucharist is consistently called 'synaxis' and considered an image of 'the state of things to come'. But little by little, the sense of the gathering of 'the whole Church' in one place (1 Cor. 14:23; Rom. 16:23) recedes, as does the eschatological character of the gathering. In the West, things reached the utter limit with the introduction and spread of the private mass, which the priest can celebrate on his own. But in the Orthodox Church too, even if celebration of the liturgy is not permitted without the presence of laity, it often happens that the laity are absent or 'symbolically' present in insignificant numbers. As it is now celebrated, our Eucharist is anything but an image of the eschatological gathering 'in one place'. Indeed, with the proliferation of eucharistic gatherings in parishes, chapels, monasteries etc., and with the bishop absent as head of the gathering of the 'whole Church' because the dioceses are geographically too large, the term 'gathering' has lost its meaning. We should be talking now about the dispersal of the faithful, rather than their gathering 'in one place'.

5. Passage through the Ascetic and Baptismal Experience

The coming of the Kingdom of God has no meaning unless the people of God have first passed through the 'catharsis' of trials, sorrows and death. The Messiah himself has to pass through these things in order to bring the Kingdom, and the people of God must do the same. A passage in Luke (22:28) is significant: those who pass through the 'trials' of Jesus are the ones to be given the privilege of eating and drinking at his table in his Kingdom. The entrance into the Kingdom is through the 'narrow gate' and 'strait way' of 'endurance', which in the first centuries meant in practice endurance of persecutions (the Epistle to the Hebrews lays particular emphasis on this), and later on meant the period of penitence and fasting which had to precede Baptism. (Great Lent, with its strict fast and its prohibition of the celebration of the Eucharist except on Saturdays and Sundays, is an indicative vestige of this, since baptism was initially performed on Easter day). In liturgical action, this was all expressed in Baptism, which already in the New

---

9   Did. 9:4.
10   See further my book, Eucharist, Bishop, Church: The Unity of the Church in the Divine Eucharist and the Bishop During the First Three Centuries, 2001.

Testament is linked with sacrifice and martyrdom (Mk. 10:39; Lk. 12:50), as also with death (Rom. 6:4; Col. 2:12), exactly as happened to Christ. The Areopagitic writings, the Cappadocians, and Maximus all speak of a stage of 'those being purified', which is identified liturgically with the catechumens who are preparing for 'illumination' (i.e. baptism), who enter into the rank of those 'made perfect' upon receiving chrismation and the Eucharist. (These ranks clearly refer to the sacraments of Baptism, Chrismation and the Eucharist and not to monks, at least in Saint Maximus.[11]

Thus the eucharistic gathering, as an image of the last times, certainly should involve only the baptized. In this sense, we are talking about a closed community which comes together 'the doors being shut' (Jn. 20:19; cf. the exclamation 'The doors! The doors!'). The Eucharistic gathering can never be a means and instrument of mission, because in the last times, which it represents, there will be no mission; anyway, mission presupposes dispersal, not a gathering 'in one place'. Consequently, it is contrary to the nature of the Eucharist as image of the Kingdom to broadcast it over television or radio, whether for pastoral reasons or for the purpose of mission (a way of broadcasting and advertising the 'richness' and 'beauty' of our worship). In the Eucharist, one participates either 'gathered in one place', or not at all. Participation at a distance has no meaning. As for those who are sick or unable to come to the gathering, the Church's very ancient practice is to bring them the fruit of the gathering (Holy Communion, antidoron, etc.), and not the gathering itself, either aurally or visually.

6. The Eucharist as a Movement and Progression

With the weakening of the temporal dimension of the Eucharist as icon of the Kingdom which we look for, *which is to come*, there has also been a gradual loss of the sense that in the Divine Eucharist there is a movement 'towards the End'; the journey of the world, in Maximus' phrase, towards the Kingdom, and the coming of the Kingdom to the world. This terrible falsification has come about with the complete disappearance of the dimension of *entrance* within the Eucharist. Yes, the so-called 'entrances' (great and little) have been preserved in the Liturgy; except that 'entrances' is precisely what they are not. In reality they are circles made by the celebrant when he 'enters' into the altar where he was before. Since the prothesis and skevophylakion ceased to exist as special annexes of the church building,[12] the

---

11   See Maximus's *Scholia* (PG 4:168-9).

12   *Translator's note*: Early church would have a separate building or annex where sacred vessels and

clergy have gone into the altar (all that remains of the church proper) to do the proskomidia and put on their vestments. But then what is the point of the entrance, little or great? In fact it has no point, since the Eucharist has ceased to signify the journey to the Kingdom or the coming of the Kingdom, and become something static that takes place in space without reference to time.

From this point of view, it is interesting to look at the interpretations of the entrance in liturgical sources from the period when the entrance was a real entrance of the clergy and people, headed by the bishop, into the church and the altar. These interpretations are dominated by a typology which has the entry of the bishop as an image of Christ's first coming to earth in the flesh, with a clear description of the progression to the eschaton. In the seventh century, as Saint Maximus demonstrates in his *Mystagogy*, this early typology still survives.[13] For this Father, the bishop's entry into the church to celebrate the Eucharist is an image of the Lord's first coming to earth, and everything that follows leads directly to the eschatological setting of the Kingdom: the sacred readings, and in particular the Gospel, represent 'the end of this world', after which 'the bishop comes down from the throne' for the judgement, with the dismissal of the catechumens and the closing of the doors. From that moment on, everything takes place before the throne of God in His Kingdom.

> [The] entry of the holy and venerable mysteries [clearly the so-called 'Great Entrance'] is the beginning and prelude to the new teaching about God's economy towards us which *will* be imparted in heaven [note once again the future tense, which distances us from a Platonic type of correspondence between the heavenly and the earthly]... For God the Word says, I will not drink... any more of the fruit of the vine, until that day when I shall drink it new with you in my Father's Kingdom.

The kiss of peace also has an eschatological meaning, indicating 'the concord that *will prevail* [again, a reference to future time] amongst all at the time when the ineffable good things which are to come are revealed'. Even the Creed, despite its historical content, leads us to the future:

> The confession by everyone of the divine Creed points forward to the mystical thanksgiving which *will be rendered in the age to come* for the

---

vestments were kept, and where people would leave their eucharistic offerings on their way into church. The bread and wine for the Eucharist were selected from among these and prepared in the same place.

13   PG 91:688ff. — all quotes in this paragraph come from this section.

most marvellous principles and ways of God's most wise Providence towards us, by which we have been saved.

The hymn 'Holy, Holy, Holy' also leads us spiritually to the *future* state: 'It indicates the union and equality in honour with the bodiless spiritual powers which *will be manifest in the future.*' The Our Father also represents the future adoption 'in which all the saints *shall be called and shall be* sons of God through the grace which will come upon them'.

There exists, then, a continuous progression within the Eucharist; a progression which, according to Maximus at least (things change somewhat in later Byzantine commentators on the Liturgy) literally *moves us along* and sets us in the Kingdom which is to come. Everything in the Liturgy moves forward: nothing is static. The symbolism in the Liturgy is not that of a parable or allegory. It is the symbolism of an *icon* as that is understood by the Fathers of the Church, meaning participation in the *ontological content* of the prototype. And the prototype in this case, as can be seen in the passages of Saint Maximus just quoted, is the Kingdom which is to come, and our ultimate reconciliation and union with God when we are incorporated into Christ.

From all this one can understand how significant is the dimension of movement and progression in the typikon of the Liturgy. It is a pity to give the impression that everything in the Liturgy is performed in a static manner. The abolition of the entrances is a great liturgical loss. It is true, certainly, that the church architecture which now prevails does not permit the priests to make a real entrance as they did in the ancient Church. The bishops, however, are able to make an entrance, and it is a shame that they no longer do it, clearly because they no longer appreciate its significance.[14]

II. Part Two

1. The Sacrifice of the Paschal Lamb

The Divine Eucharist is a *sacrifice*. The patristic tradition in both East and West lays great stress on this aspect of the Eucharist. So, for instance: Cyril of Jerusalem, Gregory the Theologian, Cyril of

---

14   It makes no sense for the bishop to go into the sanctuary, put on his vestments there, and come out of the altar so as to go in again at the Little Entrance, when he could be vested outside the altar during matins — when matins is celebrated together with the Liturgy, or just before the beginning of the liturgy when it is not — (without the exclamations of the relevant verses, if it is not a festive liturgy). In all the Slavic Orthodox Churches this order is observed, thus preserving the character of the Little Entrance as a genuine entrance. In the Greek-speaking Churches, however (with the possible exception of the Church of Cyprus), it is not observed. And yet the significance of these despised liturgical details is real.

Alexandria, and John Chrysostom, as well as the Divine Liturgies of Saint John Chrysostom and of Saint Basil the Great which are celebrated in the Orthodox Church, call the Eucharist a sacrifice which is 'unbloody', 'reasonable', etc.[15] This sacrifice is none other than the death on the cross of Christ, whose body and blood are offered 'for many' (Mk. 14:24; Mt. 26:28); in other words, they have the effect of deliverance from sins, which are 'forgiven' thanks to this sacrifice and the 'communion' of the 'many' in it, which is the fount of 'eternal life'.

This sacrificial character of the Divine Eucharist is indisputable both in biblical consciousness and theology, and in that of the Fathers and the Liturgy. The point that we often tend to overlook or underestimate is the connection and relationship between this sacrificial character of the Eucharist and the coming of the Kingdom of God, the 'last times'. The Eucharist is indisputably the very sacrifice of the Lord upon the cross. But what is the relationship of this sacrifice with the coming of the Kingdom? This question is of vital importance for theology, and also for the way in which we as believers experience this great mystery of the Church.

All the indications from the story of the Last Supper, handed down to us by the Gospels and the Apostle Paul, testify that with the words 'this is My Body and this is My Blood' Christ was referring to Himself as the *Paschal Lamb* (cf. 1 Cor. 5:7f., 'for Christ our paschal lamb has been sacrificed for us'). This identification of Christ with the paschal lamb was so widespread in the early Church that it was repeated without elucidation, not only by the Apostle Paul but also by other texts from the apostolic age, such as 1 Peter (1:19), Revelation (5:6, 12; and 12:11), Saint John's Gospel (1:29, 36), *et al.* So it is not by chance that in the language of the Church's liturgy, the portion of the eucharistic bread which is changed into the body of Christ at the Divine Eucharist came to be called the Lamb.

The sacrifice of the paschal lamb has its roots in the exodus of Israel from Egypt, as described in the Book of Exodus (12:6). In the case of the Last Supper, however, it is clear that we have not merely a remembrance and repetition of the sacrifice of the lamb in Exodus, such as took place at every celebration of the Jewish Passover, but the sacrifice of the *perfect, eschatological* paschal Lamb. This is borne out by many

---

15   Cyril of Jerusalem (*Catechesis* 23.8, 9), Gregory the Theologian (*Oration.* 2.95 and 4.52), Cyril of Alexandria (*On the Mystical Supper* 5), and John Chrysostom (*On the Epistle to the Hebrews* 17.3). Chrysostom insists particularly on this aspect of the Eucharist, which he connects with the Last Supper and the sacrifice of Christ on the Cross, and *also with heavenly worship and the Kingdom*. See *On Hebrews* 11.2.3 and 14.1.2; *On the Priesthood* 3.4, and elsewhere. As to Latin Fathers, see for instance Ambrose (*On the Duties of the Clergy* 1.248, *On Faith* 4.124, and elsewhere), and Augustine (*Confessions* 9.32; *Enchiridion* 110; *On Psalms* 21 and 33; *City of God* 10.20 etc.).

elements in the story of the Last Supper in the Gospels, as also by the liturgical practice of the early Church. Let us refer to some of these as examples.

We have already underlined, at the beginning of this study, the fact that the Lord clearly links the Last Supper with the Kingdom of God, according to the account given us by the Gospels. What we must note here is the connection of the sacrifice to which Christ refers there with the New Covenant. It has already been observed by biblical scholars that the term 'covenant' should be regarded as equivalent to the term 'Kingdom of heaven'.[16] The sacrifice of Christ as the Paschal Lamb is the fulfilment of the eschatological purpose of the sacrifice both of the original paschal lamb in Exodus, and of all the subsequent sacrifices performed by the Jews in imitation of the sacrifice of that lamb. So when Christ says at the Last Supper, and the Church repeats in the course of the Eucharist, that 'this is my blood, the blood of the new covenant', our thoughts are directed towards the coming and establishment of the Kingdom of God, and not simply towards an event which took place in the past. The sacrifice of the Lord upon the cross cannot be isolated from its eschatological significance. Remission of sins is itself linked in the New Testament with the coming of the Kingdom (Mt. 6:12; Lk. 11:4; Jn. 30:23; etc.), and this surely applies especially to the remission of sins which stems from the sacrifice of Christ as Paschal Lamb.

Things are still clearer in the Book of Revelation, which without a doubt contains elements or fragments of ancient eucharistic liturgy.[17] In this book the description of Christ as the Lamb occurs repeatedly, and, without any doubt, in connection with the paschal lamb of Exodus 12:6. The eschatological significance that Revelation gives to the Lamb comes across clearly from the following remarks, which are of profound significance:

(a) The 'lamb that was slain' has the authority to open book with seven seals, the contents and meaning of which are revealed only at the end of history.

(b) The sacrifice of the Lamb does not concern only the people of Israel, but people 'from every tribe and tongue and people and nation' (Rev. 5:9). The universal character of this salvation suggests the end of history and the dawning of the 'day of the Lord' (1 Cor. 1:8; 1 Thes. 5:2; etc.). It is characteristic that the Apostle Paul, who awaits the

---

16   See J. Behm, '*Diathēkē*', *TDNT*, II, 1935.
17   See P. Prigent, *Apocalypse et Liturgie*, 1964. On the influence of this book on the Orthodox Liturgy see P. Bratsiotis, 'L'Apocalyse de saint Jean dans le culte de l'Eglise greque orthodoxe' *RHPR* 42 (1962), 116–121.

Second Coming of Christ imminently, regards as its 'first-fruits' the return of the gentiles and their grafting into the trunk of Israel (2 Thes. 2:13). Thus the fact that the blood of the Lamb is shed 'for all' refers us to the 'servant' of God in the book of Isaiah (chapters 52 and 53) who 'bore the sin of many and was given up for their sins' (53:12, LXX), but who also in the last times *will bring together the scattered Israel* and will be 'a light to the nations, that my salvation may reach to the end of the earth' (Isa. 49:6), because 'many nations will wonder at Him... for they that have been told of Him shall see, and they that have not heard shall understand' (Isa. 52:15, LXX).

(c) In particular, we should note the connection in the book of Revelation between the Lamb that was slain and the 'new song', the 'alleluia' which is repeated three times by a great multitude and by the whole of creation ('like the sound of many waters') in the context of the marriage of the Lamb and the worship of him (Rev. 19:1-8).

The fact that this 'alleluia' is an eschatological hymn is made clear by the reason given for it in the text itself, 'For the Lord our God the Almighty reigns' (Rev. 19:6): in other words, the Kingdom of God has been established. This is also why, despite the fact that the lamb has been *slain*, the prevailing tone is one of joy: 'let us rejoice and be glad' (Rev. 19:7), recalling the 'in gladness' of Acts (2:46) in connection with the celebration of the Eucharist by the first Christians.

These observations take on even greater interest if this hymn is connected with the Last Supper itself. The Gospels note (Mt. 26:30; Mk. 14:26) that immediately after the supper and the words of Christ, which connect it with the Kingdom, 'when [Christ and the Disciples] *had sung a hymn,* they went out to the Mount of Olives'. As scholars indicate, this refers to the *hallel* which followed the Jewish paschal meal, in other words the singing of Psalms 114-118 (113-117) antiphonally, with one of the group reading the text aloud while the others (cf. the 'multitude' or the 'people' in Revelation) would respond with 'alleluia' after the middle of each verse. Already in Christ's time these psalms had an eschatological-messianic meaning for the Jews. But does not the same apply to us Orthodox, who preserve faithfully the liturgical tradition of the ancient Church which carries on the worship of the first Church? The verses which end Psalm 118 (117) — 'This is the day which the Lord has made; let us rejoice and be glad in it' — are clearly eschatological in Orthodox worship, since 'this day' for us is the day of the resurrection. The final verses of that psalm ('Blessed is he that comes in the name of the Lord... the Lord is God and has appeared unto us', etc.) have the same eschatological character.

Conclusion: the Last Supper and the Lamb slain for our salvation cannot be understood without reference to the 'last day', the 'day of the Lord', the Parousia and the establishment of the Kingdom of God. In the words of Saint Cyril of Alexandria, the Eucharist is not simply 'the performance of the dread sacrifice' but 'the gift of immortality and a pledge of life without end'.[18]

This conclusion is reinforced and confirmed by another observation; the ancient Church never celebrated its Mystical Supper, the Divine Eucharist, on the same day as the Lord's death but *after* it. It is known from history that Christians in Asia Minor in the second century celebrated Easter on the fourteenth of Nissan, the same day as the Jewish Passover. It is significant, however, that they did not celebrate the Eucharist except at dawn the next day, in other words after the Jews' paschal meal, during which the Christians fasted. The fact that even today the Orthodox Church, following the ancient tradition, waits for the Jewish Passover to pass and only then celebrates its own Passover (Easter) is not simply due, as is often held, to an anti-Jewish stance on its part; apart from anything else, it is due to the fact that the Passover of the Church, which is associated with joy and gladness, cannot precede the moment in time at which, historically, the Last Supper took place and the crucifixion followed. That time is a time of fasting, while Easter is a time of *festivity*.

Have we ever seriously thought why the Church dissociated not only its Passover, but also its Eucharist, from fasting, and linked it with the radiance of the resurrection? It is significant, as we noted earlier, that celebration of the Eucharist on fast days was forbidden by the Church. (The exception of the Exaltation of the Cross and the commemoration of the Forerunner does not negate the rule). This has been confined, of course, to the period of Great Lent,[19] but the sense remains: the Eucharist is an eschatological event, and cannot be other than festive, joyful and radiant. Its sacrificial character is transformed into the joy of the resurrection, which means eschatological joy. In Christ there is no such thing as sacrifice without deliverance. And deliverance does not just mean remission of personal sins, in accordance with the Western spirit, Latin and Protestant, but the ultimate transfiguration of the world, the overcoming of corruption and death. This is what we celebrate when we perform the Eucharist a sacrifice on the cross which takes its meaning from the resurrection, as the first realization in history of the Kingdom which is to come.

---

18   PG 77:1028.

19   According to the testimony of the historians Socrates (*Church History* 5.22) and Sozomen (*Church History* 7.19), in the early Church, at least in Alexandria, the Eucharist was not celebrated on any fast day throughout the year, and not just during Lent.

2. A Festival of the Resurrection

The most eloquent proof of the eschatological character of the Eucharist and its identification with the foretaste of the Kingdom of God is the fact that from the beginning it has been associated with Sunday, as the most appropriate day for its celebration. We referred above to the Quartodecimans in Asia Minor in the second century, who celebrated Easter on the fourteenth of the month of Nissan. This, of course, involved celebration of the Eucharist on a day other than Sunday, at least on Easter day. As is well known, this custom gave rise to the paschal controversy which threatened to divide the early Church because, apart from anything else, it created variations in the time of fasting in places such as Rome, where Easter was celebrated on Sunday by the local Church, and not according to the practice of the Quartodecimans, who came from Asia Minor and were living in Rome in the second century. But it was not long before this custom gave way, and the celebration of Easter and performance of the Eucharist on Sunday became general. Evidence for connection of the Eucharist with Sunday could start with the Acts of the Apostles (20:7) and the First Epistle to the Corinthians (16:2) and proceed to Revelation (1:10), the *Didache* (14:1) and Justin (*First Apology* 67) who is clear on this question.

But why Sunday? What led the Church to this practice? What is the deeper theological meaning of this practice?

Sunday is the day of the *resurrection* of Christ. The Christians regarded it thus from the beginning,[20] on the basis of the biblical evidence that the resurrection took place 'on the first day of the week' (Mk. 16:2; cf. Mt. 28:1 and Lk. 24:1). But the meaning that they gave to the resurrection of Christ from the beginning was very profound, and was necessarily carried over both to Sunday and to the Eucharist which was celebrated on that day. It is worth noting some of the fundamental aspects of this meaning in order to understand better the relationship between Eucharist and Kingdom.

As the day of the resurrection, Sunday is the *eighth day*. The reason is that the 'new creation' begins on this day, when 'our Christ appeared risen from the dead, it being forever, however, the first in terms of its significance. For Christ, being the firstborn of all creation, again became the chief of another race, that which is regenerated by Him...'.[21] Saint Basil the Great throws light on the eschatological

---

20   See, for example, Ignatius (*Magn.* 9; *Epistle of Barnabas* 15.8ff.); Justin (*Apol.* I, 67; *Dialogue* 41 and 138); Tertullian (*On Prayer* 23); and Eusebius (*Church History* III.27.5; *Apostolic Constitutions* 2.59; 5.19, 20, etc.).

21   Justin, *Dialogue* 138.

character of the 'eighth day' in his work *On the Holy Spirit*, when he writes the following highly significant words, which we must not forget when we speak about the Divine Eucharist:

> Thus we all look to the east at our prayers, but few of us know that we are seeking our own old country, Paradise, which God planted in Eden in the east. *We pray standing on the first day of the week*, but we do not all know the reason. *On the day of the resurrection* we remind ourselves of the grace given to us by standing at prayer, *not only because we are risen with Christ and are bound to seek those things which are above, but because that day seems to us in some sense an image of the age which we expect*. Therefore, though it is the beginning of days, it is not called by Moses 'first' but 'one'... as though the same day often recurred. Now 'one' and 'eighth' are the same, in itself distinctly indicating that day which is really 'one' and truly 'eighth'... *the state which follows after this present time, the day which knows no end or evening, and no successor, that age which does not end or grow old*. Of necessity, then, *the Church teaches her own foster-children to offer their prayers on that day standing, in order that through the constant reminder of the endless life* we may not neglect to make provision for our removal thither. Moreover, all of Pentecost is *a reminder of the resurrection expected in the age to come*. For that one and first day, if seven times multiplied by seven, completes the seven weeks of the holy Pentecost... And so it is a likeness of eternity... *On this day* the rules of the Church have educated us *to prefer the upright attitude of prayer, for by their plain reminder they, as it were, make our mind to dwell no longer in the present but in the future*.[22]

We have quoted this lengthy passage in its entirety because it gives us quite clearly the eschatological meaning of Sunday and of the Eucharist which is celebrated on that day. We note in particular that for Saint Basil, the avoidance of kneeling on Sunday[23] is necessitated not only by the fact that it is the day of the resurrection, but also by the *expectation of the age to come*, so that our minds are made to dwell 'no longer in the present but in the future'. This strong impetus *towards what is to come*, not simply towards what is above, brings the dimension of *time* into eschatology, and recalls what we have said above in commenting on the relevant passages of Saint Maximus: the eschatology of the Divine Liturgy, like that of Sunday, is not a Platonic type of representation of a heavenly state, but a *movement and progression* towards the future. Maximus and Basil concur on this point.

---

22   27.66.
23   The prohibition of kneeling on Sunday goes back to ancient times, as Irenaeus testifies in his lost work, *On the Pascha*. See fragment 6 in the series *Library of the Greek Fathers*, V, 1955, p. 174.

It is noteworthy, again, that Saint Basil refers to praying towards the east. For the east was not only the place of the original paradise, but also the direction from which the Lord is expected to appear at his Second Coming. As Saint John of Damascus says, summarizing the reasons for praying towards the east: there are many reasons, and they include the future coming of the Son of Man from the east according to the Gospel passage (Mt. 24:27), 'as the lightning comes from the east and shines as far as the west, so will be the coming of the Son of Man'.[24] So after quoting this passage, Damascene concludes, 'Waiting for Him with longing, we worship towards the east' — in other words, because we are awaiting Christ's final coming in glory, we pray facing east.

This resurrectional and eschatological character of the Eucharist has another consequence, too: during the Eucharist, the Church is *bathed in light and adorned with all available splendour*. A Eucharist in dimly-lit churches, ostensibly for the sake of devout concentration, is antithetical to its very nature. Unfortunately, the pietism which has crept into our consciousness and our worship has misled us into the mistaken idea that richness in vestments and in the decoration of churches is a bad thing. Just one simple observation shows how alien to the Orthodox tradition this idea is: the richest and most splendid vestments in our Church are to be found in our monasteries, and particularly on the Holy Mountain, the most important and authoritative monastic centre for Orthodoxy. Why, then, does the genuine Orthodox monk, who according to the Sayings of the Fathers should wear such a shoddy and threadbare *riason* that he could hang it outside his cell door in the certainty that no one would be tempted to steal it — why during the Liturgy does this same man, as celebrant, put on the most splendid vestments, yet without being scandalized or scandalizing anyone else? Quite simply, because the eschatological character of the Eucharist remains vivid in his consciousness: in the Eucharist, we move within the space of the age to come, of the Kingdom. There we experience 'the day which knows no end or evening, and no successor, that age which does not end or grow old', in the words of Saint Basil.[25] We have every possibility for practicing our humility outside the Liturgy. We do not have the right to turn the Eucharist into an opportunity to show off our humility, or a means to psychological experiences of compunction. Besides, 'he who offers and he who is offered', the real celebrant, is Christ, and indeed the risen Christ as he will come *in his glory* on the last day, and those who celebrate the Liturgy are nothing more than

---

24   *Exposition of the Orthodox Faith* 13 (PG 94:1136).
25   *Hexaemeron*, Homily 2.

icons of this eschatological Christ. And, of course, 'the honour paid to the icon passes to the prototype'.

Thus, once again, much depends on whether in the Eucharist we simply refer back to the past, or whether we look to the last times, to the future. How resolutely the Church refused to link the Eucharist with sorrow and compunction is shown by the fact that even on the days when the martyrs are commemorated, when she recalls their martyrdom, she celebrates the Divine Eucharist with the same splendour as on Sundays. It is known that from the first centuries it became the practice to celebrate the Eucharist on the feast-days of the martyrs,[26] and subsequently of all the saints. What is often overlooked is the fact that from the beginning the martyrdom the saints was seen not just as a repetition of Christ's sacrifice on the cross, but as a *revelation of the glory of his Kingdom*. Already the description of the martyrdom of Stephen in the Acts of the Apostles (7:55-60) makes clear the eschatological character that the Church recognizes in it: '…he gazed into heaven and saw the glory of God, and Jesus standing on the right hand of God; and he said, "Behold, I see the heavens opened, and the Son of Man standing at the right hand of God."' (The reference to the 'Son of Man', who is considered an eschatological figure in Scripture, is characteristic.) The same goes for the 'Acts' — the martyrologies — of all the martyrs of the early Church.[27] The celebration of the Eucharist on saints' days cannot be separated from the eschatological character of the Eucharist, which for that reason is always celebrated with particular splendour and involves the lifting of the fast.

3. Remembrance of the Future

The Eucharist is a *remembrance*. But what is meant by 'remembrance'? In psychology, remembrance means recalling the past. The basis for this meaning is Platonic, and in general ancient Greek. For Plato, in particular, all truth is stored up in the soul. Nothing new can happen 'under the sun', as the saying goes. Truth (*a-letheia*) is an escape from forgetfulness (*lethe*), a manifestation of what *already* exists. For

---

26   A. Fytrakis, *Relics and Tombs of the Martyrs in the first three centuries* (in Greek), 1955, pp. 77f.

27   A moving passage, and one that reveals the eschatological character both of martyrdom and of the Eucharist, is the following extract from the martyrdom of Saint Agathonike, published by Adolf von Harnack (*Die Akten des Karpus, des Papylus und der Agathonike*, Texte und Untersuchungen, III, 3/4, 1888, pp. 451f.: 'A certain Agathonike was standing beside them (during the martyrdom of Papylus and Carpus); and seeing the glory of the Lord which Carpus said that he saw, and contemplating the heavenly invitation, at once she lifted up her voice: "For me too is this supper [*ariston*, or 'dinner'] prepared. And I too must eat my share of this glorious meal."' The association between martyrdom and the Eucharist is clear, as is the eschatological character of both.

this reason, the teacher does no more than to prompt the pupil to remember once again what he already knows, to extract the truth from him (Socrates' method of acting as 'midwife').

This understanding is also based on common sense. None of us can comprehend what it means to 'remember the future'. This is because time, in our experience since the Fall, is *fragmentary*, and is inevitably divided into past, present and future in a sequence which cannot naturally be reversed because of death which has entered the world with the fall of man. Thus the future naturally comes after the past and present, making it meaningless to 'remember' it.

But what happens in a time which is freed from this fragmentation because death has been abolished? In such a case, the future is not separated from the past and present. If indeed the future is that which gives meaning both to the past and to the present, it is then transformed into a source from which both equally draw their substance. The future acquires 'substance' (Hebrews 11:1), and can be 'anticipated' so as to become part of our memory. Thus it is possible to talk about remembrance of the future. The fact that this is precisely what happens in the Divine Eucharist is as evident to the careful student of the Eucharist as it is unknown to those who approach it without an awareness of its eschatological character. Let us take a closer look at this very important subject.

The Anaphora of the Divine Liturgy used in the Orthodox Church, both that of Saint John Chrysostom and that of Saint Basil, includes the following phrase which is a stumbling block for common sense: 'remembering then this saving commandment, the cross, the tomb, the resurrection on the third day, the ascension into heaven, the sitting at the right hand *and the second and glorious coming again*, offering to Thee Thine own of Thine own, we hymn Thee' etc.

To remember past events (the cross, the resurrection etc.) is 'natural'. But to 'remember' something that has not yet happened (the Second Coming) cannot be explained unless it is transferred to an existential plane on which the fragmentation and necessary sequence of the three elements of time (past, present, and future) have been healed. This is precisely what happens in the Kingdom of God. In this Kingdom, everything is not turned into 'present' — that would be a typically Platonic deliverance from death — but into the 'future age which does not end or grow old', as Saint Basil calls the Kingdom, which being the state which ultimately prevails, the 'truth' in the words of Maximus the Confessor, is logically prior, since it is this that gives 'substance' and meaning to both past and present. The 'end' constitutes the 'reason' for which both the past and the present 'subsist', according to Saint Maximus; and in consequence the 'future age which does not end' becomes, as we have already established from passages of Maximus, not an effect, as happens in time as we know it after the Fall, but the *cause* of all past and present events.[28] Consequently, remembrance of this 'endless' future is not only possible but also ontologically definitive in the realm of the Eucharist as icon of the Kingdom. This is attested both in the Gospel descriptions of the Last Supper and in the liturgical practice of the Church.

In the description of the Last Supper in Luke (22:20), a prominent place belongs to the Lord's words to his disciples which are repeated by Saint Paul (1 Cor. 11:24-25) and by the Eucharistic liturgies down the ages: 'Do this in remembrance of me.' According to our common logic, bounded as it is by our experience of time since the Fall, as described above, the meaning of this phrase would be: 'Do this, *in order to remember me*.' The question, however, is whether the Lord was interested in perpetuating his memory in the minds of his disciples (or of human beings generally) through the celebration of the Eucharist, or whether he wanted, through the celebration of the Eucharist by his disciples (and by the Church), to link the Eucharist with the eternal memory of God in the Kingdom which he would establish.

This question has generated much debate among biblical theologians since Jeremias, in the work referred to earlier, refuted the first view with serious arguments and supported the second, to the point of formulating the extreme position that Christ gave the commandment that the Eucharist should be celebrated in order that God should remember him (as Messiah) at the Second Coming. We shall not concern ourselves with this discussion, which is anyway not immediately relevant to our theme in all its aspects. What interests us is whether the remembrance of Christ at the Eucharist is a psychological, human remembrance of an event in the past, or whether it is linked with the future, with the Kingdom, and not just psychologically, but *ontologically*.

If we want to use Saint Paul as our interpreter for the phrase 'in remembrance of me', we shall be led without a doubt to the conclusion that the eucharistic remembrance is orientated towards the Second Corning. The explanation Paul gives for the phrase 'in remembrance of me' is that ('For') in the Eucharist, 'you proclaim the Lord's death until he comes' (1 Cor. 11:26). As Jeremias notes, 'until he comes' is used repeatedly in the New Testament in reference to the last times (Rom.

---

28 *Questions to Thalassius* (PG 90:621). This matter had already been raised in the second century in connection with the annulment by the New Testament of certain provisions of the Mosaic Law (circumcision, sacrifices, etc.) The answer given by Saint Irenaeus remains the basis for Maximus' thinking: a future event (the coming of Christ) can annul an event in the past (for instance, the sacrifices of the Old Testament), not because the latter was evil and had to disappear, but because it existed solely for the sake of the future event, which gives it meaning and substance.

11:25; 1 Cor. 15:25; and Lk. 21:24), and its meaning in this particular case is that in the Eucharist, the Lord's death is not proclaimed as an event in the past, but *in the perspective of the Second Coming*. This explains the connection of the Eucharist with the very early Aramaic liturgical exclamation *maranatha*, which Paul knows, and the significance of which we have already mentioned.

At the Eucharist, consequently, we place the events and persons of the past and the present within the context of the Kingdom which will come, and that not simply psychologically (through a movement of our imagination towards the future) but *ontologically, i.e.* with the purpose of giving these events and persons substance, so that they are not destroyed (by time and death) and live eternally. This eternal survival of events and beings *cannot be secured by placing them in human memory*. Human memory comes and goes, because it is a created memory. When we pray as the Church that someone's memory may be eternal, we do not mean that this person should live on in our own human memory, because this would have little meaning since human memory, being created, passes away. We mean that this person lives on *in the memory of God*. Only what exists in the thought of God, really exists. When God pronounces the terrible words, 'I do not know you' (Mt. 25:12), the consequences are not psychological but ontological; so also when He says 'I will remember their sins no more' (Heb. 8:12; 10:17), the consequences are of ontological significance for those particular sins. Conversely, when God 'remembers' something or someone He is not operating psychologically — it is meaningless, anyway, to introduce psychology into God's being, as Augustine did with his trinitarian theology — but is performing a creative and ontological activity whereby that particular being is existentially affirmed.[29]

This brings us to the eucharistic Liturgy. A basic and essential element in any eucharistic Liturgy is the *commemoration*. There is no such thing as a Eucharist which does not commemorate, in one way or another, events (principally the creation of the world and the events of Christ's life on earth), and also names. What is the meaning of this commemoration of names in the Eucharist?

As our Liturgy has developed, it is difficult to make out the meaning of the commemoration of names. There are three principle points at which names are commemorated in the Liturgy today. One is at the Proskomide, *i.e.* when the faithful hand over their gifts to the celebrants (priests and

---

29   The words 'Remember me, O Lord, when Thou comest in Thy Kingdom', which we have been
      repeating in the Church since the time of the thief at the right hand of Jesus on the cross, bear
      witness that the *Kingdom* is the space in which our being is secured, by reason of the fact that *God*
      commemorates us, and not merely human beings (Remember, *O Lord...*).

deacons) *before* the Divine liturgy, so that the Eucharist can be prepared from them. For practical reasons, this point has come to be the preeminent moment for names to be commemorated, when the particles for those commemorated are cut out, to be placed on the paten beside the Lamb, and finally put into the chalice with it.[30] The whole service as it is now performed is devoid of obvious reference to the Kingdom which is to come, and its symbolic references are mainly to the sacrifice of Christ on the cross. This service was introduced gradually, beginning already from the eighth century, but it does not form part of the eucharistic Anaphora which, as the offering and sacrifice of the eschatological Lamb, takes place later. Thus the words 'Remember, O Lord' which accompany the cutting out of the particles at this time should not be regarded as the main commemoration of those mentioned, whether living or fallen asleep.

The other moment at which names are today commemorated is at the Great Entrance, principally when a bishop is celebrating. The fact that a celebrant bishop commemorates names at this time, when he receives the gifts of the people from the priests and deacons, should be connected with the fact that the bishop is not present during the preparation of the gifts (the Proskomide), since he comes into the church only at the Little Entrance. Thus this commemoration of names, too, should not be considered as the proper eucharistic commemoration, but as an extension of the commemoration at the Proskomide, which was initially performed at that time[31] and which is also not part of the Anaphora in the strict sense.[32] It is nevertheless worthy of note that the

---

30   There is considerable debate over whether the particles for the Mother of God, the saints and the faithful ought to be placed in the chalice together with the Lamb at the time of communion. Judging by historical and literary criteria, it seems that such a mixing is not favoured by the historical evidence (see Fountoulis, 'Answers to liturgical, canonical and other queries' (in Greek), *Ephemerios* 43 (1994), pp. 208, 239f.) Be that as it may, from a theological viewpoint this mixing is important. The body of Christ in the Divine Eucharist is a body *inclusive of the 'many'* (1 Cor. 10:17), in the first instance of the saints and faithful who are commemorated and for whom the particles are cut out to show the *personal* character of each one of them. Communion in the body of Christ at the Eucharist is at the same time communion with the saints and faithful who have been commemorated (see John of Damascus, *Exposition of Orthodox Faith* 13 [PG 94:1153]: 'It is called communion and such indeed it is, because through it we commune with Christ... and we commune and are united with each other through it... and become members one of another, being of the same body with Christ'). The cutting out of particles is certainly a later practice, but it is unintelligible apart from their incorporation into the body of Christ. Without such a communion, neither the commemoration nor the placing of the particles next to the Lamb makes sense. What 'washes away' the sins of those remembered is not 'contact' with the Lamb, but *their incorporation into him*. (A different matter, of course, is the elevation of the Lamb, who as the 'one holy, one Lord', as head of the body, is elevated and worshipped alone.

31   See Fountoulis, *Answers to Liturgical Queries* IV, 1982, pp. 289f.

32   As a result of the non-canonical entry of the bishop into the sanctuary before the Little Entrance in order to be vested (see section 6 of this study) it has become the practice for the bishop celebrating to complete and 'cover' the proskomide during Matins. It is not without significance

commemoration of names at this point makes a clear reference to the Kingdom: 'May the Lord God remember in His Kingdom'.

There thus remains the third moment of commemoration, which is also the moment of eucharistic 'remembrance' *par excellence*: this is the moment of the Anaphora. It is a real misfortune that the commemoration of names has ceased to take place at that time, and has been shifted almost exclusively to the Proskomide for practical reasons: because the entire theological meaning of this act is thereby destroyed. What is this meaning? If we go back again to the Church Fathers, as we always do in this study, we shall find some valuable information in Cyril of Jerusalem's *Mystagogic Catechesis* 5. Interpreting the eucharistic Anaphora, Saint Cyril regards it *in its totality* as a commemoration (remembrance). In the prayer of the Anaphora, which begins immediately after 'Let us give thanks to the Lord' and the people's response 'It is meet and right', '*we commemorate*', he says, 'heaven and earth and sea... and *all creation, rational and non-rational...* angels, archangels, etc.'; in other words creation, which through this commemoration participates in a certain way in the mystery of the Eucharist. After the invocation of the Holy Spirit and the change of the elements into the body and blood of Christ, 'upon that sacrifice of propitiation' we commemorate first the living (Churches, kings, armies, the sick and 'in a word all who are in need of help', and then those who have fallen asleep, 'patriarchs, prophets, apostles, martyrs,... bishops, and, *in a word, all who have fallen asleep before us*, believing that it will be of the greatest advantage to the souls for whom the prayer is offered *when the holy and most awful sacrifice is set forth*'.

From these words and what Saint Cyril writes in continuation, it follows that *the commemoration both of the living and of those who have fallen asleep is organically connected with and takes its meaning from* 'the holy and most awful sacrifice *which is set forth*', *i.e.* the sacrifice which is being offered up to God *at that moment. That*, in consequence, is the moment for commemoration of the living and the dead which brings 'the

---

that earlier bishops never did this, but 'commemorated' and completed the Prothesis during the Cherubic Hymn. This order, being older, is an indication both that the service of the proskomide was originally performed at that time, and also that the bishop was not in the sanctuary prior to the Little Entrance. In general, it is doubtful whether the bishop originally had any contact or connection with the proskomide, even when this service was introduced, given that the Skevophylakion or Prothesis, where the gifts were handed over and preparation took place, was, at least in Constantinople, a special, separate building next to the church (T. Mathews, *The Early Churches of Constantinople*, 1971, pp. 13–18, 158f.). Besides, it is at the time of the Cherubic Hymn, not during Matins, that the washing of the bishop's hands should take place *in front of the people*, as a *public* act of cleansing and forgiveness in view of the celebration of the Eucharist. This public washing of the hands is wrongly omitted. It has a real meaning, and is attested in very ancient sources (Cyril of Jerusalem *et al.*).

greatest advantage' to them.[33] Because then, at the holy anaphora of the sacrifice, those who are commemorated are placed before God 'for an eternal memorial'; thanks to the sacrifice of the Lamb, they are not only forgiven, but also receive 'eternal life, in other words true substance. To the question, 'What does it profit a soul that departs this world with sins, or without sins, if it is commemorated during the offering?' (in other words, the perpetual rationalistic question which makes the freedom of divine grace — and the power of the Eucharist, which it disparages as a supposedly 'magical' act — subject to the laws of sin), Saint Cyril gives the categorical answer: we 'believe' unshakably that through the Eucharist we 'propitiate our God who loves mankind on behalf of them (that is, those who are commemorated) and of ourselves' even if they are sinners, because 'we offer Christ who was slain for our sins'.

At this point we come to the matter of the Diptychs, and the ultimate fate of this very essential element in the Eucharist. The problem of the historical appearance and shaping of the Diptychs will not concern us here.[34] We shall simply make some remarks of a general nature which throw light on the subject of our study.

It has become the practice today for the so-called 'Diptychs' to be recited only when heads of autocephalous Churches are celebrating or, according to the official Calendar of the Church of Greece, when a bishop is celebrating at a great feast. This restriction serves to encourage the disuse, with the passage of time, of a very essential element in the Eucharist. In the early Church, the Diptychs had a central place and importance in the Divine Liturgy, as Chrysostom and Maximus,[35] among others, testify; and as can be deduced from the case of Chrysostom's exile, at least Constantinople, Alexandria and Antioch recited the Diptychs at the Anaphora, immediately after the Epiklesis. This place that they had in the Liturgy is clear evidence that the Diptychs not only had the very important purpose of showing mutual recognition and communion between the Churches (as shown by the business of removing Chrysostom's name from them); they also formed an organic part of the eucharistic *commemoration* to which we referred above.[36]

---

33 A note on the so-called 'episcopal memorial service': it has become the practice to have 'episcopal memorial services' when the bishop is not celebrating. But if the bishop does not offer up the Sacrifice and does not commemorate during the Anaphora the person for whom the memorial service takes place, then the whole point of the episcopal memorial service disappears. It becomes an episcopal 'trisagion'. (Within the jurisdiction of the Ecumenical Patriarchate, it has always been unthinkable to celebrate an episcopal commemoration without an episcopal Liturgy.)

34 The most thorough study on this subject is that by Robert Taft, *The Diptychs*, 1994.

35 Cf. Chrysostom, *On Acts* 21:4 (PG 60:170); and Maximus, *Explanation of Movement* 5 (PG 90:117).

36 Metropolitan Nikodimos of Patra (*Diptychs of the Church of Greece* (in Greek), 1994) is correct in maintaining that the exclamation 'Many Years' has no place in the Diptychs, precisely because

Clearly since the first of these two reasons prevailed (proclamation of the unity and communion of the various local Churches), it was finally considered sufficient for the Diptychs to contain bishops only, and to be read only when heads of autocephalous Churches were celebrating. Yet the second reason (commemoration of bishops, kings and faithful people, living and departed) is equally important. The eucharistic Anaphora, as we have seen (cf. Cyril of Jerusalem, above), requires this commemoration by its very nature.

From a single glance at the text of the Divine Liturgy which is used today in the Orthodox Church, it can be seen that at this point, at the commemoration after the Epiklesis, there has been considerable confusion in the manuscripts and generally in the liturgical material.[37] In any case, what seems beyond doubt is that in our Church *two* categories of faithful are commemorated after the Epiklesis and the consecration. On the one hand are those who have fallen asleep, whose commemoration begins with 'especially for our most holy... Lady', and on the other hand are the living, whose commemoration begins with 'Among the first remember, O Lord, our archbishop...'.[38] What we have, clearly, is a form of Diptychs which also forms the preeminent place for the eucharistic commemoration. That is when the names should be commemorated, or at least some of them, such as names of those for whom a memorial Liturgy is celebrated, and, if the names are many, there should be a general reference to those who have been commemorated during the Prothesis. All these things are not mere formal rules: they underline the fact that the 'remembrance' of Christ in the Eucharist includes within it all the saints and members of the Church on whose behalf this 'reasonable worship' is offered.

The commemoration of the departed begins with 'especially for our most holy... Lady'[39] and includes the recognized saints along with all the faithful. The fact that the Eucharist is also offered *on behalf of* the Mother

---

'they are dependent on the clause 'again we pray Thee, *remember, O Lord...*'". The Diptychs are an organic part of the prayer for remembrance in the Anaphora, and not only indicative of ecclesial communion. The 'Many Years' undoubtedly comes from a confusion of the Diptychs with the 'Phimi', and their restriction to the names of bishops only.

37   Thus the apostles, martyrs, etc., are commemorated before 'especially for our most holy... Lady', and this is repeated after 'especially...'. In the same way, before 'Among the first...' we commemorate 'the whole episcopate of the Orthodox Church, the priesthood', *etc.*, along with the departed, whereas these belong to the commemoration of the living, which is repeated after 'Among the first...'.

38   The reading of Diptychs of the departed only is mentioned in the Areopagitic writings, but, as we have seen, the evidence for Diptychs of the living as well is ancient. Cf. also Maximus the Confessor, *Scholia* (PG 4:145).

39   According to Taft (118), this was introduced by Saint Gennadios of Constantinople (458–471), and formed the beginning of the exclamation of the diptychs of the departed without the hymn

of God, the Forerunner and the saint of the day as well as 'for all those who have fallen asleep in faith, ancestors, fathers, patriarchs, prophets, apostles, preachers, evangelists, martyrs', *etc.*,[40] demonstrates that *all the saints* stand in need of the Eucharist and have to be incorporated into it. The question had already been put by Saint John Chrysostom: why do we offer the sacrifice on behalf of the martyrs, he asks, since they are already saints?[41] Despite the fact that they are saints, we make commemoration *on their behalf*, he replies, because the Lord is present at that moment, and it is a great honour for them to be commemorated at that time. The important point in this case is that in the body of the Eucharist, the sacrificed and risen body of the 'new creation', the Church with her Eucharist places *together* the saints and the sinners on behalf of whom — saints and sinners alike — she offers the sacrifice, the one case in order to honour them and to show that the saints too are saved only as members of his body, and in the other case in order to seek their salvation, always by means of the communion of all in the one body of Christ.

The commemoration of the living, in the other hand, begins with the phrase 'Among the first...', in other words with the local bishop in first place.[42] *He* is the head of the living, as the Mother of God is

'It is truly meet', which was added much later, once it had already become the practice to read the names silently (after the eleventh century and, according to Taft, not before the sixteenth).

40   This section today appears in the text before 'especially...'. See note 39, above.

41   *On Acts* 21.4 (PG 60:170).

42   The omission of 'Among the first...' in the case where the head of an autocephalous Church is celebrating is justified — and actually occurred in history (Taft) — only when the Diptychs came to be viewed as commemorating bishops alone. But as we have stressed above, 'Among the first...' is the beginning of the Diptychs of all the living (kings, lay people, etc. [cf. Maximus]), and in consequence it is essential for the presiding bishop, when celebrating, to exclaim 'Among the first remember... the whole episcopate', thus demonstrating that *before all* the living we commemorate the body of bishops. On the particular ecclesiological significance that this can have, see Maximus the Confessor (PG 90:117C-D). A problem is created when a bishop celebrates. In this case, the question arises as to whom celebrant bishop will commemorate. This question remains a mere formality if we do not take care to give a *theological* grounding to our answer. What must be emphasized is that, while the priests of a local Church celebrate the Eucharist in the name of the local bishop, the bishop always celebrates in the name of his own hierarchical superior and never of the local bishop, and commemorates him alone wherever he celebrates. If the bishop celebrates in someone, else's diocese, then the local bishop 'concedes' the presiding place at the Eucharist to him ('apart, however, from sitting on the throne'), and consequently during that liturgy his name alone is commemorated. When bishops concelebrate, it again makes no sense for a celebrant bishop to commemorate the local bishop (whatever his rank), because this suggests that the commemoration of his own 'superior' is suspended, and also that one bishop is subject to another, something that runs counter to the fundamental ecclesiological principle that bishops are equal. (The problem of 'assistant bishops' creates a complication because this is a crass ecclesiological aberration, since we have here a bishop *dependent* on another bishop. The most canonical solution would be for him to commemorate his own 'superior' wherever he celebrates, and not, as is usually done, the local bishop in each case). Consequently, when a bishop celebrates in another diocese it is he, and not the local bishop, who (by concession, of course, of the latter) who is the

of the departed. Even if there are members of the Church holier than the bishop, they are not commemorated 'among the first' because the body of the local Church has only one head: the bishop. The living are saved only in union with their bishop, and apart from him they have no relationship with the body of Christ, which is offered 'for eternal life'. Anyone who does not commemorate his bishop at this time in the Eucharist cuts himself off from the roll of the living. For this reason, a Eucharist which is not celebrated in the name of the local bishop, or of another bishop to whom he has yielded precedence, is without salvific significance for those who perform it.

In all we have said in the above paragraph, we have wanted to stress that (a) the Eucharist is the supreme commemoration of the living and the departed; (b) the subject of this 'commemorating', *i.e.* the one who does the remembering, is not simply a human being but God himself ('Remember, O Lord...'); (c) this remembrance is not psychological but ontological in its significance (it is concerned with transcending death and with substantive, true 'eternal being' in Christ); and (d) this commemoration stems from the Passion of Christ and his sacrifice on the cross,[43] but refers to and is fulfilled in the Kingdom of Christ which is to come ('Remember me, Lord, when you come into your Kingdom'). Thus the eucharistic remembrance becomes also a remembrance of the future, *i.e.* of the 'second and glorious coming again'.

We are truly alive only to the degree that God will remember us and will ultimately give us 'substance' (*hypostasis*) in the Kingdom of his Son. The Eucharist, transferring us to this Kingdom, offers us the sacrifice of Christ 'unto remission of sins' and also 'unto eternal life', in other words as 'being, eternal being and well-being',[44] our hypostatic-personal being in the 'age which does not end or grow old'.[45]

III. Part Three

1. The Structure of the Church's 'Institution'

The Eucharist is not only an icon of the Kingdom, but also a revelation of Church itself; and this because, contrary to what Western theology

superior and head of that eucharistic gathering, and that Eucharist is celebrated *in his name*. This is not a usurpation, because it takes place by the canonical concession of the local bishop. It is a basic ecclesiological principle that the bishop, wherever he celebrates, is the head of that particular eucharistic gathering, and is never incorporated into another local Church, nor does he suspend the commemoration of his own 'superior'.

43   In reality, it contains and sums up the whole history of salvation, the divine economy. Cf. Theodore the Studite, *Antirrheticus* 1 [PG 99:340].

44   Maximus, *Centuries on Love*, 3.23.

45   Basil, *Epistle 44*.

has maintained at various times, the Church is not confined exclusively to the period between Christ's earthly life and the Second Coming but preexisted,[46] being linked with the pre-eternal will of God concerning the course and outcome of the divine economy and will extend 'unto ages of ages' as the Kingdom of God.[47] The Church is a many-sided mystery and its definition — if it is not impossible to define — is itself many-sided and complex.[48] A 'definition' which refers us not to intellectual conceptions but to actual experience is the well-known one given by Nicolas Cabasilas: 'The Church made known in the mysteries.' If one can ever see (not 'define') the Church it will only be in the Divine Eucharist: 'If anyone is able to see the Church of Christ... he will see nothing other than this body of the Lord's *only*... It is therefore in no way unfitting that the Church should be made known here through the mysteries.'[49] According to Cabasilas there exists between Church and Eucharist not an 'analogy of likeness' but an 'identity of reality' — this is how far the holy writer goes! This allows him and other truly Orthodox dogmatic theologians to write — without fear of being condemned for 'one-sidedness' — that the Church is changed into Eucharist (so Cabasilas) or, in the phrase of Florovsky and Karmires, 'the Eucharist makes/constitutes the Church'.[50]

But as Florovsky writes, '*sacramental* (communion/community) means nothing less than eschatological'.[51] In constituting the Church, the Eucharist reveals it as the *communion and community of the last times*, since 'the Church bears in general an eschatological character and lives continuously in the "last hour"'.[52] The import of this truth is not only *anthropological* (salvation and deification of man through the mysteries

---

46 See I. Karmires, *Orthodox Ecclesiology* (in Greek), 1973, pp. 19f.

47 The Church 'comes into being in this life and takes its beginning from here, but is perfected in the future when we attain to that day' (Nicolas Cabasilas, *On Life in Christ*, 1-4 [PG 150:493 and 501]).

48 It requires a measure of arrogance to maintain that one's own definition is *the* definition of the Church when throughout the whole patristic period there is no definition of the Church to be found, and Orthodox ecclesiologists, such as I. Karmires (*Ecclesiology*, 1973, p. 11), not only avoid giving a 'definition' but speak of a 'vague and imperfect expression and explanation of the inexpressible and inexplicable mystery of Church'.

49 PG 150:452-53. It is a wonder that no one has yet condemned Cabasilas for 'eucharistic monism' (!) after this position of his that 'only' in the Eucharist is the Church revealed. It is noteworthy, however, that both he and Maximus prefer to use the language of the image ('to see') rather than giving a definition of the Church.

50 Georges Florovsky: 'the sacraments constitute the Church', ('The Church: Her Nature and Task', in *The Universal Church in God's Design*, WCC, 1948, p. 47). More specifically, Karmires writes: 'It has rightly been observed that the Eucharist makes the Church' (p. 94).

51 Florovsky, p. 54.

52 Karmires, p. 164.

and within the Church) but also *cosmological*[53] and *ecclesiological*. We shall dwell particularly on this last point.

The Church is a community with a particular *structure*. It is not simply a 'community of faith and hearts', as Protestant theology would have it (see the Augsburg Confession) and as it is also understood, unfortunately, by many contemporary Orthodox, who present Orthodoxy principally as a system of ideas or a form of 'religion', a religious experience of the heart, avoiding its institutions and especially bishops and conciliarity. But whence does the Church derive its structure? Since it is in its nature an eschatological community, how is its structure connected with the Kingdom of God?

As has happened with the Eucharist itself, so also with the institutions of the Church the entire effort of academic theology has focused on showing how the Church's various institutions and ministries are or are not connected with the earthly life and teaching of Christ and the Apostles (or indeed with Tradition). Very little effort has been put into showing how these institutions and ministries relate to the Church's eschatological perspective. And yet the fact that these ministries stemmed and continued to stem from the Eucharist[54] demonstrates that it is impossible for them not to be closely connected with the eschatological community of which the Eucharist is an image.

But what relation can the Kingdom of God have with *structure*? The concept of structure has been given a bad name not only by pietism, which puts all the emphasis on what is within man or his ethical behaviour, but also by modern philosophy and thought which tends to regard any structure as an alienation of the person and his freedom.

If, however, we do not give 'structure' the legal character of an authority imposed from without but connect it with the *otherness of personal relationships*, then it becomes a different matter. In the Kingdom of God *otherness of relationships will exist*, and this creates the variety and hierarchy of ministries.

To be more specific: on the evidence of Scripture and patristic writings the eschatological community, the Kingdom of God, will include the following basic elements, which constitute otherness of relationships and in this sense a structure which is existential in character:

(a) A *gathering* (*synaxis*) of the scattered people of God, and by extension a uniting 'in one place' of the world which was fragmented by corruption and death. As we have already seen (section 4, above),

---

53   See my *Creation as Eucharist* (in Greek), 1993.
54   For more detail see my *Eucharist, Bishop, Church*.

this gathering forms an essential element in the last times, in the Kingdom of God.

(b) A gathering *centred on the person of Christ* who on the one hand embodies the very presence of God in the world as 'the image of the invisible God' (Col. 1:15), and on the other incorporates and unites 'the many' in his person as the 'Servant of the Lord' and the eschatological 'Son of Man', or as the 'firstborn of all creation... firstborn from the dead', as 'the head of the body, which is the Church' (Col. 1:15-20).

(c) A gathering centred on Christ who, however, is *surrounded by the 'Twelve'* (*the Apostles*), who will 'sit upon twelve thrones judging the twelve tribes of Israel' (Mt. 19:28; Lk. 18:31).

In consequence the Kingdom of God, the eschatological community, will be a *gathering* (of the 'people of God' and the 'many') in which, however, there will be no otherness of relationships determined by the difference between the three elements, at least, to which we have referred: the people (or 'the many' or even 'all things'), Christ, and the Apostles. Without these elements the eschatological community and, by extension, the Kingdom of God, is inconceivable. The Kingdom is not simply an interior experience of 'hearts',[55] but a unity of all in the person of Christ who is 'the image of the invisible God'; but Christ as the Apostles make Him known and hand Him down to us, not as each individual would like Him to be or imagines Him.[56] Furthermore, within the people itself or the 'many' there will be a variety of gifts, because it is not conceivable that everyone should be levelled out in the Kingdom of God. The variety and multiplicity which does not break up the unity of the body but holds it together (1 Cor. 12) will assuredly be a characteristic of the Kingdom as it is of the Church.

All these things are 'imaged' by the Divine Eucharist as an image of the Kingdom. Thus the following observations take on an especial significance:

(a) All ordinations to the basic *structural* ministries of the Church (layman, deacon, priest, and bishop) necessarily take place within the Divine Eucharist.[57] Baptism and Chrismation are the 'ordination' of

---

55   The Lord's saying 'The Kingdom of God is among/within you' (*entos humon*; Lk. 17.21) means, as is evident from the context: the Kingdom of God is in your midst (obviously with the presence of Christ himself).

56   It should be noted that in the last times 'many false christs will arise' (Mt. 24:24; Mk. 13:22), and therefore the witness and judgement of the genuine apostles is of decisive significance not only historically, but also eschatologically.

57   Ordinations to the diaconate are often performed at the Liturgy of the Presanctified. This arose out of the reasoning that since at the full Liturgy the deacon is ordained shortly before Holy Communion, and the Presanctified is a service whose main purpose is the receiving of communion, such an ordination can therefore take place in the course of it. This reasoning overlooks the fact that the performance of an ordination within the Eucharist is bound up with

lay people — because 'lay' does not mean unordained, as is commonly thought, but denotes someone who through Baptism and Chrismation is a regular member of the eucharistic gathering with all the rights and obligations that this entails; and these two mysteries were united with the Eucharist in the early Church and were unthinkable apart from it, as with ordinations.

(b) In contrast with the rites whereby people are 'set apart' for all the other orders (subdeacon, reader etc.), which take place outside the Eucharist (at the end of Matins, usually) because they do not involve *structural* ministries, these ordinations have been regarded even from the time of Ignatius of Antioch as involving ministries which 'image' the elements which, as we have seen, 'construct' the eschatological community: the 'multitude', i.e. the people in a *gathering*, the throne of God which is occupied by the bishop, and the Apostles, represented by the presbyters, with the deacons as an intermediate ministry. In situations where the bishop represents the Father, the deacons represent the 'servant of God', Jesus (Ignatius); where the bishop represents Christ who occupies the Throne of God, they represent the 'ministering spirits sent forth to serve' (Heb. 1:14), the angels, as Byzantine tradition and iconography perceived and described the deacons.

The conclusion, which is of significance for our subject, is that the Eucharist as an image of the last times — with precisely that property — provided and continues to provide the basic structure of the Church, without which, as Saint Ignatius says, 'it cannot be called the Church'.[58] These structural elements of the Church are essential and relate to its *being* (not merely its *well being*), because they *touch upon its nature as an image of the Kingdom*. In other words, the disruption of this basic structure of the Church distorts the image of the Kingdom which the Church is meant to manifest in history, and presupposes an eschatology which either (i) does not allow the *imaging* of the last times in history, or (ii) does not have structural elements, in the existential rather than legal sense of the term which we referred to above. Or (iii) it contains structural elements — an otherness of relationships — different from

the entire imaging of the Kingdom, which happens only at the complete Liturgy, as is shown in the liturgical practice of the early Church (Hippolytus, etc.). Besides, it is doubtful whether the bishop can preside at a liturgy which does not contain an Anaphora. It not fortuitous that at the service of Vespers — and the liturgy of the Presanctified is nothing other than Vespers in its structure — bishop never presides as celebrant, but 'is present' or stands by the choirs. In general, all the services which are not connected with the Eucharist (Matins, Vespers, *etc.*) are the task of the presbyters, and it is doubtful whether they should be celebrated by bishops. This is important, because it shows apart from anything else that the task of the bishop *par excellence* is the offering of the Eucharist, in other words, the celebration of a liturgy which includes an Anaphora.

58   *Trall.* 3.1.

those handed down to us by our scriptural and patristic tradition and of which we gave a summary description above.[59] In this case, we should be told what these different elements are and why they should replace those that we have received from tradition.[60]

Viewing the Church's ministries and institutions as an image of the Kingdom has the consequence that the institutions cannot be understood and cannot function except *in relationship* with one another. Since each institution and each ministry *forms a part of an image*, if one of these ministries isolates itself and exalts itself so as to say to the others, 'I have no need of you' (1 Cor. 12:21-24), the result is *a distortion of the whole image*. The image of the Kingdom is a unified one, and the ontology of the ministries requires interdependence and relationship between them, as Saint Paul emphasizes dramatically in his First Epistle to the Corinthians (Chapter 12). It is not possible, for instance, for the bishop to exist without the presbyters and the people, nor for the presbyters and people to exist without the bishop. This protects the Church both from episcopal 'despotism' or 'clericalism' and 'presbyterianism', and also from 'laicism' — aberrations which have come into being historically when the iconic-eschatological approach contained in eucharistic ecclesiology has given way and been replaced by an individualistic and legalistic ontology of the ministries. Proof of this is to found in the fact that in the Orthodox Church, *the Eucharist alone* has preserved the interdependence of the Church's ministries, theoretically at least, since it is forbidden to celebrate the Eucharist without a gathering of the people,

59   The Greek newspaper *Kathimerini* (22.7.94) recently carried an article by a Mr Malevitsis entitled 'The Bishops' in which he called for abolition of the institution of bishops because their squabbles and their gold-trimmed attire are offensive, and for making do with the institution of priests (though why should we need them either?). One would have expected from Mr Malevitsis a better knowledge of theological matters. But perhaps the responsibility belongs ultimately to the Church and to theology, which for all these years have not made it their business to show why these institutions in the Orthodox Church have 'ultimate' truth and meaning. Symptoms such as Mr Malevitsis's article will keep on appearing all the more as long theology does not carry out its duty to interpret our dogmas and institutions and show their more general significance. When there are Orthodox theologians who regard the interpretation of dogma as a 'Protestant' (!) peculiarity, one can understand why such things occur. If the Fathers of the Church had done the same and left dogmas with no interpretation as to their significance for our existence, Christianity would have been relegated to the dustbin of history long ago.

60   For instance, why confine ourselves to the priest alone? Protestantism rejected bishops because it could not find them in the New Testament, in accordance with the axiom *sola scriptura* (it is now tentatively beginning to re-examine the issue). However, to choose the priest out of tradition and to reject other elements purely and simply because they are psychologically or morally offensive is not good theology — even Protestant theology. We suspect that such ideas conceal a view of the Church as an establishment serving religious needs, experiencing 'the sacred' and relating to 'the divine'; in which case, indeed, priest is both essential (cf. ancient Greek and Eastern religions) and also sufficient for this purpose. Is, however, Christianity a 'religion', and can there be a kinship between it and other religions on the basis of the idea of 'the sacred' and 'the divine'?

without the people's 'Amen',[61] and without priests and a bishop — even if it is only with the bishop's antimension and the commemoration of his name. None of this makes any sense outside the Eucharist, where every ministry (lay people and clergy) operates without any gathering or interdependence. The Eucharist as a gathering of the people around the bishop and the presbyters preserves and expresses in history the image of a world which will have transcended its death-bringing fragmentation and corruption thanks to its union and incorporation into Him who, according to the testimony of His Apostles, has by His Cross and Resurrection united what was sundered, gathered His world 'into one' and thus established His Kingdom.[62]

This is the image which the Church ought to show, both to itself and to the world, as it celebrates the Eucharist and composes its institutions. This is the greatest vision and the most important proclamation that the Church has to offer; a vision and proclamation of faith, hope and love. This is why it should guard this image 'like the apple of its eye' against any deviation or distortion.[63]

2. Communion of the Holy Spirit

It is not by chance that according to one of the hymns for Pentecost, the Holy Spirit is he who 'holds together the whole institution of the

---

61   What Cyril of Alexandria writes is characteristic (PG 74:893): the presence of the laypeople's 'Amen' at the Eucharist is essential, 'In order that what seems to be lacking in the priests may be supplemented by the measure of the laity, and that God may as it were accept the small with the great as a unity of the Spirit'. The 'Amen' is the sacred right of the laity, and it is wrong that it is usually exclaimed by the clergy during divine services. It goes right back to the first apostolic Churches (1 Cor. 14:16) and to the first centuries (see Justin, *Apol.* I, 65).

62   It is not by chance that in the patristic tradition (Maximus, Anastasius of Sinai, Theodore the Studite, *et al.*), 'synaxis' is a technical term and denotes the Eucharist without any explanation. This follows from the connection between the Eucharist and the Kingdom, which is also a 'synaxis' (see section 4, above).

63   The distortions which the Church can undergo often extend even to the structure of the prayers in the Divine Liturgy and the order in which these are read by the clergy. Thus it has become customary for the Litany of Fervent Supplication and dismissal of the catechumens to be read secretly during the Trisagion, whereas their place is after the Gospel, as the conclusion to the section of the liturgy at which the catechumens are allowed to be present. In this way it becomes almost a joke, when the celebrants (as if they themselves were the catechumens) whisper among themselves 'Ye catechumens, bow your heads unto the Lord', *etc.* (!), or again whisper among themselves the petitions of the litany which manifestly call upon the people to respond with the triple 'Lord, have mercy'! But where one really has the sense that everything has been turned upside down is when the prayer of the Anaphora which begins 'It is meet and tight to hymn Thee…' has already been read secretly by the celebrant before he gives the exhortation, 'Let us give thanks to the Lord' (usually during the Creed); or when there are several priests celebrating and they 'share out' parts of the Anaphora between them, reading them all simultaneously! Thus the sequence and structure of the eucharistic Anaphora are destroyed, and this is why it is necessary to correct deviations of this sort.

Church'. The thing that often escapes us is that, in the New Testament, the Spirit is given *after* Christ's Resurrection (Jn. 7:39), precisely because his coming into the world signals *the coming of the 'last days' in history* (Acts 2:17). It is no exaggeration to identify the Kingdom and the Holy Spirit: 'Thy Kingdom come: that is, the Holy Spirit.'[64] So the linking of the Holy Spirit with 'holding together the whole institution of the Church' suggests that both the 'institution' of the Church and the framework within which it becomes a reality, the eucharistic synaxis in other words, derive their meaning from the Kingdom of God.

The Divine Eucharist is normally approached from a christological point of view, while the Holy Spirit usually plays only a subsidiary role in eucharistic theology. This is due to Western influence. The dispute over this question between the Orthodox and the Latins after the Schism is well known. The question cannot be solved merely through history, because there are indeed ancient Liturgies in which the Epiklesis is either absent, or appears in a secondary position. The issue is above all *theological*, and its significance touches on the question which concerns us here.

If the Eucharist were simply a repetition of a past event, then one wonders why the action of the Last Supper is not copied exactly at the Liturgy: at the Last Supper, Christ first blessed the bread and wine and then spoke the words 'Take, eat...', while in the Liturgy the order is reversed. It is obvious that in the Eucharist we are not copying a historical event. As Nicolas Cabasilas writes, the description of the Last Supper at the Eucharist — and the repetition of the Lord's words 'Take, eat...' — takes place 'in the form of a narrative', while the work of transforming the Gifts into the body and blood of Christ belongs to the Holy Spirit.[65] The transformation of the gifts requires the descent of the Holy Spirit, and the Holy Spirit in his coming brings the 'last days' into history (Acts 2:17). The presence of Christ in the Eucharist cannot exist outside this pneumatological and eschatological framework. The 'real presence' of Christ in the Eucharist presupposes and entails the gathering 'in one place' of the eschatological community which the Spirit holds together. Only within the framework of this gathering does the transformation of the elements into the body and blood of Christ take place.

This observation gives rise to certain important conclusions:

(a) The Eucharist is a gathering and a *liturgy*. It is a great mistake to speak of the Eucharist without reference to the Liturgy. Academic theology makes this mistake frequently. The theologian concerned with

---

64   Maximus, *On the Lord's Prayer* (PG 90:885).
65   Cabasilas, *Commentary Divine Liturgy*, 29.

the doctrine of the Eucharist should be a liturgiologist, or at least well informed in liturgical questions. For the mystery of the transformation of the gifts and the 'real presence' of Christ cannot be separated off and examined in isolation; it has be examined as an organic unity with all the basic liturgical actions which make up the recapitulation of the divine economy and the imaging of Kingdom. We have seen that this is the way Ignatius, Maximus (above all) and other Fathers view the Eucharist. The basic liturgical rubrics and actions are not ornamental trappings of the mystery: they are the very backbone of mystery.

(b) As a gathering, the Eucharist presupposes the presence and participation of all 'orders' and ministries.[66] All these together image the eschatological community, as also the transcending of all divisions, both natural (age, race, sex, etc.) and social (rich, poor, different professions, etc.). A Eucharist just for students, for children, for lawyers or doctors, for members of 'societies', etc., distorts the image of the Kingdom and is not justified for any reason whatsoever, whether pastoral or any other.

(c) The Eucharist is a *communion* and *partaking* of the blood of Christ, which is *'full of the Holy Spirit'*.[67] We partake of Christ but, at the same time, 'in the communion of the Holy Spirit' (Liturgy of Saint Basil). 'And *unite all of us* who partake of the one bread and the one cup one to another *in the communion of the one Holy Spirit*', as the Liturgy of Saint Basil prays to the Father at the sacred moment of the Anaphora. The Spirit does not come down only 'upon these gifts here set forth' but also 'upon us' (the celebrants and the eucharistic gathering). Thus the 'real presence' of Christ is broadened to the head and the body in one unity in the Holy Spirit. The Eucharist as communion of the Holy Spirit becomes a 'communion of the holy' in a double sense: communion

66   For this reason, it is unthinkable in our Church that the Eucharist should be celebrated by the priest or bishop or lay person on his own (on the last point, see the interesting evidence of the *Spiritual Meadow* of John Moschus]PG 87:2869-71]). The presence and participation of all these 'orders' is essential, because only thus is the Eucharist brought to completion as an image of the Kingdom. When the bishop is not physically present, his presence is absolutely essential in the form of the 'appointed time' which the priest takes from the bishop's throne, the Antimension signed by his own bishop, upon which he performs the Eucharist, and the commemoration of this bishop during the Anaphora at 'Among the first remember, O Lord...'. Thus each Divine Liturgy presupposes the basic structure of the Church: bishop — priest (— deacons) — people of God. A Liturgy without the presence of the bishop, either direct or indirect in the form we have alluded to, is as unthinkable as one at which no laity are present. These things are not mere formalities, but touch upon the very being of the Church.

67   Characteristic is the phrase 'The fullness of the cup of faith of the Holy Spirit' which the celebrant pronounces every time he places the portion of the Lamb in the Holy Chalice before Holy Communion. He repeats the same thing when he pours in the Zeon (warm water). During the discussions between Latins and Orthodox after the Schism the latter regarded the Zeon as a serious point of disagreement, because its symbolism in Byzantium was connected with the Holy Spirit.

in the holy things, and communion of saints (*i.e.* holy people).[68] The Eucharist thus becomes the *mystery of love*.

> Love never ends; as for prophecies, they will pass away; as for tongues, they will cease; as for knowledge, it will pass away. For our knowledge is imperfect and our prophecy is imperfect; but when the perfect comes, the imperfect will pass away... So faith, hope and love abide, these three; but the greatest of these is love (1 Cor. 13:8-13).

The eschatological character of the Eucharist is essentially linked to the eschatological character of love, which is the experiential quintessence of the Kingdom. All asceticism and all cleansing from the passions is in essence a *precondition* for the Eucharist, because the Eucharist cannot be understood apart from love. Love is not simply a virtue; it is an ontological category, not simply an ethical one. Love is that which will survive into the 'age which does not end or grow old' when all the gifts which impress us today, such as knowledge, prophecy, etc., will pass away.[69]

Of all the forms of love, the most significant from the viewpoint both of the Eucharist and of the last times is *love for our enemies*. This love is not simply a matter of ethics (imitation of Christ and obedience to His commandment), but has *ontological* content directly connected with the Eucharist and its eschatological character, as Saint Maximus tries to show in a profound analysis of the petition of the Lord's Prayer 'forgive us our trespasses...', which he connects with the previous petition, 'give us this day our daily bread'. The argument is complex, like the whole of his language, but the following points from his *Interpretation of the Our Father* deserve our attention:

The essence of the ontological character of love for our enemies resides in the fact that if remembrance of the wrongs our enemy has done us becomes 'stamped on our mind', this *sunders* nature 'according to the will (*gnome*)', because through remembrance of wrong one appears to be, and indeed is, 'separated from some other man, while being oneself a man'. Love for enemies, in consequence, is actually a

---

68   On this double meaning of 'communion of the holy', see the minutely detailed examination of patristic sources in W. Elert's *Abendmahl und Kirchengemeinschaft in der alten Kirche, Hauptsächlich des Ostens*, 1954.

69   A phenomenon worth noting, and particularly evident today, is the way people go running after impressive spiritual gifts such as foresight, clairvoyance, etc., and consider these the supreme indications of holiness and of the presence of the Holy Spirit. These people remind us of the Jews who 'seek after sign' in order to believe. But these gifts — which, much to Saint Paul's sorrow, the Corinthians of his time also considered the most important (see 1 Cor. 12-13) — are much inferior to love because, as Saint Paul writes unlike love they will not survive into the last times.

union of the will and the principle of nature ('the will being in union with the principle [*logos*] of nature'). Through this love, human nature ceases to rebel against itself because of the will, and this leads also to reconciliation with God, because 'once the will is in union with the principle of nature, the free choice of those who have achieved this is not in a state of rebellion against God'.[70]

Much in consequence depends for us on free will, if our nature is to be able to transcend division and death. This requires dying to the 'present age' and passing over to the 'life which does not grow old':

> He who prays for the bread of spiritual knowledge [i.e., the bread of the Kingdom] having forgiven his debtors their debts, *as he knows that he is by nature mortal... anticipates nature according to his will... in order not to take with him any mark of the depravity of the present age when he departs to the life that does not grow old....*[71]

If one does not forgive one's enemies, one submits to nature as it is in the 'present age', in other words to division, to its 'rebellion' and to death, and endangers its true being which the bread of the Eucharist offers to man as the bread of the 'age to come' of the Kingdom: 'For I think that by "today" it means this age... That bread which Thou didst prepare for us in the beginning *that our nature might be immortal* do Thou give us today, *while we are in the present life of mortality...* that it may conquer death, etc.'[72]

After these remarks, it is not surprising that in the patristic texts one finds interpretations of the Eucharist which place an almost excessive emphasis on forgiveness of enemies, focusing our attention on this point. Saint Anastasius of Sinai (†608?), commenting in his *Homily on the Holy Synaxis* on the Divine Liturgy (which like Maximus he calls simply 'Synaxis'), says among other things about the petition 'Forgive us our trespasses....'

> Therefore, I pray you, let us flee this wicked and unpardonable sin (of remembrance of wrong). And if you want to learn that the darkening from remembrance of wrong is worse than any other sin, then listen. Every other sin takes a brief while to commit and is soon over, as when someone commits fornication, and afterwards realizes the enormity of his sin and comes to consciousness of it; but remembrance of wrong has a passion which never ceases to burn... Where remembrance of wrong

70   *Philokalia* II, p. 301 (PG 90:901).
71   *Philokalia* II, p. 301-2 (PG 90:904).
72   *Philokalia* II, p. 299 (PG 90:897).

has put down roots, nothing is of any avail; not fasting, or prayer, or tears, or confession, or supplication, or virginity, or alms, or any other good thing. For remembrance of wrong towards our brother destroys everything.

I often hear many people saying, 'Alas, how shall I be saved? I haven't the strength to fast, I don't know how to keep vigil, I can't live in virginity, I couldn't bear to leave the world — so how can I be saved?' How? I will tell you how. Forgive and you will be forgiven... here is a short cut to salvation. And I will show you another. What is that? Judge not, it says, and you will not be judged. So here is another path without fasting or vigil or labour... He who judges before Christ's coming is Antichrist, because he abrogates the position that belongs to Christ...[73]

These 'exaggerated' words of Anastasius, combined with those of Maximus,[74] not only explain why the Church has from the beginning regarded reconciliation with our enemies as an inviolable precondition for participation in the Eucharist (Mt. 5:23); they also show us how firmly the Eucharist is bound up with the Kingdom of God. The crucial point in the whole business is that we have to encounter the other person not as he was yesterday or is today, but *as he will be in the future in the last times*, which means as a member and our neighbour in the Kingdom. Because the future gives all things their true substance: their place in the Kingdom. And this is precisely what eludes our judgement, because it belongs exclusively to God and to the other person's freedom: 'You perhaps see him sinning, but you do not know in what sort of end he will pass from life'.[75]

Thus the eschatological orientation of the Eucharist creates its own ethos: the *eucharistic ethos*, the ethos of forgiveness, which is not merely an inner state but is experienced as *gathering* and *coexistence with the person who has hurt us*, in a future which we do not control and which

---

73   PG 89:825-849.

74   It is profoundly striking what Saint Maximus writes about slander, both in matters of 'life' and matters of 'faith' (it seems that the saint endured both): 'There is no pain of the soul that weighs more heavily than slander, whether one is slandered as to faith or as to life. And no one can scorn this except only the man who, like Susannah, looks to God who alone is able to rescue him from calamity as He did her, and tell people the truth, as He did about her, He can also comfort his soul with hope. As he prays from his soul for the person who has slandered him, in that same measure God too reveals the truth to those who have been scandalized' (PG 90:1069). There is always a strong temptation to counter-attack the slanderer so that souls are not scandalized. Maximus does not seem to approve this approach: he runs the risk of people being scandalized so as to secure the love and forgiveness (i.e. non-punishment) of the slanderer, leaving it to God to inform those who have been scandalized. How alien all this sounds to our modern mentality, even a modern 'Christian' mentality!

75   Anastasius, PG 89:845.

has no end, the 'age which does not end or grow old'. In order for the Eucharist to be 'for forgiveness of sins and unto eternal life' for those who take part in it and receive Communion, it must also be for forgiveness on our part of the sins of others and 'unto eternal life' with them in the gathering of the Kingdom.[76]

3. Transfiguration of the World

'Always, now and ever and to the ages of ages!' With this exclamation, in front of which celebrants unfortunately add 'Blessed is our God',[77] the Holy Things are taken from the altar to be transferred to the table of preparation at the end of the Liturgy. Whatever interpretation may be given to this exclamation, the fact that it was not originally connected with the phrase 'Blessed is our God' refers us to the eschatological perspective of the Eucharist: either — as favoured by many interpreters of the Liturgy in the form of Christ's promise that He will be with His disciples in the Church 'unto the end of the age', or in the sense that in the Liturgy we enter upon the 'age which does not end or grow old' in Saint Basil's words ('ages of ages' signifies the endless duration of time). In either case, this exclamation shows that the Eucharist, and all that it entails and offers, is not confined within our fragmented time but extends unto the age which has no end.

The consequences for our existence of this extension of the Eucharist 'unto ages of ages' are momentous. They signal transcendence of the tragic state which has tormented us since the Fall and offer us the taste of a life fitting to the uncreated God.

By being an 'image of the Kingdom', the Eucharist inevitably

---

76 Many spiritual fathers do not allow people to receive Holy Communion if they have not been reconciled with their enemies. This is not only in conformity with Christ's commandment (Mt. 5:23), but also follows from the fact that the Eucharist is an image and foretaste of the Kingdom, in which we shall be called to coexist with our enemies eternally. The exhortation 'Let us love one another, that with one mind we may confess' is an essential element in the Divine liturgy. The unity of the faith, which again is an essential and inviolable precondition for eucharistic communion, is formally manifested in the recitation of the Creed; this is also eschatological in character according to Saint Maximus, as we saw above (section 6). Thus faith and love are united in the same eucharistic event, which images the future Kingdom of God within the world and history.

77 According to liturgiologists (Trembelas, Fountoulis, et al.), the phrase 'Blessed is our God' did not originally belong at the beginning of the exclamation but was added later, and, if nothing else, should not be said aloud. See Fountoulis, Answers II, p. 350f. We consider this very significant from a theological point of view. The addition of 'Blessed is our God' changes the sense of the exclamation so that it becomes doxological (it should be noted that 'Blessed...' occurs at the beginning and not the end of the divine services), whereas without this addition it denotes the extension of the Mystery into the age of Kingdom 'that does not end or grow old', which is also the purpose of this exclamation at the end of the Liturgy.

underlines the paradox of 'already, but not yet' which is contained in Christian eschatology. The Resurrection of Christ has signalled the final victory over corruption and death, but this victory has not yet been realized in history. Death remains the *last* enemy (1 Cor. 15:26), in other words the enemy who will be defeated last of all, since his sting is still wounding creation. This is of course a sting which, as we know, does not ultimately put us to death (1 Cor. 15:55), and we know that this makes the death of those who participate in the body of the risen Christ into a 'falling asleep'. But this does not remove the expectation with which we look for the last times, when the resurrection of Christ will become the resurrection also of our own bodies, as we confess in our Creed. This intense *looking forward*, this longing for the Second Coming and the resurrection of the body — which we tend to forget — is not done away with or destroyed by the Eucharist. On the contrary, the Eucharist makes it more intense: *maranatha*, 'Yea, come, O Lord' (Rev. 22:17). If the Eucharist as an image of the last times is used as a sort of 'painkiller' to help us forget that evil and sin still torment creation, that will be a grave misunderstanding The eschatological character of the Eucharist does not attenuate but rather intensifies the struggle against the evil which surrounds us, both 'moral' evil as it is usually called, and 'natural' evil. As an image of the Kingdom, the Eucharist makes us appreciate more deeply the contrast between the world as it is, and the world as it will be in the last times. What the Eucharist destroys is the 'being-unto-death' of existentialism, the ontological coupling of being and non-being, life and death, a coupling which leads either to despair or to indifference concerning the transfiguration of the world.

The Eucharist calls us to look not only 'upwards' but also 'forwards'. It does not call upon us to go out of space and time, but to believe that thanks to the economy of the Holy Trinity which has been realized in the person and the work of Christ, 'with the cooperation of the Holy Spirit', space and time are capable of receiving transfiguration; and that the Kingdom of God is not something that will displace material creation but will transfigure it, cleansing it from those elements which bring about corruption and death. The Eucharist gives us the assurance that matter is sacred and worthy of every honour since the time when the Son of God became incarnate,[78] and that time too is sanctified by His incarnate presence. Thanks to the eschatological character of the Eucharist, it is clearly shown that the problem faced by created beings lies not with matter or with the time and space in which they live, but with their cleansing and transfiguration so that these elements become

---

78   '...and I do not cease to venerate matter, through which my salvation was brought about' (Saint John of Damascus, *Against those who attack the Holy Icons* [PG 94:1245]).

carriers of life rather than death. Thus the Eucharist as 'communion of the last times' reveals to us that the whole of creation is destined by God's love to be set free at last from corruption and death and to live 'unto ages of ages', having as its head the 'last Adam', Him who made a reality what the 'first Adam' refused and failed to do: the communion of what is created with God.

Conclusion

In approaching the Eucharist principally as Liturgy — for this is how members of the Orthodox Church experience it — we have tried to see, with the help of testimonies both from Scripture and from the Fathers, what it means for the Eucharist to form an image of the Kingdom of God — a manifestation, a prefiguration and a foretaste of that Kingdom. Our aim has been to show that it is not permissible for either academic theology or liturgical practice to play down or in various ways obscure the eschatological character of the Eucharist. This character is to be found throughout Holy Scripture and patristic thinking, and indeed in our liturgical typikon — often despised by dogmatic theologians — despite the alterations that this has undergone at various times as a result of the indifference or ignorance of our clergy; and it proves that what we have in the Eucharist is not a flight or deliverance from space and time or from history, but the biblical perspective of the *transfiguration* of space and time, as indeed of all the creation which God's love made 'very good'.

Our aim has also been to do what we can to help rid our people of conceptions and 'experiences' of the Eucharist influenced by Western pietism a pietism which has corroded our worship more than we ever imagined which tend to deprive our Liturgy of its resurrectional and festive character or to turn it into a medium for individual piety and psychological compunction and an instrument of mission or pastoral work.[79] In a period when our local Churches are fragmented, we have also considered it essential to stress the communal and 'catholic' character of the Eucharist as a 'gathering in one place' of the whole of the local Church; because the Kingdom of God is a *gathering*, but a

---

79 The argument put forward to justify the inept and novel practice (introduced just this century) of shifting the sermon from its natural position after the reading of the Gospel to the time of the Communion Hymn, by which time the Anaphora has been accomplished and our communion with God's eternal life is imminent, is revealing. The argument that more people have gathered by that time shows that the missionary or pastoral criterion has prevailed over that of structure and imagery: it does not even cross our minds that by making this shift we are altering the image of the Kingdom and turning back to front the whole movement and progress from history towards the Kingdom, and it is like putting the first act of a play after the final act!

gathering which is *structured* in a particular way, with Christ as its centre and head, surrounded by the Apostles. This structure, imaged in the Eucharist and transferred to the structure of the Church itself as a unity of the people of God around the bishop, is rooted in the eucharistic imaging of the Kingdom and for this reason contains an ultimate truth which may not be overlooked for the sake of a supposedly 'spiritual' understanding of the Church.

Our aim, finally, has been to demonstrate the anthropological and cosmological consequences of the eschatological character of the Eucharist, consequences which are often forgotten under the influence of the same individualistic tendencies which have invaded the territory of our Church. These consequences call upon us to draw from the Eucharist an *eschatological consciousness and ethos* (something which has tended to disappear, imprisoned as people are — even people in the Church — in a perspective which is confined to the world and to history, in both our personal and communal lives). But the person who 'lives in the Eucharist and through the Eucharist', to recall Florovsky's words, (when, of course, that Eucharist is properly celebrated) becomes accustomed to looking not only 'upwards' but also 'forwards'. In other words, he gets into the habit of placing himself, his works and history itself under the light and the judgement of the Kingdom, always and in everything seeking its *ultimate* meaning ('Seek ye first the Kingdom of heaven and its righteousness' [in other words, its love], Mt.6:33), of leaving the final judgement of other people in the hands of God, and of seeing in all things the ultimate destiny of their incorporation and survival in Christ unto 'the age which does not end or grow old'. With its eschatological perspective the Eucharist heals us of self-love, the source of all the passions, shatters the very backbone of individualism and teaches us to exist in a gathering with others and with all the beings of God's creation. Thus the Eucharist ceases to be a 'religious experience' or a means to individual salvation and becomes a *mode of being*, a way of life, illuminated by the vision and the expectation of the future, by that which the world will be when it is finally transfigured into the Kingdom of God.

CHAPTER THREE

SYMBOLISM AND REALISM IN ORTHODOX WORSHIP

Introduction

The problem we shall address in this article might be described as follows:

(a) The whole of our worship, culminating in the Divine Eucharist, is interwoven with symbolism. There is not a single act of worship or liturgical action in our Church that is performed without the use of some or other symbol. Why is this, and what is the theological justification for it?

(b) The very notion of 'symbol' contains the problem of the symbol's relationship with reality, or, more accurately, with truth. There is no such thing as a symbol which does not imply simultaneously two things: that the symbol *is not fully identified with the reality or truth*, and that the symbol *is not entirely foreign and unrelated to the reality or truth*, but participates in it in a certain sense which has to be explained and pinpointed. The symbol is a form of paradox: it at once is not and is the reality.[1]

(c) Precisely because of this paradox intrinsic to the notion of symbol, the worship that makes use of it, particularly to the extent that ours does, runs the risk of being identified with *magic*. How does symbolism differ from magic? For many Christians, perhaps not at all. It is not by chance that Protestantism opposed and virtually abolished symbolism in worship, precisely because it had seen the tendency in Western Christianity during the Middle Ages to introduce magical

---

1   Characteristic is the way the symbol is referred to by Saint Cyril of Jerusalem sometimes as identical with the truth and sometimes not. Thus he writes about baptism: 'What a strange and paradoxical thing: we *did not truly* die; we *were not truly* buried; we *were not truly* crucified and raised up; but the imitation was in an image, while the salvation is in truth' (*Mystagogical Cathechesis*, 2.5). Yet further on, referring to chrismation, he writes: 'You should know that the symbol of this chrism is to be found in the Old Testament... But these things happened to them in a type, whereas for you this is the beginning of your salvation not in a type, but in truth...' (*Mystagogical Cathechesis*, 3.6).

notions into Church life. Such notions often make their appearance among Orthodox too. For this reason, there is no shortage of people who would be happy to see the worship of our Church simplified as much as possible. The Roman Catholics gave in to this way of thinking at the Second Vatican Council, and decided to shorten and simplify the Mass, except for certain solemn or 'pontifical' Masses; to do away with the rich vestments of the celebrants and replace them with simple white vestments, etc. How many Orthodox would not honestly like something similar to happen in our Church? The long services, the rich vestments and the varied symbolism are seen by many as incompatible with the 'spiritual' character of Christian worship, the simplicity of Jesus' earthly life, the virtue of humility, etc. Add to this popular piety with its extreme, almost magical manifestations, and the problem of symbolism assumes grave dimensions even in our Church. There is in our Church a latent psychological gulf between the 'intellectual' and 'conscious' and 'enlightened' Christians on the one hand, and the simple believers on the other, and every so often this comes to the surface.[2] It is essential, then, for our theology to pose and deal with the question of symbolism in our worship: how can it be justified theologically, and how can we avoid falling from the Scylla of magic into the Charybdis of rationalism?

I. The Notion of Symbol

The notion of symbol is not an invention of the Christian Church. It is a notion intimately related and inseparably bound up with that of transcendence, which to varying degrees accompanies every form of religion. The existential source of the symbol is the need in some way to bridge the gap between finite and infinite or, in our Orthodox terminology, between created and uncreated. This bridging cannot be achieved except by using the means afforded by the finite and created world which in essence are nothing other than material and, corruptible things. Even if one wants to avoid matter in bridging the gap, one will still have recourse to means which are created, and of necessity

---

2   Related to this is the question of chanting the scriptural readings in worship. From time to time, the view is put forward in the Greek press that these readings should be rendered in a speaking voice and not sung, the argument being that this makes them more understandable for the people. Indeed, some clergy in our Church already use this manner of reading for the Apostle and Gospel during the Divine Liturgy, precisely for this reason. But is this right? Is there perhaps a theological reason which requires that the readings should be chanted? Why, for instance, does the *Typikon* provide (or the readings at Vespers to be chanted when they are from the New Testament, but simply read when they are from the Old Testament? Contrary to the prevailing view, the *Typikon* with all its details is not a mere 'formality', but has theological content. It is as well, then, before we adapt the *Typikon* to our practical common sense, to seek out the theological reasons behind it. See note 31, below.

limited and inadequate, such as human reason, which the ancient Greeks used *par excellence* and whose inadequacy was demonstrated by the apophaticism of patristic theology. Words too, then, are symbols — something distinct from the truth. But the utter silence to which mystics often resort is equally a symbol — distinct from the truth and borrowed from our finite and created being — since it has to do with human feelings such as passion and love, which the mystic borrows in order to bridge the gulf between created and uncreated. So there is no relation between man and God — even if that God is within the world — which does not have need of the symbol.

The symbol, then, in its function as a bridge between the world and God, *participates* in both these realities. The degree of participation may vary from case to case, but in order to be called a symbol it has to bring together (the etymological meaning of the Greek verb *symballo*); it must participate in what is symbolized. Characteristic is the distinction made by Paul Tillich[3] between 'sign' and 'symbol': a sign is something that points to a reality without necessarily participating in it, while a symbol is something that participates in the reality it symbolizes. Also important are the remarks of the late Alexander Schmemann[4] concerning the misunderstanding of the notion of 'symbol' even among Orthodox: a symbol has come to mean something different from or even opposed to reality, which leads to the arbitrary interpretation of liturgical symbolism and contempt for the 'formalities' of the liturgical *Typikon* on the part of academic theology (see note 2, above).

If, however, we define the symbol as the means of linking the created with the uncreated, the here-and-now with the beyond, experience with truth, by ways and means which are necessarily borrowed from the created here-and-now, then we need to seek the theologically correct Christian meaning of the symbol in the very nature and manner whereby the gulf between created and uncreated is bridged *in the person of Christ*. This is where we should locate the specific difference between Christian and non-Christian notions of symbol. And only in this way shall we understand the significance of symbolism in our Orthodox worship.

II. Symbolism in the Christian Faith

The fundamental difference between the biblical faith and pagan religions as to bridging the gulf between created and uncreated lies principally in the fact that pagan religions, which ontologically confine

---

3   *Systematic Theology* I, 1951, p. 265.
4   *The Eucharist*, 1988, pp. 30ff.

God within the world, bridge the gulf with the aid of *nature*, whereas in biblical faith nature on its own has no capacity or property of bridging the gulf; instead of being bridged with the aid of nature, this gulf is bridged only through the intervention of the *person*. Thus in pagan religions, the symbol that unites the created and the uncreated makes personal freedom in a certain way subject to natural necessity (hence magic among primitive peoples, or the motion of the stars or the symbolism of the natural ages among the ancient Greeks: for example in Aristotle, Plato, the Eleusinian Mysteries, Fate among the Stoics, etc.); whereas in biblical faith, bridging the gap between created and uncreated depends solely on personal freedom — that of God in the first place, and in the second place that of man formed in his image as a creature with free will. Thus neither in the Old Testament nor in the New Testament does there seem to be a symbolism connected with nature ('observing days, and months, and seasons, and years', as Saint Paul writes dismissively in his Epistle to the Galatians [4:10]). Biblical faith has as a bridge between created and uncreated the person, in other words freedom as love.

This precisely is the basis for the incarnation of the Word, and it is on this basis alone that Christian symbolism can be grounded. The Son and Word of God, this *person* which is 'one of the Trinity', in other words a hypostasis of loving relationship, *freely* takes up the created and bridges the gulf. If this had not happened, no symbolism would be possible: the created and the uncreated would remain separated by an unbridgeable gap. But since the Son of God has become man and become flesh and the gulf is bridged, symbolism has become possible; but under certain inviolable conditions, which would never allow us to lapse into natural symbolism. These conditions are as follows:

(a) No symbolism can be based on any form of correspondence between created and uncreated characteristics. Nor is the intelligible or rational world able to symbolize or provide an image of the invisible God. Only what the Son of God has *freely* chosen as a means of bridging the gap between created and uncreated is able to become a means of symbolism. And this choice on the part of Christ should not be interpreted or understood as dependent on properties of the created, because then it would not be free.

(b) Since no symbolism can be based on natural properties but only on personal freedom, all symbolism in the Church is based on historical events, because *historical events* alone are realities of personal freedom.

(c) Given that all historical events receive their meaning not from the past but from the future, the ultimate source of every symbolism is the *eschatological* event, the Kingdom of God. Each symbol is justified only to the extent that it images the eschatological reality. This is where the truth of the symbol is to be found: not in the nature of the materials used, nor simply in reference back to events of the past, but in the participation of the symbol in eschatological reality.

Let us now see how these basic principles are applied in Orthodox worship.

III. Symbolism in Orthodox Worship

The worship of the Church begins in its fullness from the Lord's resurrection.[5] With the resurrection, the bridge between created and uncreated begun at the incarnation is brought to completion. The veneration of the risen Christ by his disciples and the worship offered to him as 'Lord', seated at the right hand of the Father after his ascension, form the axis of Christian worship. The meals which the disciples eat with the risen Lord give meaning to the Mystical Supper (Lk. 24:30-32 and parallels), and become the first form of the Divine Eucharist. All these things happen because the resurrection is an *eschatological* and not simply an historical event. It marks God's final act in history, the victory over the 'last enemy' which is death, and the dawning of the 'last day'. This 'last day', which became a reality for the last Adam, will at the Second Coming become a reality for all creation. What does all this mean for symbolism? It means that *since the resurrection, the symbolism of worship no longer moves between the natural and intelligible worlds or simply between events of the Old and New Testaments, but principally between the resurrection and the Second Coming.* Let us explain what this means.

If we rule out, as we must, the notion of symbolism as a corre-spondence between the natural and intelligible worlds, and for reasons already given base our symbolism on the correspondence between *historical* events, then we have before us two categories of symbol. One is that which connects the symbolism used in worship with historical events *of the past*. The other is that which connects worship with 'events' *of the future*, in other words with the last times. All the symbolism in the Church's worship has these two poles, and it is these that give it its theological meaning.

The first pole (connection with historical events of the past) could be called typological.[6] Daniélou, in his well known work *The Bible and*

---

5   Before the Resurrection of Christ, Christian worship was not 'in Spirit and truth' (Jn. 4:23) since 'as yet the Spirit had not been given, because Jesus was not yet glorified' (Jn. 7:39). The Spirit who is given by the Risen Christ initially to his disciples (Jn. 20:22), and through them to the whole Church, renders Christian worship 'spiritual', bringing the 'last times' into history (Acts 2:18).

6   See Cyril of Jerusalem, *Mystagogical Catechesis*, 1.3: 'Pass across then, please, from the old to the new, from the type to the truth'.

the Liturgy, gives an excellent exposition of this subject. The worship of the Church was from the beginning full of typological characteristics: Baptism had its Old Testament types in circumcision, the Red Sea crossing, the Flood, etc. The same applied to the other mysteries and rites. Two theological conclusions may be drawn from this. First, that no symbolism in worship referred to nature and its properties. For instance, the water of Baptism did not refer to water's natural property of cleansing (even though it easily lends itself to such symbolism, this symbolism is nonetheless avoided). It refers instead to historical events. And this is significant. Also characteristic is what Saint Cyril of Jerusalem writes about the exorcisms preceding Baptism: the words of the priest expel the demons for no other reason than that they are drawn from Scripture.[7] The power of the symbolism does not lie in any natural property (e.g. the holiness of the cleric who breathes upon the candidate, etc.).[8]

The second theological conclusion is that typological symbolism never refers to the past, but always to the future. Thus Baptism is not a type of the Flood, but the Flood is a type of Baptism, etc. In worship, nothing leads us to the past, except to refer us through the past to the future.

The second pole of symbolism is precisely that which moves between the Resurrection, and the future in its eschatological form. This symbolism (the presence of which Daniélou failed to discern — perhaps because it requires antennae which only Orthodox worship affords) might be called *iconological*. We shall need to give this particular attention, because it has a particularly close connection with Orthodox worship.

In contrast to 'type', the term 'image' or 'icon' is used by the Fathers principally to denote states and events of the New Testament and not the Old. The exception is the writers of the Alexandrian School (Clement, Origen and Eusebius of Caesarea), who also refer to things in the Old Testament as 'images'.[9] The author of the Areopagitic

---

7   *Procatechesis*, 9.

8   References to natural properties are not wholly absent — such as the connection of the west with darkness when the baptizand turns from the west to the east during the exorcisms (Cyril of Jerusalem, *Mystagogical Catechesis*, 1.4). But the weight of the symbolism clearly falls on the historical events: Pass across then, please, from the old to the new, from the type to the truth. There Moses was sent by God into Egypt; here Christ is sent forth by the Father into the world. There, it was to lead the oppressed people out of Egypt; here, Christ comes to deliver those in the world who are worn out by sin. There the blood of a lamb turned away the destroyer, here the blood of the spotless Lamb Jesus Christ has been made a healing of the blood offered to demons...' (*Mystagogical Catechesis*, 1.3).

9   E.g. Clement of Alexandria, *Strom.*, 4.22; Origen, *On John*, 10.16; Eusebius of Caesarea, *Eccles. Hist.*, 1.3.4.

writings, in keeping with his general approach, uses 'image' for the correspondence of earthly worship with heavenly.[10] But Saint Maximus the Confessor, in an extremely interesting corrective, without appearing to disagree with Dionysius, transfers the whole subject of imagery in the Divine Liturgy from the historical plane to the eschatological. So while Dionysius regards the Divine Liturgy as an image of the heavenly Liturgy, Maximus alters his position by interpreting it as imaging the Kingdom which is to come.[11] This is why he very characteristically gives this epigrammatic summary: 'the things of the Old Testament are the shadow; those of the New Testament are the image. The truth is the state of things to come'. And John of Damascus echoes Maximus; although he sometimes uses the term 'image' in reference to things in the Old Testament, he hastens to explain, following the Apostle Paul (Heb. 8:5), that 'the Law was not even an image, but the foreshadowing of an image'.[12]

All this means that symbolism as 'typology' and symbolism as 'iconology' are two different things. The notion of an icon requires particular attention. The subject of icons is a very broad one and cannot concern us in detail here.[13] We shall confine ourselves to just a few remarks.

(a) In contrast with a shadow or a type, an icon is grounded in the truth of the New Testament, in other words in realized rather than expected Christology. As the supporters of the icons maintained during the iconoclast controversy, the fact that Christ has become human mandates the making of icons, for no other reason than that it has made the Son of God himself an historical reality.[14] It is significant that

---

10 Dionysius the Areopagite, *Celestial Hierarchy*, 1.3; *Divine Names*, 4.4.

11 *Scholia on Dionysius the Areopagite, On the Church Hierarchy*, 3.2: 'From the effects. That is, from what is accomplished visibly to the things that are unseen and secret, which are the causes and archetypes of things perceptible. For those things are called causes which in no way owe the cause of their being to anything else. Or from the effects to the causes, that is, from the perceptible symbols to what is noetic and spiritual. Or from the imperfect to the more perfect, from the type to the image; and from the image to the truth. *For the things of the Old Testament are the shadow, those of the New Testament are the image. The truth is the state of things to come.*' The fact that these *Scholia*, which the manuscript tradition transmits with those of John of Scythopolis (between 535 and 560AD), faithfully reflect Saint Maximus's theology, is clear from the latter's *Mystagogy*, in which all the rites performed in the Divine Liturgy form an image of the Kingdom which is to come. For more on this, see chapter 2, above.

12 *In Defence of the Holy Icons*, 1.15.

13 See L. Ouspensky, *The Theology of the Icon*, 1992.

14 See John of Damascus, *In Defence of the Holy Icons*, 1.8-16: 'It is clear that when you see the bodiless one become man for your sake, then you will make an image of his human form. When the invisible becomes visible in the flesh, then you will make an image of the likeness of him who is seen. When he who is without body and without shape... takes the form of a servant and limits himself so as to take on size and quality and clothes himself in bodily form, then draw

in iconographic depiction, the emphasis falls on historicity and not on conceptual symbolism or typology. The fact that the Quinisext Council prohibits the representation of Christ as a lamb, on the grounds that this does not correspond to historical reality,[15] shows that when symbolism in the Church is iconic, it cannot but be historical.

(b) In contrast with the state of things to come, the icon is distinct from the truth, not because it is a falsehood or a delusion or a fantasy, but because it borrows its means of expression from nature which is still corruptible. Thus the whole notion of a icon depends quite literally on the notion of person and the distinction between person and nature. If the icon is not a lie or a fantasy, despite not being the truth, this is possible because of the fact that the person does not depend on the nature. Thus we can have a *personal* presence without having a *natural* presence. Saint Theodore the Studite expresses the distinction between nature and person in respect of the icon in these words: 'When anyone is depicted in an image, it is not the nature but the hypostasis that is depicted... So Christ is circumscribed according to his hypostasis, even though he is uncircumscribed in his Godhead'.[16] 'And we call Christ's image "Christ"... The icon of Christ is nothing other than Christ, *apart, of course, from the difference in essence*'.[17]

Thus with the help of the distinction between nature and person, we can understand the relationship between symbol and truth (between

a picture of him who has deigned to be seen, and display it to be looked at. Draw his ineffable condescension, his birth from the Virgin, his baptism in Jordan, his transfiguration on Tabor, his sufferings which have freed us from passion, his death, his miracles, the symbols of his divine nature... Of old, God who is without body and without shape could in no way be represented in an image. But now that God has been seen in the flesh and walked among men, make an image of the visibility of God'.

15   This prohibition appears in the well-known 82nd Canon of the Quinisext Council (692 AD), which is of crucial importance for the notion of the icon: 'In certain reproductions of the venerable images, the Forerunner is pictured pointing to the Lamb with his finger. This representation was adopted as a symbol of grace. It was a hidden figure of that true Lamb who is Christ our God, shown to us according to the Law. Having thus welcomed these ancient figures [types] and shadows as symbols of the truth transmitted to the Church, today we prefer grace and truth themselves, as a fulfilment of the Law. Therefore, in order to expose to the sight of all, at least with the help of painting, that which is perfect, we decree that henceforth Christ our God be represented in his human form and not in the ancient form of a lamb. We understand this to be the elevation of the humility of God the Word, and we are led to remembering his life in the flesh, his passion, his saving death and, thus, the deliverance which took place for the world' (from Ouspensky, *op. cit.*, pp. 92–93.

16   *Antirrheticus*, 3.1 (34) (PG 99.405). The distinction between nature and person and the connection of the notion of the icon with that of the person is so important that, for Saint Theodore the Studite at least, the whole argument against the iconoclasts depends on the notion of the person. This should be an answer to those who belittle the central place of this notion in Orthodox theology.

17   *Antirrheticus*, 3.3 (14) (PG 99.425).

symbolism and realism) in this way: an image is personal presence *without* the nature; the truth is personal presence *with* its nature. Thanks to the incarnation and especially the resurrection, the state between the New Testament and the last times allows personal presence, in other words the preservation of the person, but only in view of the resurrection of the body, i.e. of its natural presence. Until that time, the person in a certain sense borrows nature which is still corruptible, and in this way it is able to be present. Without this borrowing, the communion of the historical Church in the eschatological is impossible. Those who reject the use of images as a personal presence reject the very possibility of prayer and worship in an Orthodox manner. Worship without images is an exercise in psychology, the most flagrant self-deception and illusion.[18]

IV. Iconic Symbolism in Worship

Given that iconic symbolism in the Liturgy is, as we have seen, a matter of personal presence and not of natural presence, nature participates in it only in a secondary way and to the degree that it is hypostatized in the person. Thus place, time, matter, colours, speech, smell, hearing, etc. are used in symbolism; not, however, as the source of the symbol — the sources are always personal and historical-eschatological — but as borrowings to express the personal presence. Let us look at some examples.

The colour red naturally suggests blood. It is thus natural for it to be used symbolically, for instance for clerical vestments on feasts of the martyrs. Indeed, it has become the practice in the Church of Russia to use this symbolism, and the same can be seen also among some Greek priests. Theologically, this means that the symbolism has its source in nature, not in history or in the person. It is consequently very close to pagan symbolism, and to the representation of Christ as a lamb forbidden by the Quinisext Council. The distinctions are subtle, but important. If the colour white is used as a symbol of purity, then we have a symbolism which is pagan in inspiration. If it is used because that is how Christ is described at the Transfiguration, or the angels at the empty tomb, etc. — in other words, in reference to history and to persons — then the source of the symbolism is not some property

---

18   The tendency to regard the liturgical life of the Church (which by definition involves imagery) as a form of inferior spirituality 'for the simple faithful' in comparison with mental prayer, makes the whole of the Church's theological struggle for the holy icons meaningless. 'So if Christ does not manifest Himself in the icon, in this respect he is inactive and ineffectual: and to think that is absurd' (Theodore the Studite, *Antirrheticus*, 3.4 [PG 99.432]).

of nature but a personal, historical event. But not even in this case can the colour be binding, because iconic representation is not simply historical, but eschatological.

The veneration of icons, the recognition of supernatural properties in holy relics, sacred vessels and objects and so forth can become forms of paganism if these objects are regarded as possessing these properties *in their nature* and not in the personal presence of the saint with whom they are connected.[19] It is in consequence a dangerous view (shared by many Orthodox) that the divine energies somehow reside in the nature of these sacred objects, if we do not simultaneously stress the *personal* character of the divine energies. The divine energies are always *hypostatic*, and what sanctifies is the personal presence of the saint and not the physical contact of the object with the divine energies (impersonally and in themselves). I consider that the theology of divine energies, if it is not clearly linked with that of hypostatic energies[20] and generally with the notion of the person, can lead straight to paganism.

But the iconic symbolism in our worship is not concerned only with things and objects. All the *movements* and *actions* in worship are also icons and imagings, together with *those who perform them*. We shall confine ourselves to the Divine Eucharist, since this is the epicentre of all worship and it is here above all that the question of symbolism is decided.

The Divine Eucharist is not just one thing, one object, the 'holy things' (the precious Gifts changed into the Body and Blood of Christ). It is an action, a work, a *function*.[21] And this point is decisive for the notion of symbolism. All the patristic commentaries on the Divine Eucharist, from Maximus to Cabasilas, approach the Divine Eucharist

---

19   'I do not venerate matter, but the Creator of matter,' John of Damascus, *In Defence of the Holy Icons*, 1.16. Similarly, Theodore the Studite, *Antirrheticus*, 3.4 (11): 'The image is with the archetype, and with the archetype the image is present and is seen and venerated. It is not at all that the essence becomes identical, but the likeness becomes one, and in respect of the likeness there is one unified veneration towards both, *not divided according to the difference of natures*' (PG 99.433). The same Father is still clearer at other points in his *Antirrheticus*: 'Nor is the nature of the icon venerated, even though the person depicted is seen in it. And yet *in respect of the identity of the hypostatic likeness*, the veneration is identical, in accordance with the single, complete similarity between the two' (3.4 [7], [PG 99.432]). 'Inasmuch as the icon is similar to the prototype, so it partakes in all the veneration relating to the prototype; it does not take with it the material in which it is exhibited for veneration. For this is the nature of an icon, that it is identified with the prototype according to its likeness to it, but *differentiated* according to the principle of its essence' (3.4 [6]).

20   The significance of the hypostatic character of the divine energies in the theology of Saint Gregory Palamas is demonstrated in the doctoral thesis of S. Yiangazoglou, *Communion in Deification. Christology and Pneumatology in the Theology of St Gregory Palamas* (in Greek), 1995.

21   Translator's note: 'function' is the everyday meaning of *leitourgia* in Greek.

as a *liturgy*, a *synaxis*, and an *image*.[22] In the Divine Liturgy, everyone and everything is an image of something: the church building represents the space of the Kingdom of God, with Christ the King surrounded by the saints. The bishop represents Christ seated on the throne, as he will be in his Kingdom, The priests represent the apostles who surround the bishop Christ on the *synthronon*.[23] The deacons represent the angels who, as 'ministering spirits sent forth to serve' (Heb. 1:14), move between the people and the clergy. The people gathered together in one place and bringing the gifts (bread, wine, oil, etc.) express the scattered people of God, which in the Kingdom of God will come together around Christ and, as the crown of creation, will bring with them the whole of the material world to be sanctified and saved as well. And all this iconic symbolism is not a static tableau but a movement in time, containing within it the historical time of salvation. Thus the bishop as another Christ does not simply sit on the throne; he *comes*. His entrance into the church is a great liturgical event (though who is aware of this?)[24] because it images the coming of Christ into the world at both his first and his Second Coming, and his reception by the clergy and people at the entrance of the church is the reception of Christ: 'Come, let us worship and fall down before Christ...' All the ancient commentators on the Liturgy see the Liturgy as an image. More than all the others, Saint Maximus sees everything that is performed as an image of the Kingdom. After the readings and the closing of the doors once the catechumens withdraw, everything from then on images future events of the Kingdom: the Creed represents our eternal thanksgiving for all that God has done for our salvation. The kiss of peace represents the eternal mingling of souls in the communion of the Kingdom, etc.[25]

22   In contrast to modern academic theology, Orthodox included, which sees as the central and virtually exclusive theme of the Divine Eucharist the Lord's words of institution and the change in the Gifts (cf. the accurate criticisms of Schmemann, *The Eucharist*, pp. 30ff.), ancient commentators on the Liturgy see the Eucharist principally as a *synaxis* (a technical term for the Eucharist in Saint Maximus, Saint Germanos, Saint Anastasios of Sinai, *et al.*), and make the *whole* of its ritual and symbolism a subject for theological examination.

23   Translator's note: the *synthronon* is a raised seat in the apse with places for the bishop and priests.

24   Either through ignorance of the enormous significance of this matter or from ill-conceived simplicity and 'humility', some of the bishops of our Church today, when they are going to celebrate the Liturgy, do not come into the church by the main entrance where the clergy and people await them, but by the 'back door' of the altar, almost unnoticed, there to vest and come out at the Great Doxology in Matins, so that they can go into the altar once again at the Little Entrance. This totally destroys the meaning of the Entrance, which for the Fathers of the early Church had a vital theological significance. As to the related question of the bishop's vesting outside the altar and not entering the altar before the Little Entrance, see my comments in 'The Eucharist and the Kingdom of God' (chapter 2, above).

25   See Maximus the Confessor, *Mystagogy*, 8ff.: 'the first entry of the bishop into the holy church during the sacred synaxis is a type and image of the first coming of the Son of God, our Saviour

Later commentators give greater weight to the imaging of events in Christ's earthly life, and thus the eschatological orientation of liturgical symbolism is gradually attenuated.[26] Nicholas Cabasilas, influenced by the climate of his age, begins already to think in scholastic terms, making the Eucharistic Anaphora an image of the sacrifice of Christ,[27] which earlier had been placed at the Proskomide, and earlier still (Theodore of Mopsuestia)[28] at the preparation of the Gifts before the Great Entrance. Prior to Cabasilas, Germanos of Constantinople and Theodore of Andida, especially the first, still largely echo Maximus, but the trend of iconic symbolism is clearly getting ever further away from eschatology, whether in the direction of a correspondence between the earthly and the heavenly, or towards the representation of past events, though always those of the New Testament. All these strands are somehow synthesized in the work of Symeon of Thessaloniki, who borrows from Maximus, Germanos and Theodore, composing a detailed symbolic interpretation of the church buildings, as well as the rites performed in them and the ministers performing these rituals. Symeon's works bears witness to how thoroughly iconic symbolism had permeated Orthodox liturgical

Jesus Christ, into this world through the Incarnation. After this coming, his ascent and restoration to heaven and to his throne above the heavens is figured by the entry of the bishop into the sanctuary and his ascent to the priestly throne... The divine readings of the most sacred books indicate the divine and blessed wills and intentions of God All-holy... The spiritual enjoyment of the divine chants signifies the vivid delight of the divine blessings ... ' From the moment of the reading of the Gospel, which images 'the end of this world', with the dismissal of the catechumens and the closing of the doors, we find ourselves in the space of the Kingdom which is to come, where everything that is performed symbolically expresses things to come, our eschatological communion in the blessed life of the Trinity through our adoption as sons. Thus the Eucharist becomes an icon of the Kingdom of God and a foretaste of joy and gladness (cf. Acts 2:46).

26   For more detail see H.-J. Schultz, *The Byzantine Liturgy* (trans. M.J. O'Connell), 1986, pp. 184ff.
27   *Ibid.*, p. 191.
28   See R. Taft's exceptionally interesting work *The Great Entrance*, 1978, especially pp. 35ff. A point of great theological interest to come out of Taft's study, and earlier that of G. Dix (*The Shape of the Liturgy*, 1945, pp. 288ff.), is that in the time of Theodore of Mopsuestia (d. 428), the entrance with the Gifts images the procession with Christ already sacrificed (during the Preparation?), going to be buried on the Holy Table. 'This will eventually lead,' Taft comments, 'in the Byzantine tradition at least, to the interpretation of the Liturgy as culminating in the Resurrection from a passion or sacrifice accomplished before the Liturgy has even begun' (37). The theological problems posed in this case are significant. Clearly in the East, the moment of the Anaphora does not seem always to have been identified with the sacrifice on the Cross, as happened in the West (and in modern Orthodox theology). This explains why for Maximus and other Byzantine writers, the actions following the Great Entrance image events of the Resurrection and the Kingdom, and not of Golgotha. This is most likely the explanation for the popular reverence traditionally shown at the Great Entrance, at which, according to the Cherubic Hymn, we receive 'the King of all'. (The reading *hypoderomenoi*, 'about to receive', instead of *hoodexamenoi*, 'having received', by which many people try to solve the problem, is of little help, since we are dealing with a reception taking place *at that moment*.)

life towards the end of the Byzantine era. But what remains of all this today?

V. A Look at the Situation Today

If we take a look at the state of affairs in the Orthodox Church today, what we observe is, generally speaking, as follows:

(a) The form of the Liturgy and all the services is preserved with almost complete faithfulness and exactitude. The centuries of Turkish domination were a time of conservatism. Thanks to this period, the Divine Liturgy has come down to us basically as it took shape in Byzantium. There were just some small changes, as the symbolism of the emperor's participation in worship was transferred initially to the Patriarch and then to all bishops. Even from Byzantine times, changes had begun which were later consolidated and still apply regarding matters which had an indirect and destructive influence on the iconic symbolism of the Liturgy:

(i)   The *skevophylakion*[29] disappeared as a special building or compartment of the church, with the result that the bishop and the other clergy now vest inside the altar, and thus the Little Entrance with its important symbolism disappears. For the same reason, the Great Entrance has essentially been done away with too, since now everything begins in the sanctuary and comes back to the sanctuary in a circular movement. The disappearance of the Entrances destroyed the iconic symbolism, depriving it of the linear movement from history to the last times and thus reinforcing the imagery of 'place'[30] already present in the Areopagite and later commentators on the Liturgy.

(ii) The distinction between episcopal and presbyteral Liturgies, which was marked in the earliest centuries (second to fourth centuries), disappeared (cf. already Symeon of Thessaloniki). The result was that the notion of the bishop as icon of Christ was gradually lost from the Liturgy, and the episcopal Liturgy became simply more solemn and cluttered with pointless rubrics. Together with this the *synthronon* gradually fell into disuse, and the 'stall' was made into the bishop's throne; whereas even in the sixteenth century (cf. Hubert *Archieratikon*) this was simply a seat next to the choir (cf. the term *chorostasia*, lit. 'standing at the choir', to denote the bishop's presence at the service) which the bishop used when he attended church at Vespers or at Matins before celebrating the

29   Translator's note: the *skevophylakion* is the room in which holy vessels and vestments were kept.
30   Translator's note: 'place', that is, the earthly Liturgy as an image of the heavenly Liturgy.

Liturgy. With the loss of the *synthronon*, the iconic symbolism of the Kingdom of God in the Divine Liturgy was also lost.

(c) Under the influence of the Enlightenment, which gradually ate its way into the Orthodox Church too, the iconic ontology broke down almost totally and was replaced by rationalism and individualism. The two last are incompatible with iconic ontology, because this ontology is predicated upon relatedness and the way one thing refers to another, transcending individualism and making the person the ontological category. Thus iconic imagery became symbolism of a psychological kind, and for rationalistic thought a purely metaphorical notion. To regard the bishop as an image of Christ became pious naïveté and nonsense, since you know very well that *as an individual* he is a human being with any number of imperfections and sins; to venerate icons and relics became something like superstition and magic. So we Orthodox have come to the point of not knowing what to do with our Liturgy and our Tradition. Those who kiss the icons or the priest's hand do it out of habit, without knowing why, and under the mocking gaze of those who know better — and there are plenty of those in this Age of Enlightenment!

(d) Again, under the influence of pietism, which has also corroded our Orthodox people as an offshoot of the Enlightenment, iconic ontology has been replaced by the *ontology of qualities* and the *psychology of the inner man*, with the result that liturgical symbolism is virtually useless, since the purpose of the Liturgy is not to participate in the communion of the last times, but to create moral examples useful to society or to serve the religious needs of man, who is looking for 'peace', 'prayerfulness' and so forth. The sermon is considered so important as a source of edification that it is transferred to the time of Communion, thus making havoc of the entire eschatological image presented by the Liturgy. Vestments are simplified to be more humble ('moral perfection' demands it). Simple, humble country chapels are preferred to light-filled cathedrals as being more prayerful. The apostolic and biblical readings are not chanted but read like ordinary texts, so as to become comprehensible to human reason.[31] Episcopal liturgies are only for feasts, etc., etc. Certainly there

---

31 The question of whether scriptural readings in the Divine Liturgy should be chanted or simply read should not be unrelated to the approach, eschatological or otherwise, to the Divine Eucharist. Reading a text with a view to teaching and moral edification is radically different from reading it in a spirit of *doxology*. In the first case, the words are *grasped* and *comprehended* or 'taken possession of' by human reason. In the second case, the words 'broaden out' (hence the chanting) so that *they* 'grasp' and 'take possession of' human reason. It is obvious that this second sort of reading (the doxological) flies in the face of rationalism, which demands that human reason should 'take possession of' the truth. It is no accident that the demands for plain reading of scriptural texts arise at a time when the ambient cultural atmosphere is rationalistic, and the Church, having lost her awareness of the eschatological nature of the Liturgy, has turned it into a vehicle for teaching and edification, which naturally obliges her to undertake innovations such as plain

are still people — and many of them — who love the Church's feasts and flock to celebrate them, as well as little old ladies — fortunately, there are still plenty of these too — who kiss priests' hands, touch their vestments to receive grace, kiss the icons and holy relics with a faith that is almost 'magical' and generally preserve the traditions with piety. If they do not fall victim to wily clerics, these people are the only leaven, the little leaven available to us to preserve and restore iconic symbolism, purifying it from such magical tendencies as may exist. But in order for this to happen, we theologians and clergy have to rediscover the lost meaning of iconic ontology. A return to the Fathers without recovering the meaning of liturgical symbolism will get us nowhere; for in the Orthodox Church, the *lex credendi* has no meaning without the *lex orandi*. Only the rediscovery of iconic ontology will save us from both the paganism and the rationalism that lurk in our midst, each in its own way threatening the iconological symbolism of our Liturgy.

---

reading of the scriptural lessons so that they are better 'understood' — transferring the sermon from after the Gospel to before communion, when the church is full (so that more people can be *taught*), and similar — not to mention the grave danger in plain reading of a subjective element creeping into the delivery. This is a danger far more serious than the one usually remarked, that of the reader showing of his musical and vocal skill to the detriment of the meaning of the text when readings are chanted. It is obvious that the Church ought to train readers in the proper way to chant the scriptural lessons, rather than proceeding to abolish this practice.

CHAPTER FOUR

THE ECCLESIOLOGICAL PRESUPPOSITIONS
OF THE HOLY EUCHARIST

Introduction

The subject on which I have been asked to speak is extremely important
and vast. Although it is a subject on which I have worked for many
years, I feel inadequate to deal with it properly in a brief lecture. What
I intend to do here is to offer only some general suggestions or theses
which may be of some help in deepening further the discussion on the
subject. I therefore propose to raise and discuss briefly the following
questions:

(1) What phases has the problem of the relation between Church
and Eucharist gone through before reaching its present state? This brief
return to the past is necessary in order to appreciate the significance that
this problem carries for us today.

(2) What conclusions can we draw from a study of the ancient
Tradition, common to both the West and the East, concerning the
relation between Eucharist and ecclesiology, and more specifically, the
ecclesiological presuppositions of the Eucharist?

(3) What conclusions can we draw from all this for our ecumenical
situation today? At this point special attention will be paid to the
problem of the 'validity' of the Eucharist of the divided Churches
and the possibilities that may exist for a restoration, of eucharistic
communion between them.

I. History

Let us begin with a brief look at the historical background. The history
of the relationship between Eucharist an ecclesiology seems to involve
the following three fundamental phases:

(a) In the primitive phase, that of the ancient Church, the Eucharist
is closely linked with the mystery of the Church. Already at the time
of Saint Paul the word *ekklesia* and those terms which describe the

Eucharist signify the same reality. A careful study of 1 Corinthians 11 shows this clearly. An analysis of verses 20, 33, 34, etc. of this chapter leaves us in no doubt that for Saint Paul the terms 'Lord's Supper' (*kuriakon deipnon*), 'coming together on the same place' (*synerxesthai epi to auto*), and 'Church' (*ekklesia*) are used to denote the same reality.[1] It is true that in Paul's mind the idea of the Church as the 'people of God' in its Old Testament sense occupies a place of priority.[2] And yet, if not in a general, at least with regard to 1 Corinthians, the Church is above all a *concrete community*.[3] And what is even more important, the Church in these texts is not simply a concrete community of any kind, but the community of a city[4] united *epi to auto to celebrate the Eucharist*.[5] For Saint Paul the local community becomes the very 'Church of God' when it gathers to celebrate the Eucharist.

This Pauline ecclesiology which identifies so closely Church and Eucharist is developed even further in Saint Ignatius of Antioch. What characterizes Ignatius in particular is that for him the Eucharist does not simply make the local community into the Church, but that it makes it the catholic Church (*katholike ecclesia*),[6] that is, the *full and integral body of Christ*.[7] It would not be an exaggeration to say that for Ignatius the catholicity of the Church derives from the celebration of the Eucharist.[8] And this allows Ignatius to apply the term 'catholic Church' *to the local community*.[9] Each local eucharistic community presided over by the bishop surrounded by the college of the presbyters and assisted by

---

1   In verse 18 Paul writes: 'when you gather together (*synerchomenon*) in [or 'as'] Church (*en ecclesia*) I hear that there are divisions among you' etc. As it is evident from verse 20, Paul has in mind here specifically the eucharistic gatherings of the Corinthians: 'Therefore as you gather together (*synerchomenon*)… to eat the Lord's supper (*kuriakon deipnon phagein*)…'. Cf. also 33–34 and 29. In all these cases, the identity of the terms *ecclesia*, *synerxosthai* (*epi to auto*), *kuriakon deipnon*, etc. is obvious.

2   See L. Cerfaux, *La Theologie de l'Eglise suivant saint Paul*, 1942.

3   This is admitted also by L. Cerfaux, *op. cit.*, esp. pp. 153–161.

4   That Christianity started as a city 'religion' was noticed already by Adolf von Harnack, *Mission…* II, 1924, p. 278. Cf. R. Knopf, *Nachaposlischer Zeitalter*, 1905, p. 61; and K.S. Latourett, *A History of the Expansion of Christianity* I, 1953, p. 110.

5   See note 1, above.

6   Ignatius, *Smyrn.* 8.

7   This is the meaning of *katholike* suggested to us by the study of Ignatius, cf. my *Eucharist, Bishop, Church*. For the different views of modern Patristic scholarship on this, see the well-informed discussion by A. de Halleux, 'L'Eglise catholique dans la Lettre ignacienne aux Smyrniotes', *Ephemerides Theologicae Lovanienses* 58 (1982), pp. 5–24.

8   For an analysis of the sources see our work mentioned in n. 7 above. Cf. also my "Eucharist and Catholicity" in *Being as Communion*, 1985, pp. 143–170.

9   Ignatius, *Smyrn.* 8: 'That Eucharist should be regarded as certain (or valid: *bebia*) which is under the bishop or whosoever he would appoint. Wherever the bishop would appear there should the multitude (*plethos*) [i.e. the local Church] also appear, just as (*hosper*) wherever is Jesus Christ, there is also the catholic Church'. Cf. *Trall.* 2,3; *Phld.* 4; *Magn.* 7,2; *Eph.* 5,2 etc.

the deacons, in the presence of the 'multitude' (*plethos*), i.e. the laity, constitutes the 'catholic Church' precisely because in it the total Christ is found in the form of the Eucharist.

After Ignatius the preoccupation of the Church with the danger of Gnosticism and other heresies forced her to emphasize *orthodoxy* as the fundamental and decisive ingredient of ecclesiology.[10] Thus, the relation between Church and Eucharist seems to be weakened to some extent in the writers of the second century without being altogether absent from their thought. The situation at this stage in history is exemplified by Saint Irenaeus, who, while regarding orthodoxy as fundamental to ecclesiology combines this very strongly with the Eucharist as a criterion of catholicity: 'Our faith (belief: *gnome*) is in accordance with the Eucharist and the Eucharist confirms our faith'.[11] It is mainly for this reason that in all ancient writers before Saint Augustine each local Church is called catholic,[12] that is, the full and integral body of Christ.

Now, with Saint Augustine something seems to change in this respect. With this author, who strives to combat the provincialism of the Donatists the term 'catholic Church' acquires for the first time in history the meaning not of the local Church but of the Church *universal*.[13] This gives to catholicity the meaning of universality and with it a *quantitative* and *geographical* content instead of the original qualitative one.

This change was destined to exercise a decisive influence in the subsequent centuries in the West. And yet, as it has been shown by the remarkable studies of scholars such as Henri de Lubac[14] and Yves Congar,[15] the link between Church and Eucharist was not weakened at all as a result of this in the West up to the 13th century. The Eucharist continued to constitute the sacrament of the Church, that which expresses the Church's unity and which makes the body of Christ and the body of the Church identical. Church, Eucharist, and body of Christ continue up to that time to constitute one and the same reality in the West as is also the case in the East. In the latter, in spite of certain shifts of emphasis that led Byzantine theology to a preoccupation with

---

10   E.g. *Mart. Pol.* 16.2, and especially Irenaeus, *Adv. Haer.* 1.6.2; 1.16.3; 1.33.8: 3.3.4; 3.10.8; 3.12.5 etc. The bishop here is the *didaskalos*, while earlier in Ignatius his authority is thought to be strengthened by his 'silence'. Cf. Henry Chadwick, 'The Silence of Bishops in Ignatius,' *HTR* 43 (1950), pp. 169–172.

11   Irenaeus, *Adv. Haer.*, 5.5.5.

12   For instance, *Mart. Pol.*, inscription; Tertullian, *De prescr.*, 26.4; Cyprian, *Ep.* 49 (46) 2.4; 55 (52) 1.2; Eusebius, *His. Eccl.* 6.43.11, etc.

13   Augustine, *Ep.* 93.23: *De Unit.* 6.16, etc. Also Optatus of Milan, *Contra Parm.* 2.1. Cf. P. Batiffol, *Le Catholicisme de s. Augustin*, 1929, p. 212.

14   Henri de Lubac, *Corpus Mysticum: The Eucharist and the Church in the Middle Ages*, 2007.

15   Yves Congar, *L'Église de saint Augustin à l'époque moderne*, 1971, especially pp. 173ff.

the anthropological rather than the strictly ecclesiological dimensions of Christian faith,[16] the Holy Liturgy never ceased to occupy the centre of the Church's life and to be regarded as the ecclesiological event[17] — in the East one still speaks of 'going to Church' when going to the Eucharist, thus preserving the early link between Eucharist and ecclesiology.

(b) From the 13th century onwards the relation between Church and Eucharist entered a new phase which was destined to exercise an enormous influence on the theology of the subsequent centuries up to our own time. With the help of subtle distinctions used by the scholastic theologians of that time, the terms 'body of Christ', 'body of the Church', and 'body of the Eucharist' ceased to be identical.[18] This, together with the appearance of a sacramental theology independent of both christology and ecclesiology,[19] led to a disjunction between Eucharist and ecclesiology and to a conception of the Eucharist as *one sacrament among many*. Thus, the Eucharist was no longer identified with the Church; it became a 'means of grace' something assisting the faithful in their spiritual life, which was no longer regarded as manifesting *the total body of the Church*. As a result eucharistic celebrations could become 'private' — something unheard of in the early Church — and the sole presence of a presbyter, in the absence of the other orders of the Church, was regarded as sufficient for a 'valid' Eucharist. Church and Eucharist were thus gradually dissociated from each other both in theory and in practice.

The Reformation, although critical of many medieval practices with regard to the Eucharist, seems to have done little to restore the old link between Church and Eucharist. It is true that the Reformers were strongly concerned with the centrality of communion — i.e., communion of laity — in the eucharistic celebration. But by attributing increasingly greater centrality to the preaching of the Word in the Church's life and by opening the way to rare celebrations of the Eucharist during the year — in many cases under the influence of civil authority and in contrast with the theology of the Reformers — the Reformation weakened even further the already loose link between Eucharist and ecclesiology. In this respect it continued faithfully the

---

16 Monasticism must have contributed very much to this. A tendency to regard the ordained ministry as somewhat 'lower' than the 'spiritual fathers' or human persons transformed by holiness, is observable in Byzantine authors such as Saint Symeon the New Theologian, and others.

17 See John Meyendorff, *Byzantine Theology*, 1974, pp. 206–210.

18 Lubac, *op. cit.*, pp. 59ff.

19 Congar, *op. cit.*, pp. 161ff.

medieval post-thirteenth century conception of the Eucharist as one sacrament among other sacraments — this time two instead of seven.

The Counter-Reformation insisted on the same line and reinforced it even further in the West. The Eucharist remained a sacrament *produced by the Church* and not *constitutive* of her being. The ecclesiological presuppositions of the Eucharist were in this way understood as involving a 'valid' ministry, through ordination which implied *a character indelebilis*, and a *potestas* to perform the sacraments regardless of any other conditions, such as the presence of the community, orthodox faith, or other such factors.

At this time the East, struggling to relate somehow to the ongoing debate between Roman Catholics and Protestants, produced its own 'Confessions',[20] which assumed without any criticism the problematic inherited in the West from medieval Scholasticism, and tried to reply to the Protestant views by using Roman Catholic arguments and vice-versa. Thus, in the very centre of Orthodox theology and in spite of the continuous centrality of the Eucharist in Orthodox Church *life*, an ecclesiology developed in the academic level which regarded the Eucharist as *one* sacrament among many (usually seven), and which actually distinguishes very clearly between Church and Eucharist in its methodology. The consequences of this involved the emergence of a dichotomy between academic ecclesiology and ordinary liturgical Church life, a dichotomy which remains still responsible for many problems in today's Orthodoxy.

(c) This takes us to the third phase in the history of the relation between Church and Eucharist, which is our contemporary era. It seems that in our time the situation has changed in a radical way as a result of the revival of biblical, patristic and liturgical studies since the beginning of this century. This revival has recovered the ancient link between Church and Eucharist which was obscured, if not lost, in the Middle Ages. Thanks to the work of such scholars as Gregory Dix, Odo Casel, Werner Elert and others in the West, the *Orthodox theologians themselves* have been reminded of the patristic concept of the Eucharist as *leitourgia*, i.e. a *work of the people* and as gathering *epi to auto* to realize the ecclesial event *par excellence.*[21] The Orthodox theologian Nicholas Afanasiev[22] launched, as a result of this revival, his 'eucharistic

---

20 Such as those of P. Mogila, Dositheus of Jerusalem, Cyril Lukaris, etc.

21 G. Dix, *The Shape of the Liturgy*, 1945; O. Casel, *The Mystery of Christian Worship*, 1999; W. Elert, *Eucharist and Church Fellowship in the First Four Centuries*, 2003.

22 N. Afanasiev, 'La doctrine de la Primauté à lumière de l'ecclésiologie', *Istina* 4 (1957), pp. 401–20; 'The Church Which Presides in Love', in *The Primacy of Peter: Essays in Ecclesiology and the Early Church* (ed. J Meyendorff), 1992, pp. 91–144; 'Una Sancta' in *Irenikon* 36 (1963) 436f.; *Tserkov Ducha Svjatogo*, 1971.

ecclesiology', the main principle of which is well-known: 'wherever there is the Eucharist there is the Church'. Since Afanasiev the Orthodox are known as the promoters of the *eucharistic* presuppositions of ecclesiology and not so much of the ecclesiological presuppositions of the Eucharist. 'Eucharistic ecclesiology' seems to involve a one-sidedness calling for further clarifications and even corrections in order to do full justice to the patristic roots of Orthodoxy.[23]

This recovery of the link between Church and Eucharist seems to be a characteristic of the ecumenical situation in general in our time. With its help the Roman Catholic Church seems to have rediscovered the ecclesiological fullness of the local Church since Vatican II. At the same time even the Protestant Churches appear to attach increasingly greater centrality to the Eucharist in their ecclesiologies,[24] even to the point of reaching an amazing convergence with Roman Catholics and Orthodox on this point, as is evident from the latest work of the Faith and Order Movement.[25] It is, therefore, appropriate to deal with the implications of this new situation for our present day and Church life.

II. Tradition

This brief historical sketch shows that we have inherited in theology a problem which would have been inconceivable in the early Church. This problem is expressed in the question: *does the Eucharist make the Church or is the reverse true, namely that the Church constitutes the Eucharist?*

The theological tradition which has been influenced by Medieval Scholasticism both in the West and in East has tended to answer this question by saying that it is the Church that makes the Eucharist, and not *vice-versa*.[26] Some Orthodox theologians, on the other hand, being under the influence of the so called 'Eucharistic Ecclesiology' which was launched mainly by Afanasiev have tended to take the opposite view. The debate is not closed, and what I shall say today in this lecture is meant to be nothing but a modest contribution to this discussion.

(a) In the first place, I should like to draw our attention to the deeper theological roots of this problem. The question we have just raised is

---

23   For a discussion of the difficulties that Afanasiev's 'eucharistic ecclesiology' presents, see my *Being as Communion*, pp. 23ff.

24   The contribution of theologians such as J.J. von Allmen has been of particular importance in this respect. See his *The Lord's Supper*, 2002.

25   The most significant step forward is to be found in the document *Baptism, Eucharist, Ministry* approved by the Faith and Order Commission in Lima, Peru, in January 1982.

26   For modern Orthodox authors. see P. Trembelas, *Dogmatique de l'Église Orthodoxe Catholique* III, 1968. Cf. my 'Die Eucharistie in der Neuzeitlichen orthodoxen Theologie' in *Die Anrufung des Heiligen Geistes im Abendmahl*, 1977, pp. 163–179.

part of a broader and more fundamental question which has to do with the relation between christology and pneumatology or even between history and eschatology. Behind the position that the Church precedes the Eucharist lies the view that christology precedes pneumatology and that the institutional or historical aspect of the Church is what *causes* the Eucharist to exist. This position forms part of an ecclesiology which views the Church as the Body of Christ which is *first* instituted in itself as an historical entity and *then* produces the 'means of grace' called sacraments, among them primarily the Eucharist. The order that is suggested by traditional dogmatic manuals is precisely this: first comes Christ, then follows the Spirit, then the Church, and finally the sacraments (including the Eucharist). If this order is followed, then you must have first the ministry of the Church who actually *makes* the Eucharist. The Eucharist is a *product* of the priestly machinery. In many people's mind this is a common assumption.

In speaking about the *ecclesiological presuppositions* of the Eucharist I wish to exclude right from the start such an assumption. If there are ecclesiological presuppositions of the Eucharist — and there certainly are — these must not be understood as involving a priority of the Church over against the Eucharist. My position, which I wish to develop here, is that *the Church constitutes the Eucharist while being constituted by it*. Church and Eucharist are inter-dependent, they coincide, and are even in some sense identical.

In order to find the deeper roots of this coincidence between Church and Eucharist we must again go back to the question of the relation between christology and pneumatology. All the biblical accounts of Christology seem to speak of Christ as a being constituted by the Holy Spirit and in this sense as a *corporate person* (e.g., the Servant of God or the Son of Man).[27] The person of Christ is automatically linked with the Holy Spirit, which means with a *community*. This community is the eschatological company of the 'saints' which surround Christ in this kingdom.[28] The Church is part of the definition of Christ. The body of Christ is not first the body of an individual Christ and *then* a community of 'many', but simultaneously both together. Thus you cannot have the body of the individual Christ (the One) without having simultaneously the community of the Church (the Many).

The Eucharist is the only occasion in history when these two

---

27   On this important idea of 'corporate personhood' see: J. Pedersen, *Israel: Its Life and Culture*, 1926; H. Wheeler Robinson, *The Hebrew Conception of Corporate Personality*, 1936; A. R. Johnson, *The One and the Many in the Israelite Conception of God*, 1942; J. de Fraine, *Adam and the Family of Man* (trans. D. Raible), 1959.

28   See Mat. 25:40 and its interpretation by T.W. Manson, *The Teaching of Jesus*, 1967, pp. 265 ff.

coincide. In the Eucharist the expression 'body of Christ' means simultaneously the body of Jesus and the body of the Church. Any separation of these two leads to the destruction of the Eucharist. *Therefore, the ecclesiological presuppositions of the Eucharist cannot be found outside the Eucharist itself.* It is by studying the nature of the Eucharist that we can understand the nature of the Church which conditions the Eucharist.

(b) The body of Christ, which is the body of the Eucharist and of the Church at the same time, is the body of the *risen*, the eschatological Christ. This means that the ecclesiological presuppositions of the Eucharist are to be found in a consideration of the eschatological Christ and the eschatological community. Let me briefly mention both the basic elements which constitute this eschatological community.

(i)   The eschatological community both in its ecclesial and its eucharistic form is above all a synaxis *epi to auto* of the dispersed people of God. It is not an accident that in Paul, Ignatius, etc. the expression *synagesthai epi to auto* means simultaneously the Church and the Eucharist. It follows from this that it is impossible to have the Eucharist celebrated properly without the gathering of the people of God in one place. The laity are indispensable for the Eucharist. They *constitute* it, together with the other orders through their responses to the prayers, through their *Amen*, which is the prerogative *exclusively* of the laity.[29] It appears therefore that a fundamental ecclesiological presupposition of the Eucharist is the gathering of the laity in one place. The Eucharist is a *leitourgia*, an act of the people.

(ii)   Another characteristic of the eschatological community, which the Eucharist as the body of the risen and corporate (spiritual) Christ must portray, is its *charismatic nature*. All the members of the Church possess the Holy Spirit through Baptism and Chrismation (or Confirmation), and being a 'charismatic' means in the final analysis being a member of the Church.[30] Ordination is a bestowal of a *particular* charisma on certain people and as such it does not raise the ordained person above or outside the community, but assigns him to a particular position, an *ordo*.[31] The Eucharist includes not only the laymen but also other charismata and orders. Its proper performance, therefore, must include a variety of orders and not simply what we call the 'laity' or the 'clergy'.

---

29 Cf. P.P. Rouget, *Amen. Acclamation du peuple sacerdotal*, 1947.
30 A careful study of 1 Corinthians 12 shows that for Saint Paul charisma = membership of the Church and *vice-versa*.
31 Cf. my 'Ordination et Communion' in *Istina* 16 (1971), pp. 5–12.

(iii)   Among these orders there are three that have survived in history as constitutive for the Eucharist in addition to that of the laity. Saint Ignatius of Antioch says that 'without these the Church cannot be constituted'.[32] One of them is the Bishop with whom we shall deal separately below. The others are the *deacons* and the *presbyters*. The constitutive role of the deacons for the Eucharist has been almost lost in our time. Are the deacons necessary for the celebration of the Eucharist? Few people, if any, would be inclined to answer this question in the affirmative. The deacons have almost become a decorative element in the Liturgy.[33]

The presbyters on the other hand have assumed a eucharistic role that was not theirs originally. Since the Middle Ages they have become the *main* presidents of the Eucharist. Some would call them the *sole* ecclesiological presupposition of the Eucharist: *if you have a presbyter, you do not need anything else in order to have the Eucharist.* This widespread assumption, which has led to the practice of the private Mass, is absolutely wrong and contrary to the ancient tradition and ecclesiology. The presbyters are only part of what is necessary in order to have a valid Eucharist. Their function was originally to surround the bishop in his throne as the Twelve will surround Christ in the Kingdom,[34] and serve as a collegium, not as individuals, in the eucharistic community. The Eucharist is not presbytero–centric in its nature but *episcopocentric*.

c) Thus we arrive at the question of the Bishop as the presupposition of the Eucharist. In what sense is he such a condition? Here the following points emerge from a study of the ancient Church.

(i)   The Bishop is not a minister that exists outside or above the Church but is *part* of the community. There is no pyramidal structure in ecclesiology, and the idea that the bishops in any sense precede the community can be very misleading. The best way to understand the office of the bishop is through the biblical image of the *one* and the *many* to which I referred earlier. Just as the *one* (Christ) cannot be conceived without the *many* (the Body), so also the Bishop is inconceivable without his community. The practice of titular bishops can be misleading, if it does not imply — at least theoretically — that a bishop is part of a community.

(ii)   However, something must be immediately added to this. The Bishop has at the same time the special ministry of representing

---

32   *Choris touton ekklesia ou kaleitai* (Ignatius, *Trall.* 3.1). The word *kaleitai* can be, quite significantly, translated as both 'called' (into being, constituted) and 'named'.

33   In the Early Church the deacons were attached to the bishop and performed the significant function acting as link between him and the people in prayer and holy communion.

34   See Ignatius, *Smyrn.* 8 and *Magn.* 6.1.

Christ to the community.[35] There is the paradox in the office of the Bishop which is the very paradox of Christ's position in the Eucharist. In the Eucharist Christ represents the community to the Father. He offers the Eucharist as the first-born of the brethren, as *part* of the community. At the same time He addresses the community, especially by giving it the Holy Spirit, the charismata. In this sense he stands above the community. The Bishop does the same paradoxical work. He offers the Eucharist as part of the community and as its head. At the same time, he is the *sole ordainer*, none else can give the Spirit to the community, none else can ordain.[36] In this sense he is addressing the community; he *constitutes* it, as the ecclesial presupposition *par excellence*. The Bishop thus becomes also the ecclesiological presupposition *par excellence* of the Eucharist.

(iii) To these functions we must add another important one. The Bishop is the link between the local and the universal Church. He is part of a local community, and yet not in the same way as are the presbyters, the deacons and the laity of that community. He is ordained by more than one bishop[37] and as such his ministry transcends *the local community*. In fact it is the Bishop that makes each local Church *catholic*. And this applies also to the Eucharist.

The Eucharist would remain a local event of a local Church had it not been for the Bishop. The Bishop is necessary as a condition for Eucharist precisely because it is through him that each Eucharist becomes *the one Eucharist* of the One, Holy, Catholic, and Apostolic Church. If a Eucharist does not take place in the name of a Bishop, it risks remaining a local event without catholic significance. This is one of the profoundest reasons which account for the importance of the Bishop as an ecclesiological presupposition of the Eucharist.

Thus in the office of the Bishop we encounter at least two fundamental paradoxes which are also paradoxes of the Eucharist. One is that in him the *one* becomes *many* and the *many* become *one*.[38] This the mystery of christology and pneumatology, the mystery of the Church

---

35   In Ignatius (*Magn.* 6, 1) the bishop is the 'type of God'. Cf. Henry Chadwick's remarks on this (note 10, above). But the Christological image prevailed (cf. Hippolytus and ancient Liturgies).

36   Hippolytus, *Apost. Trad.*, 4.2 seems to speak of a participation of the presbyters in the laying on of hands during the ordination, hence the view of B. Botte, *Hippolyte, Tradition Apololique*, 1946, p. 30, that the presbyters participate in the act of ordination in an essential way. But Hippolytus makes it himself clear (9) that only the bishop ordains, precisely because he alone can *give* (a reference to the christological character of episcopacy).

37   Hippolytus, *Apost. Trad.* 2; *Council of Arles*, canon 20; *Council of Nicaea*, canons 4 and 6.

38   Cf. our 'Cristologia, pneumatologia e istituzioni ecclesiastiche' in *Cristianesimo nella storia* II, 1981, pp. 111–128.

and at the same time of the Eucharist. The other paradox is that in the Bishop the local Church becomes Catholic and the Catholic becomes local. If a Church is not *at the same time* local and universal, she is not the body of Christ. Equally the Eucharist has to be at the same time a local and a catholic event. Without the bishop it cannot be so.

d) This links the question of the ecclesiological presuppositions of the Eucharist closely with another aspect of ecclesiology, namely conciliarity. The Eucharist by its very nature transcends the dilemma 'local or universal', because in each eucharistic celebration the Gifts are offered in the name of and for the 'one, holy, catholic and apostolic Church' which exists in the whole world. In practical terms this means that if one is a member of a certain eucharistic community (or local Church), one is *ipso facto* also a member of all the eucharistic communities of the world: one can communicate in any one of these communities.

It was precisely this nature of the Eucharist and its practical implications that led to the emergence of the synodal system in the early Church.[39] Conciliarity is closely connected with eucharistic communion — both in its theory and its practice — and with its presuppositions. If two or more Churches are in schism, the eucharistic life (and perhaps also 'validity'?) of *all* local Churches is upset. Conciliarity as an expression of the unity of the local Churches in *one* Church, constitutes a fundamental condition for the Eucharist. Just as the many individual members of a local Church must be united in and through the ministry of the One (the bishop, representing Christ) in the same way the many local Churches must be united into one for their Eucharist to be proper ecclesiologically. Ecclesial unity on a universal level is essential for the Eucharist.

III. Summary

These, therefore, seem to be the fundamental conclusions that can be drawn from a study of the ancient tradition with regard to the ecclesiological presuppositions of the Eucharist. Let me summarize them:

(a) The celebration of the Eucharist requires the *concrete gathering* of the local community — not simply a symbolic or implicit representation of it in the person of a priest.

(b) The Eucharist requires the gathering of all the members of a local community including all the orders of this community. Here the problem of the *parish* arises as a very acute one. The parish is not only

---

39   See esp. canon 5 of I Nicaea. For a fuller discussion see my 'The Development of Conciliar structures to the Time of the First Ecumenical Council' in *Councils and the Ecumenical Movement*, 1968, pp. 34–51.

part of the people of a certain place, but also part of the structure of the community. It does not include the Bishop, except by implication. For the parish Eucharist to exist properly it is necessary to be understood as an extension of the Bishop's one Eucharist. The ancient practice of the Fermentum[40] indicated this very clearly, and the same is true about the Antimension used in the Liturgy in the East.[41] One would not exaggerate, therefore, if one said that the ecclesiological presupposition of the parish Eucharist is not only its celebration by an ordained priest, but its celebration *in the name of the local bishop.*

(c) It follows from this that the Eucharist requires the presidency of the Bishop for the following reasons: i) in order to preserve its character as a *gift from God* and not simply as a *gift to God*, that is, a product of a human community; ii) in order to preserve the paradoxical nature of a unity in diversity in which no member of the Church can relate to God individually, but only as a member of a body; iii) in order to preserve its paradoxical nature as a local and at the same time universal event.

If these theological conclusions are to be translated into canonical terms, it is clear that the *validity* of the Eucharist depends on the following conditions: i) the presidency (direct or indirect) of the Bishop; ii) Communion with the other Churches in the world (both in terms of space and time, that is, Apostolic succession, and conciliarity); and iii) the presence of the community with all its members and orders, including the *laity.*

IV. Contemporary Application

If we tried to apply these theological and canonical conclusions to our ecumenical situation today, it would appear that no attempt to restore eucharistic communion among divided Churches would ignore the above mentioned ecclesiological presuppositions of the Eucharist. This would mean that all Churches wishing such a restoration of communion should ask themselves whether not only in theory but *also in practice* they fulfil the above mentioned principles. It may well be that many Churches who do not accept these principles in theory (e.g. the episcopal office, Apostolic succession etc.) in fact practice them, while other Churches who profess these principles in their doctrine fall in fact short of applying them in their liturgical and canonical practice. No progress towards full eucharistic communion can be made without some kind of reformation of existing practices taking place in all

---

40   Cf. J.A. Jungmann ('Fermentum in Colligere Fragmenta' in *Festschrift Alban Dold*, 1952, pp. 185–190); and G. Dix (*op. cit.*, 105 and *A Detection of Aumbries*, 1942, pp. 16–20).
41   For a discussion of the sources see my *Eucharist, Bishop, Church,* pp. 183f.

Churches in one form or another. The eucharistic communion requires a solid common ecclesiological ground both in theory and in practice — especially in the latter.

These observations apply particularly to the relations between the Roman Catholic and the Orthodox Churches. A great deal of what has been proposed here is shared by these Churches in doctrine, especially as the common ground of the ancient undivided Church is gradually rediscovered and stressed by theologians of both Churches. It is to be hoped that liturgical and canonical practice will be adjusted to this growing theological consensus. What in the light of this paper would emerge as particularly important in this case is a proper understanding of the ministry of the Church so that the mystery of the Eucharist, which is at the same time the mystery of the Church as the *one* and the *many* may be fully expressed and experienced in eucharistic communion.

CHAPTER FIVE

REFLECTIONS ON BAPTISM, CONFIRMATION AND EUCHARIST

Introduction

There are two ways of approaching Baptism, Confirmation and Eucharist in our theological thinking. One is the way of looking at each of these three from the viewpoint of their particularities. This is the way which leads to or presupposes an understanding of the 'sacraments' as objective signs or channels of God's grace, and makes possible a clear distinction or even enumeration of these forms of grace. The other way begins from the view that there is in fact only one mystery, that of Christ, in which the entire mystery of our salvation is contained. In this approach all particularities that may be found in any of these three are seen in the light of the one mystery of Christ and never in any form of objective self-explanatory existence. Both these ways may lead to the same faith about Baptism, Confirmation and Eucharist. But each of them presupposes a different vision and may lead to quite different formulations of this same faith.

In my opinion the second of these two ways has been the characteristic approach of the East. This is indicated by the fact that it was in the East that the three rites, Baptism, Confirmation and Eucharist, remained united in the liturgical life, and that it was there too that no particular theology of any of these three developed, at least in the first centuries. The whole problem of the relation between Word and Sacrament, as well as the particular question of whether Confirmation is a sacrament at all, have been unknown to the East. This is not due to a mere traditionalism and liturgical conservatism. For the Roman Church was in liturgical matters the conservative Church *par excellence* up to at least the eighth century. And yet it was there that clear-cut distinctions, to the point of separating Baptism, Confirmation and Eucharist from one another, took place. This can be explained only in the light of a tendency to isolate and evaluate specific aspects of the mystery of the Church, a tendency which the East did not experience at least in the history of the ancient Church. It is in the light of this vision, particular to the East, that the following thoughts are submitted for consideration.

I. The Unity of Baptism, Confirmation and Eucharist

If we try to approach Baptism, Confirmation and Eucharist as isolated entities, we may be able to attribute to each of them some specific characteristics, but we shall be unable to explain many things concerning their origin and the place each of them occupied in the early Church. Thus we may say, for instance, that Confirmation is the rite of the bestowal of the Holy Spirit upon the baptized, and this would be in full agreement with the classical theological view that has prevailed. But then the question would immediately arise: is this giving of the Holy Spirit not the case with Baptism and the Eucharist as well? In the very narrative of the Baptism of our Lord the connection between the descent into the waters and the descent of the Holy Spirit is so close that one can hardly isolate the one from the other without destroying the entire scene of Baptism. It is significant that the word 'immediately' (*euthus*) is chosen by Saint Mark (1:10) to connect them. The same should be said about the descent of the Holy Spirit on the day of Pentecost. Could we isolate this from the Baptism which follows after the sermon of Saint Peter and the birth of the first Church in Jerusalem? Baptism without the Holy Spirit may have existed in the times of the New Testament, and it is certainly clearly referred to on many occasions as the 'water' or the 'Baptism of the water' especially in the Fourth Gospel (1:26, 31, and 33). But it is never understood as *Christian* Baptism. It might have been the baptism of the Jewish proselytes or of John the Baptist. But the Baptism of the Church was always a Baptism which included the descent of the Holy Spirit (Jn. 3:5). This belief survived in the Church for many centuries. Origen, for instance, identifies Baptism with the descent of the Holy Spirit when he writes in connection with Acts 8 :14–17: 'In the Acts of the Apostles through the laying on of the apostolic hands the Holy Spirit was given *in Baptism*.'[1] The same seems to be true also of Saint John Chrysostom who, in referring to the descent of the candidate into the waters for Baptism, writes: 'Through the words of the priest and his hand the visitation of the Holy Spirit comes upon you and another man arises.'[2]

Even at the very controversy on the Baptism of heretics in the third century when the first attempt was made in the West to separate

1   *De Princ.* 1.3.2 (P.G. 2, 147).
2   *Eight Baptismal Catecheses* (ed. A. Wenger), 1957, p. 147.

theologically Baptism from Confirmation, the party of Saint Cyprian supported by the bishops of the East held the view that Baptism without the Holy Spirit was inconceivable. This was exactly the basis of Saint Cyprian's argument that heretics and schismatics cannot baptize, i.e. simply because the Holy Spirit is needed for Baptism.[3] For Baptism, he argues, forgives sins, but sins are forgiven only by those who possess the Holy Spirit according to John 20:22.[4] The same observations can be made if one studies the liturgical texts of the early Church. The bestowal of the Holy Spirit is connected there even with the pre-baptismal blessing of the waters which are 'to be filled with Holy Spirit'[5] or with the candidates who are also to be filled with the Holy Spirit.[6] The same problems will arise when one attempts to isolate Baptism from the Eucharist. It is not an accident that our Lord uses the term 'baptism' in connection with his death (Mt. 20:22; cf. Lk. 12:50). The 'cup' of his death and the 'baptism' of his death to which he refers there, can hardly be understood apart from the cup of the New Covenant of the Last Supper. And in the entire Pentecostal scene described in Acts 2 the descent of the Holy Spirit, the Baptism of the three thousand people and the participation of all in the 'breaking of the bread' form one indivisible unity. There is thus an essential unity in the origins of all three, Baptism, Confirmation, and Eucharist, so that any attempt to look at them outside the light of this unity would create serious theological and historical problems. What does this unity consist of and what can one say about Baptism, Confirmation and Eucharist in the light of this unity?

The answer to this double question is not an easy one and would require a detailed theological study. What can be said here in a very general way is that the context in which Baptism, Confirmation, and Eucharist were placed in the consciousness of the early Church was that of a christology which summed up in itself the entire history of salvation as it was not only seen but also eschatologically realized through the Pentecostal outpouring of the Holy Spirit. Thus, it was hard for the early Christians to see any aspect of this history without seeing at the same time all the rest. It is quite instructive to remember here that the early Church celebrated Baptism, Confirmation, and Eucharist always on a Saturday towards Sunday, preferably on the Saturday of the Holy Week of Easter (or on the eve of Epiphany). These were the occasions

---

3   Ep. 69 [66] 10.
4   Ep. 69 [66] 11.
5   Serapion of Thmuis, *Euchologion* (ed. G. Wobbermin), 1899.
6   See, for instance, the prayer after the exorcisms in *The Barberini Euchologion* (ed. Conybeare and Maclean), 1905, fol. 170ff.

on which a real recapitulation of the whole mystery of Christ was celebrated.

II. The Reality of Baptism in the Mystery of Christ

If we now look at Baptism in the light of this unity of the one mystery of Christ we shall discover that what the Church knows and practices as Baptism cannot be understood apart from a pre-existing baptismal reality in the mystery of salvation. Such a pre-existing baptismal reality appears in the following dimensions, which are united in the person of Christ. There is first the dimension of the *historical*. It is expressed in the idea, so explicit in the New Testament, of the Baptism with water. It is a reference to the Baptism already present in the Old Covenant and described by Saint Paul (1 Cor. 10:1-2) as the Baptism of the Fathers into Moses by participation in the crossing of the Red Sea. It is also expressed in the Baptism of John the Forerunner, a Baptism which the Fourth Gospel especially is so anxious to label as with 'water', without dismissing it but, on the contrary, stating that Jesus or rather his disciples took over their own Baptism from this (Jn. 3:22 and 4:1-2). The other dimension is the *eschatological* or *pneumatological* one. It is a reference to the fact that it was only by virtue of the outpouring of the Holy Spirit 'in these last days' (Acts 2:17) that Christian Baptism could exist as the Baptism of both water and the Spirit (Jn. 3:5). Both of these dimensions had to be united in the person of Christ. The narrative of his Baptism, to which we referred earlier, shows how important it was for the early Church to combine both the historical and the eschatological in the person of Christ. When Paul speaks of Baptism as participation in the death and resurrection of Christ he does nothing but refer to the person of Christ both in the Paschal crossing of the Fathers in the sea (1 Cor. 10:1-2) and the Baptism 'of all... in one Spirit... into one body' (1 Cor. 12:13).

From this basic observation two implications seem to follow concerning Baptism. One is that all Baptism in the Church is a participation in the history and call of the People of God. This is the implication of the *historical* dimension. The other is that all Baptism presupposes a Pentecostal community (remember again Acts 2) into which Baptism takes place. It is quite important to bear in mind that 'no one can say "Jesus is Lord" except by the Holy Spirit' (1 Cor. 12:3). There is no worshipping life possible in the Church without the presence of the Spirit. Since both the historical and the eschatological are united in Christ in the Holy Spirit, Baptism appears to be in the last analysis an incorporation into this community, which is the Body of Christ, the Church.

This seems to be the primary reality, the ground of all understanding of Baptism in the Church. It is a reality which does not depend on the belief or unbelief of the individuals since it is the reality of Christ himself[7] (we are baptized always into Christ) — a reality which makes it possible even for such a paradoxical thing as 'infant Baptism' to exist.

This placing of Baptism in the context of the entire mystery of salvation led the Church very early on to the attachment of Baptism to the concept of 'enlightenment'. We see this clearly referred to by Justin Martyr.[8] This concept should be combined with that of the cleansing of the waters and the exorcisms of the demonic powers, as well as with the idea of healing which was also attached to Baptism from the early times of the Church. It is interesting to note that the miracle stories of the Gospels were organically connected with the rites of initiation and that the ancient lectionaries which survive until the present in the East place the Synoptic Gospels in the period before Easter and reserve the Fourth Gospel for the period beginning with the Easter Liturgy. The miracle stories of the Synoptics with their healings and exorcisms were fit especially for those prepared for Baptism. Enlightenment of the whole nature, healing from sickness, exorcism from demonic powers — all these, organically connected with the rite of initiation, reveal another dimension of Baptism, namely that of the *natural* or *cosmic*. This dimension is easily forgotten in the discussions about Baptism. And yet, not only did it very early form part of basic liturgical acts entailed in the rite of Baptism, but it was a fundamental element in the baptismal typology of the Primitive and Early Church. As Per Lundberg made clear some years ago, the water symbolism attached to Baptism from the beginning was taken over from the creation and the Flood, to come through the filtering of the Passion of Christ into Baptism and thus bring the whole of creation into the baptismal reality.[9] Baptism is not an act which concerns only human beings, but in its relation to the entire mystery of Christ it becomes a process of *conversion* through which all the world has to go in and with man, if it is to be accepted into the Body of Christ.

---

7   All references to Baptism in the New Testament bear this significant characteristic. Whenever the reference is made to Christ the preposition *eis* (into) is used, while in all references to the Holy Spirit that of *en* (in) is used. Baptism is always into Christ in the Holy Spirit. This is, I think, basic for any distinction between christology and pneumatology in the idea of Baptism and should be a warning to those (esp. Orthodox) who tend to overlook such distinctions in their pneumatological approach to the mystery of the Church. At the same time it indicates quite clearly that there is no Baptism which can be divorced from both these prepositions and, therefore, from a christological and pneumatological reality preceding individual Baptism and serving as its ground and context.

8   *Apol.* I, 61.

9   *La typologie baptismale dans l'Église ancienne*, 1942, pp. 10ff.

In this broader context of a Christology which through the Holy Spirit becomes an *anakephalaiōsis* of all and creation in the Church, the individual or personal Baptism finds its proper place. Here the turning of the individual's entire attitude (*metanoia*) towards God with a subsequent forgiveness of his sins (*loutron*) is what he *as a person* receives in Baptism. By dying into himself with Christ in his death and rising in his resurrection he receives a 'generation again' (*palingenesia*) or a 'regeneration' (*anagennēsis*) which equals his being acknowledged by the Father as his son, in the person of his only-begotten Son in whom he is pleased.

Thus, the *historical*, the *eschatological*, the *cosmic*, and the *personal* are all dimensions in which Baptism should be placed if it is to be properly understood.

III. The Reality of Confirmation in the Mystery of Christ

If we now turn to Confirmation and try to place it in the same light of the one mystery of Christ we will have to clear the ground of all later meanings attached to this rite. Confirmation, whether administered by the laying-on of hands or by Chrismation, was from the beginning understood as the bestowing of the Holy Spirit upon the baptized. This understanding was for a long time common between East and West. But it is important to notice that in the history of this understanding, the emphasis was gradually directed in the West towards the idea of *perfection* of Baptism by Confirmation. (The term *perfectio* for Confirmation is used in the Pseudo-Ambrosian writings.) This was expressed even more by the adoption of the term *confirmatio*, which seems to have been used for the first time (in its verbal form) by Leo the Great and officially by the Council of Riez in 430 (Canon 3). By the final adoption of this term in the West the implication was becoming clearer that Confirmation is necessary because something is lacking in Baptism, either in the rite itself or in the person who received it (age, for example). This easily opened the way towards an understanding of Confirmation as basically an opportunity of *response* of the adult faithful, especially if he had been baptized as a child.

All this history of Confirmation in the West develops within another important evolution, namely the separation of 'water Baptism' from 'Spirit baptism' as it appears in the middle third century on the occasion of the controversy over the Baptism of heretics. Once the two Baptisms are separated, Confirmation, being identified with the second, becomes a self-sufficient entity and acquires every meaning necessary for the completion of the first. At the same time the reservation of the rite to the laying on of hands and consequently to the bishop, linked Confirmation indirectly, yet essentially, to the practice of penitential discipline, and thus contributed towards a special understanding of the laity in the West.

This development remained strange to the East where no idea of a 'completion' or 'confirmation' of Baptism appeared, apparently because of the liturgical and theological unity in which Baptism and Confirmation were always kept. There, an understanding of Confirmation in such a successive role in relation to Baptism was so strange that in areas like Syria and perhaps Palestine the order of the two was in the liturgy reversed, and where, contrary to the West, Baptism itself was called 'perfection'.[10] Instead of developments of this kind the East understood and practiced Confirmation as *Chrismation*. This facilitated another understanding of Confirmation, namely as anointment with that chrism which Christ himself received (*Christos*). This idea is found explicitly in Cyril of Jerusalem and in many Eastern prayers of Chrismation.[11] But this could lead towards another direction in the understanding of Confirmation. The association of the anointing of Christians with the anointing of priests and kings in the Old Testament is made constantly in the liturgical and theological writings of the ancient Church.[12] In its baptismal context this anointing means participation in Christ's royal priesthood, by virtue of which the baptized would become himself a king and a member of the People of God 'an anointed one' (*Christos*), which is nothing else but a *layperson* in the specific sense of the word : 'Not because those who are now baptized are being ordained priests, but as being "Christians" from "Christ"'.[13] The implications of such a view of Confirmation for the understanding of the layman in the East are undoubtedly significant.

It is at this point precisely that the baptized is introduced into the Eucharist.

IV. The Reality of the Eucharist in the Mystery of Christ

If we read carefully the account of the Baptismal Liturgy of Hippolytus we are struck by his insistence just at the point between Confirmation

---

10 Ephrem the Syrian, 4th hymn for Epiphany. This may well go back to the New Testament. Cf. the theory of T. W. Manson, 'Entry into Membership of the Eastern Church', *JTS* 48 (1947), pp. 25–33.

11 Cf. *Cat.* 21.1 (PG 33, 1089). 3. For its ancient and not only Eastern roots cf. Tertullian, *De Bapt.*, 7-8: 'Christi dicti a Chrismate'. Cf. also Theophilus of Antioch, *Ad Autolycum*, 1.12.

12 See, for example, *Didascalia* 16 (ed. Connolly), p. 146: 'as of old priests and kings were anointed in Israel, do thou in like manner with the imposition of thy hand anoint the head of those who receive Baptism…'.

13 *Const. Apost.* 3.16, where a connection with both Old Testament royal anointing and — significantly enough — 1 Pt. 2:9 occurs.

and Eucharist on the idea that it is *now* and *only now*, that is, after Baptism and Confirmation, that the baptized can pray with the faithful. This seems to minimize the distinctive character of the Eucharist to the point of participation in a common prayer. And yet, the idea behind it is clear, namely that the Eucharist, as distinct from Baptism and Confirmation, is mainly a community, i.e. an *ecclesial reality* in which all that was individual in Baptism and Confirmation becomes *communal* by virtue of communion in the Body of Christ.

It is an unfortunate development which has been established in the Orthodox Church itself to offer the Holy Eucharist to the newly baptized individual outside the Eucharistic assembly. This, of course, has been the only possible solution once Baptism and Confirmation were separated from the Eucharistic liturgy, since the other alternative would be even worse, namely to postpone the first Holy Communion until the first Eucharistic liturgy after Baptism, thus dividing the unity of the three, Baptism, Confirmation and Eucharist. But in order to avoid any illusions for the Orthodox themselves it is important to underline that keeping the unity of Baptism, Confirmation, and Eucharist does not mean simply offering the Holy Eucharist to the baptized right after Confirmation; it is mainly *introducing the newly baptized person into the assembly of the faithful*. This was the meaning given to the attachment of the Eucharist to Confirmation and Baptism by the early Church. The Eucharist was not simply the food and medicine of immortality to which every baptized and chrismated individual was immediately entitled, but at the same time — and this, I am afraid, we have lost sight of — it was the synaxis of the people of God, the *ecclesia tou Theou*, in the unity of which he was asked to enter and take his place. By virtue of his Chrismation each baptized person becomes a member of the royal *laos* of God, a *laikos*. It is only natural that he enters immediately the assembly of the Eucharist in order to occupy his proper *taxis* or *tagma* ('order')[14] of the layperson in this called and summoned people of God, the *ekklēsia*.

Indeed the Eucharist as a natural continuation of Baptism and Confirmation appears to be the realm in which *order* becomes a reality and *ministry* finds its ground of existence. It is not an accident that *all ordination*, i.e. entrance into an *ordo* within the People of God, appears in the early Church (e.g. in Hippolytus and in all ancient liturgies, Eastern and Western) as of necessity *within the context of the Eucharistic liturgy*. This is a liturgical survival which bears great significance for our understanding of the ministry and the Eucharist itself. Its significance lies in the following general points:

---

14   Cf. *1 Clem.* 40.3-41.4.

(a) The Holy Eucharist in its communal and ecclesial character is the Pentecostal, eschatological community *par excellence*, a community which experiences and witnesses to the entrance of the *eschaton* into history and offers a taste of the Kingdom to come. 'We have seen the true light, we have received the heavenly Spirit, we have found true faith, worshipping the indivisible Trinity, which has saved us' is the final hymn of the participants in the Orthodox Eucharistic liturgy. Since all ministry in the Church is charismatic (the well-known division between charismatic and permanent ministry is very misleading and in any case should not lead to the inconceivable possibility of a ministry which is not charismatic) entrance into it and even expression of it can only find their proper place in this Pentecostal gathering. It is in this sense very instructive to study 1 Corinthians 11-14, where all the *charismata* together with the idea of order are placed within the Eucharistic assembly already from the apostolic times.

(b) This communal character of the Eucharistic liturgy, its being a 'common action of the entire Church' in a certain place, offers the proper context for the ordination into the ministry of the Church, because there is in fact no ministry and no *ordo* that stands in itself outside or above the community of the Church. Ordination is in the last analysis an act of the entire Church and not of a certain part of it. The fact that all ordinations have to take place within a Eucharistic context means that ordination, too, cannot be viewed as a self-explanatory sacramental entity, an objectified 'sacrament' in itself, but as part of the one and indivisible mystery of Christ. The Eucharist guarantees this *par excellence*, for it is the only act of the Church that by nature belongs to *the whole community*; it is a catholic act of a catholic Church. Entrance into an order in the Church is by virtue of its Eucharistic context not a matter of laying on of hands by a valid bishop, but a liturgical act of a certain community in its entirety.

(c) Finally, the Eucharist appears to be the only natural context of ordination into a certain ministry, because the natural ordaining person happens to be also the natural head of the Eucharistic assembly. It is not a mere accident that the bishop came to be the only person that could perform ordination. This cannot be explained by a mere reference to the concept of 'apostolic succession'. For it would then be permissible for a bishop who belongs to the chain of such a succession to perform an ordination in his study-room. The fact that he can only do this in a Eucharistic context means that it is mainly by virtue of his being the head (and originally the only head) of the Eucharistic assembly that he does so. The Eucharist is, therefore, the proper context of all order in the Church.

By entering into Eucharistic communion the baptized and confirmed person enters into the realization of the capacity of the 'lay-person' which he acquired in the first two stages of Christian initiation. From then on any other entrance into an *ordo* or ministry within the Church will take place within the same Eucharistic context. The Eucharist, therefore, following immediately Baptism and Confirmation is the expression of the summoned People of God in a certain established and charismatic order in the unity of the Body of Christ.

CHAPTER SIX

THE EUCHARISTIC VISION OF THE WORLD

Introduction

The Orthodox tradition is profoundly liturgical. For Orthodoxy, 'the church is in the Eucharist and by the Eucharist', and its concrete form is the temple in which the Eucharist is celebrated and which is also called — not coincidentally, of course — the Church. The entire universe is a liturgy, a cosmic liturgy that offers the whole of creation before the throne of God. Orthodox theology, too, is basically a doxology, a liturgy: it is a eucharistic theology.

But what is the significance of this for us today? The view of the world and of life has changed so much compared to Byzantium — and continues to change so rapidly under the influence of scientific, philosophical and sociological transformations — that we must ask: what could the Orthodox liturgical life offer us?

In light of the radical break that the modern world has made with the church in the modern era, this question is especially pressing. Western civilization, though it was nourished by Christianity, has rapidly become de-Christianized. The church, which still speaks the language and follows the issues of the past, seems less and less relevant. Especially in the West, Christians have encountered the full force of this secularization. Yet the Western tradition — a tradition which lives under the weight of the dissociation of the world into sacred and profane — multiplies the problems rather than resolving them.

In this situation, the Orthodox liturgical life presents itself as a witness of hope. In fact, the eucharistic vision of the world and of its history does not suffer the same crisis concerning the relationship between theology and life caused by the shift in contemporary thinking that is the fate of the philosophical style of theology — though, due to a lack of liturgical education, this is not always understood by the Orthodox themselves. The Orthodox liturgical life has its own worldview that not only can, but must be implemented in the present life. The Orthodox conception of humanity is particularly relevant today, for it provides, in short, an interpretation both of history and its problems and of the moral life and its possibilities.

But how do we understand the Eucharist when we speak of a 'eucharistic vision of the world'? Answering this question is fundamental, for since the scholastic era the Eucharist has been much misunderstood and its sense much distorted. Thus the use of its former patristic and Orthodox meaning requires some explanation.

I. The Eucharist as Event

In our conscience, the Eucharist is connected to the expression of a pietism that views it as an *object*, a *thing*, a *means* of expressing our piety and facilitating our salvation. However, the older understanding of the Eucharist viewed it not only or primarily as a thing, but as an *action* (and especially as an act of *assembly*), as a *liturgy* (this Orthodox term is very characteristic) and as the common (catholic) expression of the whole Church — not as a vertical relationship between each individual and God. It is characteristic that the East, which has kept this older understanding (but rather unconsciously), never introduced either private Masses nor the adoration of the Holy Gifts in a form that reduced them to the state of an object of piety and worship. The Eucharist is essentially an *event*, an act of the whole Church and not an individual action.

We often consider the Eucharist as one sacrament among others (e.g. among the seven). The ancient Church had a conception of a *single, unique sacrament*, the sacrament of Christ, as it is called in holy scripture (Rom. 16:25; Eph. 3:4; 5:32; Col. 1:27; 2:2; 4:3). The only possible understanding of the Eucharist is Christological: it is the body of Christ himself, the *totus Christus*. So we should not view it as a means of grace — an abstract grace independent of Christology (as we unfortunately still present it in dogmatic treatments). We need to view it as Christ himself, who saves humanity and the world and reconciles us with God. Therefore all the problems regarding the *elements* of the Eucharist, the debates concerning the real presence (transubstantiation), etc. which so preoccupied the Middle Ages, are secondary and bring us back to viewing the Eucharist as a *thing*. The fundamental character of the Eucharist consists in the fact that it is a gathering and an act and that *the whole mystery of Christ* (the *totus Christus*) — the salvation of the world — is revealed in it, lives in it and is concentrated in it.

If, therefore, we regard the Eucharist from this point of view, we must approach it as it stands before us in the concrete liturgy of an Orthodox church, and not in an autonomous and abstract doctrine of the sacraments. This celebration of the liturgy will reveal that the Eucharist contains a particular vision of history.

II. The Eucharist as Acceptance of Creation

The liturgy is the most positive and *active* acceptance of the world and creation. If monasticism as an act — not as a theory and as a practice — is characterized by a movement away from the world (by flight from the world), the liturgy is characterized by the opposite movement. All the faithful who go to the liturgy bring the world with them (and we mean this in the most realistic way). They bring not merely human flesh, concrete human being with its weaknesses and passions. They bring their relations with the natural world, with creation. In the ancient Church (but also today in the places where simple traditional piety has not yet been completely ousted by intellectual dissociations), the faithful not only went to church, but they brought with them the gifts of creation: bread, wine and oil. And these gifts were carried in liturgical procession (on parade) to arrive in the hands of the Bishop who was waiting at the entrance (the current 'Grand Entrance' of the Liturgy) and who would offer them to God as Eucharist. Rather than forgetting temporal needs by going to church (as one might expect), the Liturgy requires the faithful to make their contribution and to pray for 'mild weather, abundant fruits of the earth, for those who are at sea, the travellers, the sick', for the defeat of the enemies of the State, for victory for the king, etc. So, too, is the collection — this scandal for certain pious hearts — an act that reveals that what takes place during the Liturgy is precisely a *journey*, a parade of the whole world before the altar. Bringing the world as it is with them, the faithful receive a foretaste of paradise, an eschatological glimpse of the world as it will be, and then are called again to 'go in peace' back into the world.

This experience of the journey of the whole human life towards the place of the liturgy does not ignore the fact that because of sin the world is not the 'very good' reality that God saw at the moment of creation. Sin is a tragic element which returns to the consciousness of the celebrating Church on several occasions: 'None of those who are bound by the desires and pleasures of the flesh is worthy to come to You, to approach You, and to render You this worship, O King of glory....' But in the Liturgy sin is not a distressing and unsolved problem of the world. The corruption that follows creation is neither remarked upon nor denied in the Liturgy (though I will not comment at the moment on this dilemma). However, the world that enters the liturgical space is the fallen world, and this entry immediately highlights its ontological importance. But there is more. This world does not enter into the church in order to remain as it is. The liturgy is 'a medicine of immortality'[1] precisely

---

1   Ignatius, *Eph.* 20:2.

because in its acceptance and affirmation of the world, it refuses its corruption, and sanctifies the offering to the Creator: 'We offer to you these gifts from your own gifts in all and for all'.

This acceptance of the world through the liturgy shows that in the liturgical vision of creation, the world has never ceased to be the *cosmos of God*, that sin and destruction are not demiurges — as in the thought of Marcion (and Harnack!) — but that everything we are, everything we do, everything we want in the world can and must pass through the hands of the celebrant as an offering to God. Not that it might remain as it is. Not that it might be transformed into something other than creation. But to undo the distortion caused by sin and to *become* what it *truly* is.

Paradoxically, then, the liturgy both affirms and negates the world, for the Eucharist is the transformation of the world that is not its destruction and the renewal of the world that is not its creation *ex nihilo*. In this way, the Eucharist manifests the very mystery of Christ in space and time, the mystery in which the old Adam is renewed without being destroyed, human nature is assumed without being changed, and the human is deified without ceasing to be human.

The vision of the world through the eucharistic experience leaves no possibility for dissociating the natural and the supernatural, thereby avoiding the dilemma in which Western theology is locked. In our opinion, this facilitates the opening of the Church to the contemporary world, which finds this natural-supernatural distinction very difficult, if not impossible. For on account of developments in science and philosophy it no longer understands the supernatural as 'beyond' nature. Yet, under the weight of this dichotomy inherited from Western theology, the Christian mind has been led either to the complete negation of the supernatural or to an internal dissociation (that is to say to a state of schizophrenia) that sometimes accepts the supernatural (in order not to betray the faith) and sometimes pays it no notice (in day-to-day life). Now, for the liturgical vision of the world, there is no natural-supernatural distinction. What exists is the single reality of nature and creation — even to the point of the *identification* of earthly and heavenly reality ('We who mystically represent the Cherubim...'). In the eucharistic encounter, God himself cannot be understood as 'beyond' nature, because in the person of his Son, he became the one 'enthroned on high with the Father and also invisibly present *here with us*'. Thus, the Eucharist can save us from the dissociation that drives moderns to deny God — the God that theology has placed in a sphere incomprehensible to moderns.

The eucharistic vision of the world eliminates another false opposition placed before us by Gnostic and Hellenistic theology: the opposition between eternity and time. In the Eucharist, history and time (usually understood either as an evil human obligation or as the antechamber of eternity) intersect with eternity and consequently, eternity ceases to be 'before' or 'after' time and becomes exactly the dimension into which time can open. In this way we become contemporaries of the whole history of God's pre-eternal plan for our salvation in a unity of past, present and future that allows the full acceptance and sanctification of time and history. 'Remembering... this command of the Saviour, and all that came to pass for our sake, the cross, the tomb, the resurrection on the third day, the ascension into heaven, the enthronement at the right hand of the Father, and the second glorious coming, we offer to you these gifts from your own gifts in all and for all.'

All of this might very well form a fundamental answer to certain contemporary expectations.

III. The Eucharist as Anthropology

The Orthodox liturgical life still has its own vision of humanity that seems to match the needs of modern humanity. From their centuries-old theological tradition, contemporary persons have inherited the anguish of its dichotomy between body and soul, mind and matter, and the dilemma of choosing between the two, because the purely spiritual is incomprehensible. In contrast, the Orthodox liturgical life pays very close attention to the body and its needs — to the point that the bread and the wine are identified with the Lord Himself, that wood and colours become icons of saints, and that the relics of the saints also express a sanctifying personal presence. In this tradition, humans participate as *a whole* and not by closing their eyes — the Western model of piety in which one encounters God in an allegedly immaterial relationship (which is at base merely a psychological relationship). Yet how does such a denial of the unity of the human creature correspond at all with the thought of those who have ceased (and who can blame them?) to think according to the anthropological categories of Aristotle and Plato? Rather than protecting human integrity, this psychologized Eucharist is yet another factor leading to a fundamental crisis of conscience and life.

We emphasized earlier — and we have always emphasized — that the Holy Eucharist is not the place in which each one encounters God in a merely 'vertical' relationship. No, the Eucharist is essentially *social* and *ecclesial* and has been preserved — more or less lived — as such in the East. There is perhaps no other event of ecclesial existence in which Christians cease to be individuals and become Church. In the Eucharist, prayer, faith, love and charity (that is to say all that the faithful practise individually) cease to be 'mine' and become 'ours' and the entire relationship of humanity with God becomes the relationship of God with his people, with his Church. The Eucharist is not only communion between each person and Christ, it is also communion among the faithful themselves and unity in the body of Christ, 'not many bodies, but one body', according to Saint John Chrysostom's faithful interpretation. Thus, the biblical truth that sums up the path to God and implies a true path towards the neighbour is especially alive in the Eucharist, which is the most anti-individualistic act of the Church.

In this way, the human ceases to be an individual and becomes a person, that is to say, a reality which is not a fragment, the appendix of a machine or of an organization directed at its own goal — even if it be the most sacred (collectivism). The person is not a means towards an end; the person him- or herself is the goal, the image and likeness of God that finds its fulfilment in communion with God and with other persons — and only thus.

Contemporary humans live every day under the weight of the opposition between the individual and the collective. Their social life is not *communio* but *societas*. And because there is no other choice, their violent reaction against collectivism leads to individualism and *vice versa*: for, paradoxically, the one presupposes the other. Our Christian tradition generally has not provided contemporary humans with an anthropology that would substantiate them as persons because, even in the Church, humans were sometimes seen through the lenses of dualism and collectivism. In contrast, the Liturgy presupposes — and at the same time leads towards — an anthropology that understands humanity to be 'a new creation in Christ'. The liturgy is not theology, it does not specify, it shows and reveals. To the question: 'What is humanity?', it responds by showing Christ as the human *par excellence*, that is to say as the human united to God, *deified*. In the communion 'of holy things' offered 'to the holy ones', the compass is magnetized immediately towards the One — praised in the Great Doxology: 'Thou only art Holy, Thou only art the Lord, O Jesus Christ' — in whom humanity, through Holy Communion, becomes what it truly is: catholic humanity.

4. The Eucharist as Ethics

Such is the experience of those participating in the Liturgy. But what happens when they 'go in peace' and return to the world? We used to say that humanity drew upon divine — supernatural — powers through the sacrament of the Eucharist, which would help in the struggle against sin. Regardless of this transfusion of power, the Eucharist, as action and as community, gives the full and concrete meaning of the moral life.

Our theological tradition has transformed ethics into a system of rules and an independent field of theology. Thus certain forms of conduct have become disembodied and absolute dogmas — related neither to diverse historical contexts nor to human diversity — that repeatedly judge and morally condemn the world. Under this influence the relationship between man and God became a *legal* relationship, in accordance with an old temptation of the West.

In contrast with this tradition, the Eucharistic vision of the world and society neither permits nor admits an autonomy of ethics or its reduction to absolute legal rules. Rather, it holds that the moral life follows from the *transformation* and *renewal* of humanity in Christ, so that every moral commandment appears and is understood only as a consequence of this *sacramental* transformation. In such a vision of ethics — for example, that found in Saint Paul's Epistle to the Colossians — moral conduct is understood as a continuation of the liturgical experience: 'So if you have been raised with Christ... Put to death whatever in you is earthly... You have stripped off the old self with its practices and have clothed yourself with the new self, which is being renewed...' (Col 3:1-5, 9-10; note that the terms 'to strip off' and 'to put on' are here liturgical terms and that they especially, but also all the terminology of this passage, link it to the experience of baptism). It is for this reason that the Liturgy recognizes only one kind of moral terminology: the *sanctification* of souls and bodies so that — in communion with 'the Blessed Virgin... and all of the Saints' — we entrust 'ourselves, each other and all our life to Christ our God'.

In this way, the Eucharist does not offer the world a system of moral rules, but a transfigured and *sanctified* society, a leaven that will lead the entire creation by a sanctifying *presence*, and not by the compulsion of moral commandments. This *witnessing* presence does not forge intolerable chains, but *invites* them to the freedom of the children of God, to a communion with God that will bring rebirth.

Contemporary humans seem to reject, utterly and indignantly, the moral rules imposed for centuries by a Christian civilization. Putting to one side the causes of this situation, let us merely note that the structure that we have built with our good moral values with so much zeal is now seen as a human prison that threatens to ruin its very foundations.

Why the moral decadence in secular society? Why does our Christian voice resound as if in a vacuum? We have turned to moral preaching and to statements of moral principles to convince the world, and we have failed; no one hears us. We offered the *Logos* and the world did not accept it. We forget that the *Logos* is not our words, but a Person, not a voice, but a living Presence and that this personal presence is embodied in the Eucharist, which is above all *communion* and *assembly*.

This society, which was transfigured in order to transfigure, no longer exists. It was dissolved by our pious individualism, which believed that, in order to work in the world, it had no need for the parish, for the eucharistic community, and it replaced them with an 'instructive logocracy', believing that it would be sufficient to *tell* the world to change. The presence of our Church in the world has become a pulpit without a sanctuary and a group of Christians with neither unity nor community. We do not draw our moral attitudes from the new life that we enjoy at the eucharistic assembly, and society thereby has lost the leaven of the divine communion that, alone, can spark an authentic revival.

V. The Eucharist as Eschaton

We do not mean to say that a eucharistic vision will provide a solution to the moral problems of our society. Instead, it should be noted that in such a vision there is no place for the 'opium' of a 'social gospel'. Waiting for the terrestrial paradise of a morally perfect society is a creation of western rationalism that cannot be assumed from the witness of the Eucharist. For the Eucharist, in its innermost nature, has an eschatological dimension: although it enters into history, it is not transformed entirely into history. It is the most dramatic evidence of a meeting in human existence here and now between the *eschaton* and history, between the perfect and the relative. The Eucharist is witness to a morality that is not an historical evolution but an ontological grace, acquired only to be lost again, until on the last day it will be acquired definitively. This eschatological invasion is not an historical development that one can comprehend logically and by experience; it is the *descent* of the Holy Spirit, by *epiclesis* — this epiclesis that is so fundamental and so characteristic of the Orthodox Eucharist — that transfigures the 'present age' and transforms it in Christ into 'a new creation'. This descent from heaven to earth, which makes possible the ascent of the earth to the heavenly throne, fills the earth with light, with grace and with joy, and makes the feast of the Liturgy a solemn celebration from which the faithful return to the world full of joy and charism. But in crossing the threshold of the church, they find an unabated struggle. Until the end of time, they must pursue their eucharistic journey, receiving only a taste of the divine communion which soon mixes with the bitter taste of evil. The Eucharist has given them the strongest assurance of the victory of Christ over the devil, but upon this earth, this victory will ever be a victory of 'kenosis', the victory of the cross, the victory of heroic ascesis — as it has been understood and lived in Eastern monasticism.

Therefore the Eucharist will always open the way not to the dream of a gradual perfection of the world, but to the demand for heroic ascesis, an experience of kenosis and of the cross, the only way in which it is possible to live the Eucharist in the world until the victory of the Resurrection at the end of time. At the same time, the Eucharist offers the world the experience of this eschatological dimension that penetrates history in the eucharistic communion and makes possible our deification in space and time. Without this dimension, no missionary method, no intelligent diplomacy ('dialogue with the world'), no system of morality will transfigure the contemporary world into Christ.

VI. The Eucharist as Hope

Without a doubt, the crisis of the relation between contemporary humanity and Christ and the incapacity of Christianity to meet contemporary humanity is due in large part to the debased theological tradition that we teach. This tradition has alienated humanity, made us schizophrenic, asphyxiated us with dualistic conceptions and moralistic constructions — in short, it has destroyed the integrity of the human. Given this situation, the Orthodox Church dooms itself to failure if it restricts its theological witness to this tradition. If, instead, the Orthodox Church resolves the contemporary dichotomies in the Eucharist, it will appear *liturgically* as the hope of the world where humanity finds its integrity in communion with God. When the Orthodox Church becomes aware of the eucharistic vision that it conceals and that will lead it to creative theological revisions and renewed practice, then she will save herself from secularization and the world from its seclusion from God.

CHAPTER SEVEN

PROPRIETORS OR PRIESTS OF CREATION?

Introduction to the Present Situation

The development of ecological awareness and sensitivity in recent years has led to the use of various models of speaking about the relationship of the human being to nature. The prevailing one among these models is that of *steward*: the human being is the steward of creation. This terminology has become widespread not only among secular but also among religious ecologists, especially among the latter. We encounter it in almost every reference to the ecological problem by theologians.

The idea of stewardship is a useful one mainly from the point of view of what it intends to exclude, namely that the human being is the lord and proprietor of creation. Such an understanding found support in modern times mainly in two areas: the anthropology of the Enlightenment, and Western, particularly Protestant, theology.

The Enlightenment found its typical representatives in this respect in such thinkers as Descartes, Francis Bacon and even Kant. In the words of Descartes, the development of science would make the human beings '*masters and possessors of nature*', while Francis Bacon in an almost brutal way invites humanity to treat nature as its 'slave'.[1] Kant, on the other hand, understood humanity's relationship to nature as that of a 'judge' whose function is to exercise rational and moral judgement on nature, directing it in accordance with what the human being considers to be right or wrong, good or bad for it.

Protestant theology, on the other hand, particularly in its Calvinist tradition, did its best to exploit the Biblical verse 'Subdue and have dominion over the earth' (Gen. 1:28) in order to promote, directly or indirectly, capitalist views of work and economy, as Max Weber has demonstrated so clearly. Without such religious ideas the appearance of the ecological crisis would probably be difficult to explain historically.

---

1   C. Adam and P. Tannery, *Œuvres de Descartes* V (rev. ed.), 1966-1976, p. 62; J. Cottingham, R. Stoothoff, and D. Murdoch, *The Philosophical Writings of Descartes* I, 1985, p. 142.

Now the replacement of the model of proprietor and possessor with that of steward of creation may be useful in order to exclude the undoubtedly unacceptable view that the human being is the lord of creation or may behave as such a lord. Ecologists recognized this and adopted the model of stewardship. However, a closer examination of this model would reveal to us its limitations and disadvantages from the ecological viewpoint. Thus:

(a) Stewardship implies a *managerial* approach to nature. The Greek word *oikonomos* which stands behind the notion of steward points to the capacity of the human being to 'manage' a given 'property' and make 'use' of it, albeit within the limits of what has been 'entrusted' to humanity. In this sense stewardship resembles what the English mean by the function of a 'trustee'. A utilitarian implication in the relationship of the human being to nature seems to underlie this model. Equally significant is the underlying conception of nature as a 'thing' and an 'object' to be managed, arranged, re-arranged, distributed etc. by the human being.

(b) Stewardship suggests a *conservationist* attitude to nature. The steward is the 'guardian' of what is given to him or her, called to conserve it, albeit, as we have just noted, while managing it. This conservationist approach to our relationship to nature seems to overlook two important truths. On the one hand, the human being is not called only to 'guard' but also to 'cultivate' nature, i.e. to improve its capacities and help it grow and bring forth fruit. On the other hand, human intervention has already reached such proportions that it would be unrealistic and futile to speak of sheer conservation of the environment. Certain parts of the environment may still be capable of conservation, but other parts have undergone irrevocable changes, and any attempt to preserve them would be unrealistic, and in some cases even undesirable.

Thus the idea of stewardship, much as it is useful to indicate our objection to the view that the human being is the lord and proprietor of creation — a view that accounts historically to a considerable degree for the appearance of the ecological crisis — has its own limitations and would appear to be problematic from the ecological point of view. It may therefore be necessary to complement it with another model, namely with what we may describe as *the priest of creation*. Such a model seems to emerge naturally from the patristic and liturgical tradition of the Orthodox Church, but its existential meaning is universal. The word 'priest' forms part of the religious language and for this reason it may appear to have a significance limited only to religious people. We shall try to show that this is not so. But in order to do that we must first clarify our anthropological presuppositions. We cannot tackle the idea of what Man — in the sense of *anthropos*, that is both male and female — is. (From now on we shall use the word 'man' in this sense, and not in its ordinary sexist usage.)

I. Theological Anthropology

What is the being that we call 'man'? It is not only theology that tries to answer this question, but also science and philosophy. Although each of these three disciplines has something different to say, they cannot but have also something common about this matter. Otherwise there would be no common ground and, therefore, no possibility of a dialogue between them.

For science — and for biology in particular — the human being is very closely connected with what we call animals; he or she is another animal. This view has prevailed in biology ever since Darwin produced his theory of evolution. Although this may sound rather disturbing to theologians, we must bear in mind, as we will see later on, that it is important for all of us to remember this connection of the human being with the rest of the animals. Biology approaches the human being as another animal with higher qualities than those of the rest of the animals, but with many things in common, including intelligence and consciousness. Attributes such as these used to be attached exclusively to human beings in the past. But for biological scientists today, the human being is, in a certain sense, basically an animal.

Philosophy tries to give a different view of the human being. Although it admits that the human being is an animal, it distinguishes it from the animals in one important way. In the past, philosophers made this distinction by saying that humans were specially characterized by intelligence or rationality. However, ever since Darwin showed that intelligence can also be found in other animals, and that the difference is a matter of degree and not of kind, philosophy no longer insists on rationality as the special characteristic of man.

The difference seems now to lie in the fact that whereas the animals adjust to the given world — and sometimes they manage that very well, much better than the human being — the human being wants to create its own world, to use the existing world in order to make something specifically human out of it.

This is why the human being produces tools of its own, which are used in order to exploit nature. But more significantly, it treats nature as a raw material from which it creates new realities, as is evident particularly in the case of art. Only the human being can see a tree, for example, and make another tree out of that, a tree which is 'his' or 'her' tree, bearing the personal seal of the person who painted it. Thus it is creativity that characterizes the human being, and this we cannot find in the animals. Man is a creative being. This is very important, as we will see later, for ecology as well.

In his attempt to be creative and to create his own world, man is normally frustrated, because he tends and wishes to create, as God does, out of nothing, and to be fully free from what is given to him as his environment, his 'world'. It is because the human being has this tendency to use the natural world for his own purposes that he can be both good and bad for creation. The human being can exploit creation in such a way as to subject it to himself, and in this way make the natural environment suffer under his dominion.

All this indicates that what distinguishes the human being from the animals is freedom expressed as creativity, as the free creation of something new. There are two ideas here to remember which will be very important for our subject. The first we draw from biological science, and that is that the human being is organically and inseparably linked with the natural world, particularly with the animals. The second is that although he is united with the rest of creation, man tends to rise above creation and make use of it in a free way, either by creating something new or sometimes by simply destroying what is 'given' to him.

With these thoughts from science and philosophy in mind, let us now ask what theology thinks the human being is. For theology, the human being is not only related to the rest of creation, but also to another factor, which science does not want to introduce, while philosophy sometimes does, but very often does not — namely, God. For theology, God is crucial in order to know what the human being is. The human being must emerge as something different, as a different identity with regard to the animals, with regard to the rest of creation, and also with regard to God. Thus man is a link between God and the world. This is what is expressed in theological terms through the idea of the 'image and likeness of God.'

In the Bible, when man was created, God said: 'Let us now create man in our image and likeness.' What does that mean? What does it mean that the human being is an image of God? This has been discussed throughout the centuries, and I will not bother you with all this complex discussion. Instead, I will simply mention that one of the elements that the Fathers saw as expressing this 'image of God' in man is rationality (*logos*), that man is a 'rational living being' (*logikon zōon*), and that it is through his rationality that he reflects the being of God in creation.

However, *logos* or 'rationality' had a particular meaning at that time, and it had mainly to do with the capacity of the human being to collect what is diversified and even fragmented in this world and make a unified and harmonious world (*cosmos*) out of that. Rationality was not, as it came to be understood later, simply a capacity to reason with one's mind. Instead, as the ancient Greeks thought of *logos*, it is man's capacity to achieve the unity of the world and to make a *cosmos* out of it. Man has the capacity to unite the world.

There is also another element that was stressed by the Fathers as expressing the 'image of God'. This is what Gregory of Nyssa calls the *autoexousion* — the freedom of the human being. The animals do not have a *logos* in the sense of acquiring a universal grasp of reality, nor the freedom from the laws of nature; whereas the human being has to some extent both of these things, and that is very important for him in order to be, as we shall see, the priest of creation.

Another aspect of the image of God in man — or rather, another aspect of what man is or represents for theology, particularly Orthodox and Patristic theology — is that man is the 'prince of creation', and the microcosm of the whole of creation. One of the Fathers who wrote in the seventh century, Saint Maximus the Confessor, developed this idea in particular, namely that in the human being we have the whole world present, a sort of microcosm of the whole universe. Because the human being has this organic link with creation and at the same time the drive to unite creation and to be free from the laws of nature, he can act as the 'priest of creation'.

II. The Priests of Creation

The priest is the one who freely and, as himself an organic part of it, takes the world in his hands to refer it to God, and who, in return, brings God's blessing to what he refers to God. Through this act, creation is brought into communion with God himself. This is the essence of priesthood, and it is only the human being who can do it, namely, unite the world in his hands in order to refer it to God, so that it can be united with God and thus saved and fulfilled. This is so because, as we said earlier, only the human being is united with creation while being able to transcend it through freedom.

This role of the human being, as the priest of creation, is absolutely necessary for creation itself, because without this reference of creation to God the whole created universe will die. It will die because it is a finite universe, as most scientists accept today. This is theologically a very fundamental belief, since the world was not always there, but came into being at some point and, for this reason, will 'naturally' have an end and come into non-being one day.

Therefore, the only way to protect the world from its finitude which is inherent in its nature, is to bring it into relation with God. This is because God is the only infinite, immortal being, and it is only by relating to him that the world can overcome its natural finitude and its natural mortality.

In other words, when God created the world finite, and therefore subject by nature to death and mortality, he wanted this world to live forever and to be united with him — that is, to be in communion with him. It is precisely for this reason that God created the human being. This underlines the significance of man as the priest of creation, who would unite the world and relate it to God so that it may live forever.

Now, the human being did not perform this function, and here lies for theology the root of the ecological problem. The human being was tempted to make himself the ultimate point of reference, i.e. God. By replacing God with himself — that is, a finite created being — man condemned the world to finitude, mortality, decay and death. In other words, the human being rejected his role as the priest of creation by making himself God in creation.

This is what we call in theology the 'fall of man'. When this occurred, God did not want the world to die and brought about a way of restoring this lost communion between himself and creation. The incarnation of the Son of God was precisely about this. Christ is the one who came in order to do what Adam did not do: to be the priest of creation. Through his death and resurrection, Christ aimed precisely at this unity and communion of the whole of creation with God, at the reference of creation back to God again. It is for this reason that Christ is called the 'second Adam', or the 'last Adam', and that his work is seen as the 'recapitulation' (*anakephalaiosis*) of all that exists, i.e. of the entire creation.

Now it is this role, which Christ performed personally through his cross and resurrection, that he assigned to his Church, which is his Body. The Church is there precisely in order to act as the priest of creation who unites the world and refers it back to God, bringing it into communion with him. This takes place in the Church particularly through the sacraments.

The meaning of the sacraments, for example that of baptism, is that through it the attitude of the fallen Adam is reversed. Man dies as to his claim to be God in creation, and instead recognises God as its Lord. Through the path of asceticism, the Church educates man to sacrifice his own will, his self-centredness, and subject himself freely to the will of God, thus showing that man has reversed the attitude of the first Adam. Finally, through the Eucharist, the Church proclaims and realizes precisely this priestly function of humanity. The Eucharist consists in taking elements from the natural world, the bread and the wine which represent the created material world, and bringing them into the hands of the human being, the hands of Christ who is the man *par excellence* and the priest of creation, in order to refer them to God.

At this point, it is important to remember — especially those of us who belong to the Orthodox Church and are familiar with the Orthodox Liturgy — that the central point in our Liturgy is when the priest exclaims: 'Thine of Thine own we offer unto Thee'. This means precisely that the world, the creation, is recognised as belonging to God, and is referred back to him. It is precisely the reversal of Adam's attitude, who took the world as his own and referred it to himself. In the Eucharist, the Church does precisely the opposite: the world belongs to God and we refer it back to its Creator through the priestly action of Christ as the real and true man, who is the head of the Body of the Church.

III. Being a Priest of Creation in Our Time

Let us now look briefly at the ecological significance of all this.

(a) The understanding of the human being as priest rather than steward of creation means that the role of man in creation is neither passive (conservationist) nor managerial, that is, 'economic' (the notion of 'economy' is deeply linked with that of management — the idea of arranging things according to and for the sake of *expediency*, not only in political but also in ecclesiastical language). The human being is related to nature not *functionally*, as the idea of stewardship would suggest, but *ontologically*: by being the steward of creation the human being relates to nature by what he *does*, whereas by being the priest of creation he relates to nature by what he *is*. The implications of this distinction are very significant. In the case of stewardship our attitude to nature is determined by ethics and morality: if we destroy nature we disobey and transgress a certain law, we become immoral and unethical. In the case of priesthood, in destroying nature we simply *cease to be*, the consequences of ecological sin are not moral but existential. Ecology is in this way a matter of our *esse*, not of our *bene esse*. Our ecological concern becomes in this way far more powerful and efficient than in employing the model of stewardship.

(b) The idea of priest of creation gives to ecology a *cultural* dimension. The word culture must be taken in its deepest meaning, which is the elevation of an otherwise transitory and ephemeral entity to something of lasting and even eternal value. When an artist creates, he or she wishes to bring about something of eternal value and significance. The priest is in this sense an artist: he takes the material world in his hands (the bread and the wine, for example, in the case of the Eucharist, which are perishable by nature) and lifts it up to acquire eternal divine meaning. In such an approach the entire *raison d'être* of ecology undergoes a profound change. We do not ask people to respect the environment simply for negative reasons, such as the fear of destruction etc. — this would be an ecology based on fear. We ask people to take a *positive* view of ecology, something like an attitude of *love* towards nature. As priests rather than stewards we *embrace* nature instead of managing it, and although this may sound romantic and sentimental, its deeper meaning is, as we stated above, ontological, since this 'embracing' of nature amounts to our very being, to our existence.

(c) Such a cultural dimension of ecology implies that the protection of nature is not contrary to the *development* of nature. The human being is the priest of creation in the sense that the material world he takes in his hands is *transformed* into something better than what it is *naturally*. Nature must be improved through human intervention; it is not to be preserved as it is. In the Eucharist we do not offer to God simply grain or wheat and grapes, but bread and wine, that is, natural elements developed and transformed through the human labour, in our hands. Ecology is not preservation but development. The model of priest is in this sense far more suggestive and rich than that of steward. It does not, however, bring us back to the model of proprietor, since in the case of priesthood the development of nature through the intermediary of the human hands does not end up with the human being and its interests, but is referred to God.

Ecology and development have always been, as we all know, two terms that require some kind of reconciliation. (There is always the fear among developing countries that ecology has been 'invented' as a means of keeping them underdeveloped). This is indeed the case if the development of nature has as its ultimate purpose the satisfaction of human needs. But in a priestly approach to nature we develop it not in order to satisfy our needs as human beings, but *because nature itself* stands in need of development through us *in order to fulfil its own being* and acquire a meaning which it would not otherwise have. In other words, there is a development of nature which treats it as *raw material for production* and distribution, and there is a development which treats nature as an entity that must be developed *for its own sake*. In the latter case, although the human being is not passive, simply preserving or sustaining nature, he is developing nature with respect for its, and not his, interests, taking care of its fragility and its 'groaning in travail', to remember Saint Paul's moving expression in Romans 8.

Conclusion

I have tried to describe the model of priest of creation in its ecological significance. I hope I have shown some of the advantages that this model may have for ecology compared with other models, especially that of stewardship. I am fully aware of the fact that the way things are going with regard to ecology none of these models would save us. I nevertheless think that the moralistic approach to the ecological problems expressed through such words as 'responsibility' etc. has to be complemented with a cultural approach. Our ecological crisis is due not so much to a wrong ethic as to a bad ethos; it is a *cultural* problem. In our Western culture we did everything to de-sacralise life, to fill our societies with legislators, moralists and thinkers, and undermined the fact that the human being is also, or rather primarily, a *liturgical* being, faced from the moment of birth with a world that he or she must treat either as a sacred gift or as raw material for exploitation and use. We are all born priests, and unless we remain so throughout our lives we are bound to suffer the ecological consequences we are now experiencing. We must allow the idea of priest of creation to re-enter our culture and affect our ethos. For, an ethic which is not rooted in ethos is of little use to ecology.

CHAPTER EIGHT

PRESERVING GOD'S CREATION

Introduction

The subject of these lectures has to do with one of the most pressing and critical issues of our time. It is becoming increasingly evident that what has been named 'the ecological crisis' is perhaps the number one problem now facing the world-wide human community. Unlike other problems, this one is marked by the characteristic that it is a global problem, concerning all human beings regardless of the part of the world or the social class to which they belong, and a problem that has to do not simply with the well-being but with the very being of humanity and perhaps of creation as a whole. It is, indeed, difficult to find any aspect of what we call 'evil' or 'sin' that would bear such an all-embracing and devastating power as this ecological evil. This way of describing the ecological problem may still sound to some ears as a gross exaggeration, and yet there are hardly any serious and responsible scientists and politicians today who would not agree with it. If we follow the present course of events, the prediction of the apocalyptic end of life on our planet at least is not a matter of prophecy but of sheer inevitability.

In view of this situation what does theology have to offer to humanity? The first obvious thing to be mentioned is that theology cannot and should not remain silent on an issue like this. If faith is about ultimate things, about life and death issues, this particular problem certainly falls within that category. Christian theology and the Church can hardly be excused for staying silent for such a long time on this matter; particularly since, and not without good reason, they have both been accused of having something to do with the roots of the ecological problem. Church and theology have to speak on this matter not so much in order to apologize and offer explanations in view of such accusations, but in order to offer their constructive contribution to the solution of the problem. For they must have something constructive to say on a matter like this. Otherwise they risk being irrelevant and unable to live up to their own claim to the Truth. For a truth which does not offer life is empty of all meaning.

If we try to identify the direction in which our Western societies are going regarding possible solutions to the ecological problem, we shall immediately realize that all our hopes seem to be placed in ethics. Whether enforced by state legislation or taught and instructed by Churches, academic institutions, etc., it is ethics that seems to contain the hopes of humankind in the present situation. If only we could behave better! If only we could use less energy! If only we could agree to lower a bit our standards of living! If, if... But ethics, whether enforced or free, presupposes other, more deeply existential motivations in order to function. People do not give up their standards of living because such a thing is 'rational' or 'moral'. By appealing to human reason we do not necessarily make people better, while moral rules, especially after their dissociation from religious beliefs, prove to be more and more meaningless and unpleasant to modern man.

The experience of two world wars and their destructive consequences in our century came as a blow to the optimism of the eighteenth- and nineteenth-century prophets of the Enlightenment who thought that the way things were going, with the cultivation of reason and the spread of knowledge, the twentieth century would be the era of human paradise. Humanity does not always behave rationally and cannot be made to behave so either by force or by persuasion. There are other forces, besides the human intellect, that decide the direction in which the fate of the world moves. Theology and the Church ought to embrace areas other than the ethical — that is, the rational prescription of behaviour — if they are to be any use in this case. Such areas must include all that in the pre-Enlightenment world used to belong to the mythological, the imaginative, the sacred. We did our best in the post-Enlightenment world to destroy the mythological, to leave the non-rational to the *Belles Lettres*, which we separated sharply from hard thinking philosophy, and we thus destroyed the 'world-view' (the accent on world), the understanding of the world in which we live as a mysterious, sacred reality broader than the human mind can grasp or contain, a 'cosmic liturgy' as the seventh-century Greek Father Saint Maximus the Confessor would describe the world.

Of course, the fear of paganism and all that it implies can justify a great deal of the attitude that led to sheer rationalism. But there could be, as indeed there have been, other responses to this fear than the total dichotomy between nature and history, the sacred and the profane, reason and myth, art and philosophy, etc., which have marked our modern way of thinking in the West. Certainly the Church and theology ought to have found better ways to respond to such a fear than the way of separating the rational from the mythical, the sacred from the secular. For they are, after all, claiming that faith in Christ implies a unity between the transcendent and the immanent, and an *anakephalaiosis* of all in the person of Christ. Appealing, therefore, only to the ethical solution, as so many Christians seem to do today, would only reinforce the reasons that led to the ecological crisis in the first place. If we try to solve the ecological problem by introducing new ethical values or re-arranging the scale of the traditional ones, I fear that we shall not go very far in reaching a solution.

In the course of this chapter I shall try to show why I think we stand in need of a new culture in which the *liturgical dimension* would occupy the central place, and perhaps determine the ethical principle. If I were to give an overall title to this effort, a key notion for what I shall be trying to say to you here, this would probably be that of *man as the priest of creation*. I used this expression in Patmos last summer in the context of the International Environmental Conference that took place there in connection with the 900th anniversary of the founding of the Monastery of Saint John, the author of the Book of Revelation. I feel that our culture stands in need of a revival of the consciousness that the superiority of the human being as compared with the rest of creation consists not in the reason it possesses, but in its ability to *relate* in such a way as to create events of communion whereby individual beings are liberated from their self-centredness and thus from their limitations, and are referred to something greater than themselves, to a 'beyond' — to God, if one wishes to use this traditional terminology. This the human can do, not as a thinking agent but as a *person* — a notion that needs to be defined further in the course of this chapter. The notion of 'priesthood' must be freed from its pejorative connotations and be seen as carrying with it the characteristic of 'offering', in the sense of opening up particular beings to a transcending relatedness with the 'other' — an idea more or less corresponding to that of *love* in its deepest sense. In all this the underlying assumption is that there exists and an interdependence between *man* and *nature*, and that the human being is not fulfilled until it becomes the *anakephalaiosis*, the summing up of nature. Thus man and nature do not stand in opposition to each other, in antagonism, but in positive relatedness. This cannot be achieved in any other way except through liturgical action, because it is only through such action that nature is involved itself in the very event of this positive relatedness. Man has to become a liturgical being before he can hope to overcome his ecological crisis.

But before we come to an analysis of this thesis, we must become aware of the factors that have led to the present crisis and of the tools that history offers us toward its overcoming. A quick look at history is therefore our immediate task in this chapter.

I. Part One

1. The First Centuries

The American historian Lynn White, writing about the historical roots of the ecological problem in 1968, was quite categorical in attributing this problem to the Western intellectual tradition with its rationalistic view of humanity, and in assigning to theology and the Church an important role in this development.[1] Regardless of the extent to which one agrees or disagrees with this judgement of a contemporary historian, it can hardly be disputed by anyone that history must have something to teach us about the roots of the present crisis and that religion, and Christianity in particular, being a dominant force in the shaping of our culture throughout the centuries — at least up to the Enlightenment — must have had some role to play in the background of this crisis It will be necessary, therefore, to go back to the earliest stages of Christian history and to try to identify the forces that may have led to the subsequent developments up to our time.

If we accept the view that classical Christianity took shape in the context and perhaps under the influence of two cultures, the one dominated by the Hebrew or Semitic and the other by the Hellenic way of thinking, it would be instructive to try to see in what ways these two cultures conceived humanity's relationship to nature, and the place that God occupied in this relationship.

With regard to Hebrew and Jewish culture which formed the original milieu of Christianity, historians on the whole agree that the Hebrew mind tended to attach decisive importance to history (the history of the elect people of God in particular) and to see God as revealing Himself mainly in and through His acts in history. Nature played a secondary role in this revelation, and very often such a role was totally denied to it under the influence of an obsession with the fear of paganism that threatened the specific identity of the people of Israel.

This preoccupation with history rather than nature resulted in the development of prophetism at the expense of cosmology in Hebrew culture. Prophetism looked at the events marking the history of Israel, or other peoples — the 'nations' — and often of individuals, and was concerned with the final outcome of these events. God was expected to reveal Himself in the final event that would supersede and at the same time gave meaning to the previous events, and this final event — the *eschaton* as it came to be called in the Greek-speaking Jewish communities of the New Testament period — would be all that mattered to the Hebrew mind.

---

1   *Machina ex deo: essays in the dynamism of Western culture*, 1968.

Greek culture, on the other hand, attached little significance to history. In fact very soon in the circles of philosophers and scientists of classical Greece history was even looked upon with distrust and suspicion as the realm of change, flux and disorder. Nature offered to the Greek the sense of security he needed, through the regular movement of the stars, the cyclical repetition of the seasons, and the beauty and harmony which the balanced and moderate climate of Attica (at *that* time) offered. Cosmology was the main concern of the Greek philosophers who saw God present and operating in and through its laws of cyclical movement and natural reproduction. Even minds as cultivated and as reflective theologically as Aristotle could not avoid worshipping the stars, while Plato, the theologian *par excellence* of classical Greece, could reach no further than a creator God who would be an artist creating a universe in accordance with pre-existing matter, space, and ideas.

This comparison between Hebrew and Greek attitudes to nature, allowing of course for all qualifications necessary to a generalized presentation of things such as the present one, implies, among other things, two points that are of immediate interest to our subject.

(a) The Hebrew mind seems to lack cosmological interest, while the Greek lacks prophetism. If Christianity were to make use of both Hebrew and Greek cultures it ought somehow to arrive at what may be called 'cosmological prophecy'. It is this that I believe we find for the first time in the book of Revelation in which a Christian prophet following the best of typical Hebrew tradition rises above history and views the fate not of Israel alone but of *creation*, that is, of the *natural world*, from the angle of eschatology, of God's final act in history. Cosmological prophecy is thus seen as a new type of prophecy, and this marks the beginning of a new approach to humanity's relationship with nature, which the Church would pick up and develop further later on.

(b) The comparison between these two cultures that lie at the root of classical Christianity reveals that whereas for the Greek the world was a reality which contained in itself sufficient energy to live forever — hence the understanding of the universe as eternal — for the Hebrew the world was itself an *event*, a gift that must to be constantly referred back to its Creator in order to live. At this point the Early Church had to combine a world-view that trusted nature for what it was — that is, believed in its rationality, its *logos* or *logoi* and one that regarded it as a *gift* and an *event*, constantly dependent upon its Creator and Giver. It is out of this combination that early Christianity developed its 'eucharistic cosmology', which like cosmological prophecy took a view of the world as *finite* and subject to its limitations in its nature, nevertheless as trustworthy and capable of survival in and through its being referred back to its Creator. Thus, in a typically Greek fashion the world would be conceived as good and beautiful and would occupy a central place in man's consciousness, but its beauty and permanency and centrality in man's preoccupation would constantly depend on an event of reference back to what is not the world or nature, that is, to God. Thus, the earliest eucharistic prayers of the Church being composed in the best of typically Hebrew liturgical tradition, would involve a blessing over the fruits of the earth, but this would be done in such a way as to involve also an affirmation of faith in the survival of Creation and nature, as if this survival — and not simply the survival of a people or of the human being — were central in the Church's consciousness.

To sum up this point, both cosmological prophecy and eucharistic cosmology, which emerged out of the encounter between Hebrew and Hellenic thought on Christian soil, involved the view that the world is an *event* and not a self-explainable process, but that owing to another *event*, namely its being referred to the eternal and unperishable Creator, it can be said to *be* permanent and to survive. It is at this point that the responsibility of humanity as the one who refers the world back to the Creator and forms the basis of what we have called here his capacity to be the 'priest of Creation'.

But we shall discuss this point later on in the course of this chapter. At the moment let us continue with our brief look at history.

What we have said so far shows that in primitive Christianity cosmology an interest in nature occupied a central place in the Church's consciousness, but this was done without falling into paganism, owing to the fact that the reality or nature of the world had to be conditioned by an *event* — the event of referring the world to God. Thus, whereas in paganism faith in the survival of the world emerges from faith in the world's eternal and inevitable self-perpetuation, in Christian cosmology the world is contingent and contains in itself no guarantee of survival except in so far as it is in communion with *what is not world by nature* — not what is part of nature — namely God as understood in the Bible. The crucial point, therefore, in the survival of the world lies in the act or the event of its communion with God as totally other than the world. Man's responsibility becomes in this way crucial for the survival of nature.

2. The Middle Ages

All this describes the situation with regard to the first two or three centuries of the Christian era. Things, however, seem to change gradually, and the Church is eventually led to a seriously modified consciousness with regard to the relationship between man and nature.

Very briefly the decisive steps in this development can be described in the following way:

(a) A strong influence of Platonic and Gnostic dualism in the second and third centuries had the result of undermining the importance of the material world and regarded it at best as irrelevant and at worst as evil. The Christian Gnostics of Alexandria, above all the extremely influential Origen, represent classical examples of this development. Origen, in particular, who was widely read by the monks of Egypt, influenced a considerable part of Eastern Monasticism, which was fortunately rescued from this influence by monastic forces such as that of Macarius of Egypt and Saint Maximus the Confessor.

(b) In the West similar developments tended to introduce a dichotomy between man and nature by regarding the former as superior to the latter, and as the centre of everything. Typical examples of this development are to be found in Saint Augustine and Boethius, who defined the human being, or even the divine being, in terms of reason and intellect, and introduced consciousness and introspectiveness as the supreme aspects of human and indeed divine existence. Thus the human being was singled out from nature as being not only a higher kind of being but in fact the sole being that mattered eternally apart of course from the angels who, owing to their spiritual and immaterial existence, were of an even higher value than the human souls. The kingdom of God in Saint Augustine's vision of the last things has no place for nature; it consists of the survival of spiritual beings, of the eternal souls. The Church was gradually losing consciousness of the importance and eternal value of the material creation, and this was particularly evident in the way it treated the sacraments and the Eucharist in particular: instead of being a blessing over the material world, the fruits of nature, and a reference of it with gratitude and dedication to the Creator, the Eucharist soon became primarily a memorial service of the sacrifice of Christ and a means of grace for the nourishment of the *soul*. The dimension of the cosmos soon disappeared from sacramental theology in the West giving its place to a soul- or spirit-centred world-view.

(c) The Middle Ages and the Reformation did little to change this situation, having in fact reinforced through Scholasticism the idea that the *imago Dei* consists in human reason. The sacraments still remained to a large extent in the West irrelevant to the material world, and the gap between man and nature widened even further. Descartes following the Augustinian tradition made the thinking subject the centre of everything ('*cogito ergo sum*'), while the Enlightenment strengthened even further the view that the thinking rational being is all that matters in existence. Romanticism, while paying attention to nature, reinforced the dichotomy between the thinking, conscious subject and the non-thinking, non-conscious nature, clearly giving superiority to the former and allowing the latter to be of value only in so far as it contained in itself the presence of the former. Pietism, mysticism and other religious and theological movements still operated without any reference to nature, while Puritanism and mainstream Calvinism exploited to the utmost degree the Genesis verse urging man to 'multiply and to dominate the earth', thus giving rise to capitalism and eventually to technology and to our present-day civilization.

3. Modern Times

To this human-centred and reason-dominated world-view, to which Christian theology has contributed the main factor, our modern Western world managed to produce two intellectual forces that acted as antibodies, both however outside the area of theology and the Church, which even remained for the greatest part hostile to these forces.

(a) The first of them was Darwinism. A blessing in disguise as we might call it, Darwinism pointed out that the human being is by no means the only intelligent being in creation — a blow to the Scholastic view that the image of God in man is his reason and intellect — and that consciousness, even self-consciousness, is to be found in animals, too, the difference between them and Man being one of *degree* not of *kind*. Thus, Man was thrown back to his organic place in nature, and the question remained open as to what constitutes his difference from the animals, given now the fact that reason is no longer the *special* difference. The Church by defending on the whole its reason-centred culture failed to respond constructively to the challenge of Darwinism and preferred either to enter into antagonistic debate with it, or to succumb to it by accepting its downward looking anthropology and refusing to seek in areas other than reason the difference of the human being. But Darwinism by having virtually won the science of biology for itself is still there, and theology has to make the best use of it — both positively and negatively — not least for the sake of overcoming the ecological crisis.

(b) The second set of antibodies to this inherited human-centred and reason dominated culture of ours came in modern times from the area of natural philosophy through *Einstein* and the subsequent schools of modern quantum-physics. Here the blow was of a different and perhaps deeper kind. In the first instance it signified the end of the dichotomy between *nature* or substance and *event*. Everything that *is* at the same time *happens*, space and time coinciding one with the other. The world itself is an event, and cannot be conceived apart from an *act*, one might say a ritual, that takes place all the time. In addition, we have the blow to the subject–object structure dealt by quantum-mechanics. The observer and the observed form an unbreakable unity, the one influencing the other. The universe in its remotest parts is present in every single part of it. Even what is called by a certain school of natural philosophy 'the anthropic principle', in spite of its anthropocentricism, cannot apply to a world-view in which man can be isolated from the rest of the universe. Natural science as well as biology press hard on theology in our time, demanding a review of our traditional theology. I believe that this pressure can be of decisive benefit to the Church in its attempt to face the ecological problem. This, however, presupposes a creative use of all the new developments in the areas of biological and natural sciences in connection with whatever Christian tradition can offer for the same purpose. Such elements from the Christian tradition can be drawn from the following areas of classical theology, especially from that of the patristic era.

4. Positive Elements from Tradition

From the liturgical experience of the ancient Church, the following elements must be underlined:

(a) All ancient liturgies, especially in the East, involve a sanctification of matter and of time. There is no introspective and self-conscious attitude of the human soul in the ancient liturgies; everything is aimed at the involvement of the praying individual in an event of communion with the other members of the worshipping community and with the material context of the liturgy. Apart from the bread and wine, themselves parts of the material world, the ancient liturgies tried to involve all of man's senses in the liturgical event: the eyes through the icons and the liturgical vestments; the ears through hymns and psalmody; the nose through the smell of incense, etc. In addition to that, the prayer for 'seasonable weather, for an abundance of the fruits of the earth, etc.' places the liturgy right in the middle of creation.

(b) All ancient liturgies seem to be centred not so much on the consecration of the elements, even less so on a psychological anamnesis of the cross of Christ, as on the *lifting up of the gifts of bread and wine to the Creator Father*, what is called in all the ancient Greek liturgies the *Anaphora* (literally, 'the lifting up'). Liturgiologists today tend to stress this forgotten detail, which can be of particular significance for a theology of creation. For it attaches at least equal centrality — if not more — to man's act as the priest of creation as it does to God's act of sending down the Holy Spirit to transform the offered gifts into the body and blood of Christ. This forgotten aspect was so central in the consciousness of the Early Church as to lend itself for identifying and naming the entire eucharistic service: in the ancient Church the service was called, not without significance, purely and simply *Anaphora* or *Eucharistia*, both terms having to do with man's priestly action as representative of creation.

In this connection it must be also underlined that all ancient Eucharistic liturgies began their eucharistic prayer or canon with thanksgiving for *creation* in the first place, and only afterwards for redemption through Christ. In certain cases, like that of the eucharistic liturgy commented upon by Saint Cyril of Jerusalem in his *Mystagogical Catecheses*, the thanksgiving for creation seems to be the only point of the eucharistic canon with no mention at all of the sacrifice of Christ. Of course, this was not the norm, but it can serve as an illustration of how central the reference to creation was in the ancient liturgies. The priestly aspect of the Eucharist — and this is worth underlining — did not consist in the notion of sacrifice, as it came to be understood in the Middle Ages, but in that of *offering* back to God his own creation. It is a great pity, indeed, that sacrificial notions came to occupy the meaning of priesthood for centuries. It is a pity not so much because this gave rise to endless controversy between Roman Catholics and Protestants, preventing them from reaching a common mind on the Eucharist even today, but mainly because it has meant the loss of the dimension of creation from the notion of priesthood. It is important, therefore, to recover and restore this dimension for the purpose of facing the ecological problem.

A second area besides the eucharistic liturgy in which the ancient Church can help us recreate our theology today is that of *asceticism*. Here things need some explanation, for asceticism has been normally associated with hostility or, in the best of cases, with contempt towards the material world. With the exception of certain trends in ancient monasticism that were under the direct influence of Origenism, asceticism was by no means associated with neglect or contempt of the material creation. In the earlier *Gerontikon* (collections of stories about monks and their sayings) we encounter stories of ascetics who wept over the death of birds or who lived in peace with wild animals. Even today on Mount Athos one can encounter monks who never kill serpents, but co-exist peacefully with them — something that would make even the best of Christians among us shiver and tremble.

Besides this respect for nature, it must be noted that it was in the circles of the desert theologians especially that the idea developed in the East that the 'image of God' in man is to be found also in his *body*, and not simply in his mind. Indeed, asceticism was accompanied in the early Church by the breaking of one's own selfish will so that the individual with his or her desires to dominate the external world and use it for

amazon.com

Returns Are Easy!
Most items can be refunded, exchanged, or replaced when returned in original and unopened condition. Visit http://www.amazon.com/returns to start your return, or http://www.amazon.com/help for more information on return policies

Your order of December 25, 2012 (Order ID 111-9492339-8963442)

Qty.	Item	Item Price	Total
1	**The Eucharistic Communion and the World** Zizioulas, John D. --- Paperback (** **P-2-A44E830** **) 0567326608	$29.39	$29.39

Subtotal	$29.39
Shipping & Handling	$ 3.99
Promotional Certificate	$-3.99
Order Total	$29.39
Paid via credit/debit	$29.39
Balance due	$0.00

This shipment completes your order.

Have feedback on how we packaged your order? Tell us at www.amazon.com/packaging.

0/D4D1STdgN/-1 of 1-/-/SP-NOMA/sss-us/9483782/1231-01:30/1227-12:10

A0

their own satisfaction may learn not to make the individual the centre of creation. This is a spirit which is needed in order to teach modern man how to solve the ecological problem. But it should not be taken as part of an ethical education, for then it would lead nowhere. It can only be meaningful if, combined with the liturgical experience, it creates an *ethos* rather than a prescribed rule of behaviour, and it is in this sense that it can be useful to theology, which in turn can be helpful in facing the problem of our time.

One could add to the list of elements borrowed from tradition many others, such as the use of space and matter in architecture, the use of colour and shape in painting, of sound in music, etc. In general, it is, as I said at the beginning, a matter of *culture* which theology must aim at. But for the purposes of this section, it may suffice to stop at this point. We have seen how history has contributed to the emergence of the ecological problem and how it can contribute to its solution. But history cannot be repeated and reconstituted intact. Nostalgic voices for a return to Byzantine forms of art are abundant today among the Orthodox. We do not intend to offer here any support to such voices: our modern world has passed through changes that make a return to the past impossible, and therefore undesirable. Theology today must use the past with respect, for it has indeed managed to overcome paganism without falling into gnosticism, and it must try to learn from that. But it must try to adjust it to the present by creatively combining it with whatever our contemporary world has achieved or is trying to achieve in all areas of thought — science, art, philosophy, and the rest.

II. Part Two

In the remaining sections we shall attempt to discuss in some depth the aspects of tradition that we believe can be of positive value in facing the ecological crisis today. We shall try to say something more about the idea of man as the priest of creation, and about how this can affect our or a moment that the ecological crisis culture. We do not, of course, claim for a moment that the ecological crisis will be solved at the end of this chapter. But we hope that these modest reflections may not be altogether irrelevant to the task facing theology in these critical times of ours.

1. Liturgical Culture and World-View

In the previous sections we emphasized the seriousness of the situation with which humanity and indeed our planet as a whole, are faced because of the ecological problem, and tried to look briefly at history in order to see to what extent (a) Christian theology could be regarded as responsible for the ecological crisis of our time, and (b) Christian tradition could be of help in our attempt to deal with this crisis. Our brief and inevitably generalized historical survey has led us to the conclusion that the Christian Church and its theology have indeed been to a large extent responsible for the emergence of the ecological problem in our time, and that, in spite of that, they possess resources that can be of help to humanity in its present crisis. The ecological problem, therefore, although being a problem of science and to a large degree of ethics, education and state legislation, is also a theological problem. As it is evident that certain theological ideas have played an important role in the creation of the problem, so it must be also the case that theological ideas can help in its solution. Theology cannot and should not be irrelevant to the creation of culture.

It is unfortunate that Christian theology has often in our time taken a negative view of culture, science, etc., very much in contradiction to its fundamental claims and beliefs. And it is equally regrettable that, owing to the pressures from the Enlightenment, theology and the Church were marginalized in our Western society and became incapable of doing harm as well as good to modern culture. One would suspect from the way things are developing in our modern world that the absence of theology from our culture will be felt very deeply, as science, ethics, etc., will appear increasingly unable to handle situations such as the one created by the ecological problem. For it is necessary to repeat the point I tried to underline in the previous section, namely that without a world-view that involves religious and what we may call *liturgical* attitudes to creation, it will be impossible to reverse the alarming situation the world is facing today.

How does Christian theology view creation and Man's place in it? This is the question to which we must now address ourselves. If Christian theology has somehow led the world to its present crisis, by what ideas can it now help the world to deal with it?

In order to answer this question we propose to deal first with the way Christian tradition views the reality we normally call creation. The next step will concern more specifically the role humanity is called to play in creation. It will then be, we hope, possible to draw some conclusions as to what Christian theology and the Church can offer to man in the difficult crisis he faces in our time.

2. Doctrines of Creation in the First Centuries

'Creation' is a term which Christian theology found from the beginning to be convenient in order to express its world-view. It is a term which indicates that the world as we know it is a *work* or a *product* of someone, the result of a certain personal cause. Normally the Greek term corresponding to 'creation' is *demiourgia*, although the Christian writers of the first centuries, for reasons to which we shall refer presently, would prefer to use the term *ktisis* — a word that brings to mind images of craftsmanship, or rather of building and raising an edifice.

Now the view of the world as a 'creation' by someone was by no means a Judeo-Christian invention. The idea was widespread at the time of the rise of Christianity that the world was created by some creator, and what the Church had to do was not so much to insist on this idea as to offer its own interpretation of it. True, there were still around some atheists in the first and second centuries AD who would either attribute the world to certain laws inherent in its nature and be happy with this explanation (such were the 'physiologists' whom Plato had in mind) or those who, like the Epicureans, would attribute the world to pure chance. But all these were negligible, almost marginalized in the intellectual milieu in which the early Church found itself, and it is for this reason that the Christian writers did not bother very much about them. The main views of creation that the Church had to face and from which it was seen to dissociate itself were of two categories. One was the *Gnostic* interpretation of creation, and the other was what we may call the *Platonic* or classical Greek philosophical view. To these two we shall briefly turn in order to see in what way the Christian concept of creation took its shape in this early period.

Gnosticism took the view that the world in which we live is so penetrated with evil, pain, suffering, etc., that it could not have been created by the God — the Father — whose goodness would have never allowed him to create such a world. Thus, in order to keep God the Father free from any responsibility for the evil that permeates the world Gnosticism attributed creation to the lowest of the intermediaries between the ineffable Father and the world. This it called *Demiurge* (literally 'Creator'), and made him responsible for creation. Gnosticism believed that creation is bad by definition and had no interest in saving it, particularly in its material form. Man was created (according to certain Gnostic myths) before the material world was made, and his present material state of existence constitutes his fall. Salvation is achieved through knowledge (*gnosis* — hence the name of this heresy), a secret knowledge of the truth taught by the teachers of the Gnostic schools. It is through an escape from time and space that man can be saved. Caring for this material world is the most absurd and in fact sinful thing there is. The sooner you get away from the material world the better.

It is well known to all that the Church took a very negative attitude towards Gnosticism. Great theologians of that time, in particular Saint

Irenaeus, bishop of Lyon at the end of the second century, wrote treatises against the Gnostics. The result of this anti–Gnostic polemic was to have a statement included in the early baptismal creeds of the local churches, which finally became part of the Creed we all use in the liturgy, declaring that it is *God the Father* who made the material world believe in God the Father, maker of heaven and earth. Consequently the material world ('all things visible and invisible') is good, since it was made by God the Father himself. Evil is of course a problem. But this should not lead us to the conclusion that the world is bad by nature and that it is not God's creation. The Church had to find other ways of explaining the presence of evil without attributing it either to God or to the material world. On this matter we shall have an opportunity to say more later on.

Thus Gnosticism introduced a gap between God and creation. Platonism, however, and mainstream classical Greek though took up the opposite position. For them not only the gap between God and the world was narrowed to the point of often disappearing altogether, but in fact the world was penetrated by divine presence in all its parts. 'Everything is filled with gods', as the famous saying in put it. Some identified the world with God to the extent of not needing a doctrine of creation at all. Others, like Plato, believed that the world was created by someone, whom Plato called Father, or Mind (*nous*) or Creator (*demiourgos*) and who made the best possible world — not absolutely perfect to be sure — given the fact that it is a world made from matter and enclosed in space, which have inevitably acted as limitations upon the Creator. Thus the material world, in the Platonic view of things, is good and beautiful, yet only insofar as it partakes of the absolute goodness and beauty which is to be found outside this material world in the world of ideas to which we can ascend through contemplation and intellectual *katharsis*, moving from the sensible to the spiritual, to the ideal world. Pure Platonism took a positive view of the material universe because it provides us with a ladder to ascend higher. It was Neoplatonism, a little later, that showed a distrust for the material world and regarded it negatively.

Now the Church did not react to Platonism in the same polemical way as it did in the case of Gnosticism. She seemed to like the idea that the world was attributed to a 'creator' (even called the Father-God by Plato) and some of her greatest theologians, such as Justin Martyr in the 2nd century, came out strongly in favour of Plato on almost all counts, including creation. Yet it would be a mistake to regard the Church of the first centuries as having accepted the Platonic or the ancient Greek view of the world. For the differences were very deep, and relate directly to the subject we are discussing in this chapter. Let us consider them briefly.

3. Creation with a 'Beginning'

If we look carefully into the issues that divided the Church form ancient Greek philosophy as a whole in what concerned creation, we can perhaps locate the heart of the problem and the crucial difference in the question of whether the world has had a *beginning* or not. This question, as we shall try to show in this lecture, has such far reaching implications, that it can be said to constitute one of the most important aspects of the relation between Christian theology and the ecological problem.

That the world should have a beginning in any absolute sense of the word seemed to be utter nonsense and absurdity to all ancient Greek thinkers. As Professor Richard Sorabji states in his study, *Time, Creation, and the Continuum*, 'the view that the universe has had a beginning was denied by everybody in European antiquity outside of the Judeo-Christian tradition'.[2] For all ancient Greeks the world was eternal. One may argue that Plato in his *Timaeus* (the famous work that deals with creation) accepts the idea of a beginning in creation, but the fact is that this beginning, as indeed all notions of beginning in ancient Greek thought, was not absolute, since it always presupposed something *from* which the world (or anything for that matter) was created. In the case of Plato's *Timaeus* this presupposes 'something' which the creator used in order to create the world was *matter, ideas,* and even *space (chora)* all of which acted as conditions limiting the creator's freedom. Creation was therefore beginning-less, and the world, though particular beings in it could be said to have beginnings, has had no beginning when taken as a whole.

The Church and the Fathers reacted negatively to this view. They felt that this limited God's freedom in creating, since he had to work with pre-existing matter and other conditions, and it also made God and the world eternally somehow 'co-existent'. They had, therefore, to modify Platonism in this respect if they were to remain in some sense 'Christian' Platonists. Such a modification had already been made in what we call 'Platonism' (the Platonic Schools of the first two centuries AD before Neoplatonism appeared in the 3rd century) and by Philo, the famous Jewish philosopher of Alexandria, in the 1st century AD. The modification involved the rejection of the idea that matter was not created by God, and the suggestion that Plato's ideas on the basis of

---

2   Richard Sorabji, *Time, Creation, and the Continuum*, 1986, p. 194.

which God formed creation were thoughts in the mind of God. This modification removed to a large extent the crudest and, to the Christian mind, most provocative aspects of Plato's doctrine of creation, but left still enough to make Platonism unacceptable to the Church on this subject. Where did the problem lie?

The real problem became evident when Christian Platonists such as Origen in Alexandria (3rd century) put forth the view of an eternal creation on the basis of his belief that the ideas or *logoi* with which the world was created were thoughts in the mind of God, thereby answering the question, 'How could God be almighty eternally, if he had no world on which to exercise his power?' This not only led Origen to the view, officially condemned by the Church a few centuries later, that souls were eternally pre-existing, but it also showed clearly the danger involved in any doctrine of creation which does not presuppose a radical and absolute beginning. As the late Father Georges Florovsky put it, Origen's doctrine of creation implied that besides God there was always, eternally a non-ego, a non-God, which means that God was a creator by necessity and not freely. Without creating the world God would remain unfulfilled, he would not be God. The notion of God and the notion of creation thus overlap, and paganism makes its appearance disguised under the form of Christian doctrine.

Thus the idea that the world has had a beginning ought to be taken in an absolute sense. But how could this absolute sense be described? And how could it 'make sense' without leading to an absurdity, as the ancient Greeks thought? Above all how does such an idea of absolute beginning affect our existence in this world and eventually the world's fate? These are the questions to which we shall now turn.

4. Creation 'Out of Nothing'

The idea that the world has an absolute beginning could only be expressed through the formula that the world was created 'out of nothing', *ex nihilo*. But what does 'nothing' mean in this case? Can there *ever* be something out of nothing? The ancient Greeks replied categorically in the negative. The Christians had to find ways of making sense out of this statement. Some of these ways did not always maintain the absolute character of nothingness, but succumbed indirectly to the logic of Greek thought, which could not accept this idea and found it absurd. Such an understanding of 'out of nothing' is to be found already in the Neoplatonists, who understand it in the sense that a beginning-less creation could be produced by God without its coming *out* of anything. Thomas Aquinas in the Middle Ages gave a meaning to 'nothing' which amounted to more or less a source out of which creation came, while Karl Barth in our time, if studied carefully, seems to understand 'nothing' as a sort of void which God *rejected* in opting for Christ pre-eternally as the one in whom and through whom he created the world. All these interpretations of 'out of nothing' should not be confused with what Saint Irenaeus and other Church Fathers meant by it. The purpose of this expression for them was to indicate that nothing at all existed previously to creation, no factor whatsoever apart from God's free will was at work or contributed in any way towards the creation of the world.

In order to make sense of this understanding of 'out of nothing' the ancient Christian theologians had to make one thing clear: time and space are categories which come into being *together with creation*. It is meaningless to ask, 'What did God do before creating', for there is no such a thing as 'before' and 'after' before creation. Time and space are notions that have to do with beginning, and whatever had no beginning could not be measured with such categories. Thus it seems that by accepting the view that the world has had a beginning the Christians opted for a notion of time which (i) is tied up with space organically — something that Platonism, for example, would not consider — and (ii) characterizes exclusively the created world — as space does too — and together with space affects the existence of the universe throughout and decisively. There is no way, therefore, for the world to escape from space and time or from the pre-condition of beginning which lies behind its being. Created being by definition is subject to these conditions, which not only mark the difference between God and the world, but also determine the world existentially. It is to the existential conditions of being created out of nothing that we shall not turn our attention, for they have to do directly with our subject.

What does being created out of nothing imply existentially? How does the world 'experience', so to speak, the fact that it has had a beginning? We can reply briefly to this question by making the following points:

(a) If we take the world as a 'whole', as an entity in itself, which we *can* do if we regard it, as we do, as *finite* and as *other* than God, the fact that the world has had a beginning forces us to put a line of demarcation, a point of departure, at least at its beginning. A classical logical axiom would oblige us to put a line of demarcation, a stopping point also at the end, for according to this axiom, whatever has had a beginning will have also an end. But even leaving aside this axiom, the idea of *finitude* attached to that of creaturehood by definition implies that in the very concept of creaturehood there lies together with the idea of the beginning, also that of the end. All this means that creation *taken in itself* (this condition is of decisive importance for, as we shall see, things are different if creation is not taken 'in itself') constitutes an entity surrounded and conditioned by *nothing*. It came from nothing and will return to nothing.

I have called this implication of creaturehood 'existential' not because I have in mind certain modern philosophical schools that bear this name, but because there is in fact no other way for us to speak of the universe except by somehow personifying it and attributing to it categories stemming from our experience. We cannot, for example, avoid associating the disappearance of a certain thing with the experience of death, and *vice versa* the experience of death with the disappearance, the extinction of something. If the universe is conceivable as a finite particular entity, the very possibility of conceiving it in our minds implies putting lines of demarcation around it. But lines of demarcation allowing for conception mentally, imply existentially the experience of a 'before' and an 'after', the experience of the beginning and of the end of the thing conceived, therefore something analogous to the experience of the birth as well as the death of something. In this way of speaking, therefore, the notion that the world has had an absolute beginning implies that, taken in itself, it hangs in a void and cannot avoid the threat of death. The universe is not eternal, neither in terms of its beginning nor in terms of its end; it is mortal, and mortality in this case is as absolute as the use of the term 'nothing'. It signifies total extinction.

(b) If we do not take the world as a whole, as an entity in itself, but look instead at its interior, at what happens, so to say, inside it, we observe the same consequences of the fact that it has come into being out of nothing. Just as the world in its totality has had a beginning, so also each particular being that makes it up is conditioned by a beginning which threatens it with extinction. The space-time structure of the universe is 'experienced' by everything and everyone in the world as the means by which entities acquire their being and at the same time their non-being. My father was united with me through time, and through the same time he is divided from me by his death. The same space that unites me with you at this moment also separates me from you. Things are brought together and are separated by the same means. Space and time are the exclusive characteristics of creation, and this is expressed in every simple being that can be said to have an identity of its own. No individual thing can exist without space and time,[3] and this — unless space and time were always there, that is, they were beginning-less — proves them in the end to be non-entities.

One could say, therefore, that the nothingness out of which the

3   Cf. P.F. Strawson, *Individuals*, 1959.

world came into being permeates it and affects every single being within the universe. Death is experienced as a return to nothingness, in spite of the fact that new entities may emerge out of the old ones that have died. For neither the fact that species procreate can change the fact that a concrete progenitor no longer exists after his death as a particular identity, nor, worse even, can the return of a corpse to the earth in order to become the basic natural elements for other forms of life be a consolation for the loss of a particular being. Death amounts to the extinction of particular beings precisely because the world, having come out of nothing and being penetrated by it, does not possess any means *in its nature* whereby to overcome nothingness. Plato had to make use of the idea of immortality as a *natural* characteristic of the soul in order to secure the overcoming death in the universe, and Aristotle, having at some point denied this belief of his master, had to rely on the immortality of the species through procreation. In these ways the world as a whole would achieve immortality, yet at the expense of particular beings. But a Christian? What could a Christian do to secure the overcoming of death as the extinction of particular beings, given the fact that there was no eternal and immortal element in the nature of creation, all things — including souls, species, and matter — having had a beginning? It is tragic, but once we accept the doctrine of creation out of nothing we are unable to find anything in this world that is not subject to death, and — what is even more significant — we cannot understand death as anything less than total extinction. Here I find the worlds of Unamuno to be quite revealing: 'For myself I can say that as youth and even as a child I remained unmoved when shown the most moving pictures of hell, for even then nothing appeared quite so horrible to me as nothingness.'[4]

These words may be easily taken as sheer psychologizing and therefore dismissed by hard thinking individuals. But the psychological aspect of death — which may or may not play an important role, depending on the particular individual and his mood at the time — is not all there is in this quotation. This quotation conveys faithfully the message of Christian theology that the world as a whole, like every part of it, exists under the threat of nothingness because it was created out of nothing in the absolute sense of the word. The world possesses no natural power in itself which would enable it to overcome this situation, for if it did it would be immortal and eternal by nature; it would have had no beginning in the absolute sense, as the ancient Greeks rightly observed. A Christian who wishes to have both his doctrine of *creatio ex nihilo* and a faith that the world possesses in its nature some kind

4   Quoted in Sorabji, *Time, Creation, and the Continuum*, 175.

of means for eternal survival is bound to be logically inconsistent. For what such a combination implies is that the eternal God created an eternal world, i.e. another God by nature, which amounts to the total denial of the doctrine of creation out of nothing and at the same time to the abolishment of the distinction between created and uncreated being — a distinction on which the entire Patristic tradition insisted.

5. Towards a Christian Answer to the Question of Death and Nothingness

Now in saying all this I can sense the reaction coming to the minds of some of you: if things are the way we have described them here, does this mean that the world was created by God in order to disappear one day? Was God so cruel as to bring about beings other than himself without taking any measures to secure their survival? Do we not believe in a God who is 'the God not of the dead but of the living' and who loves the world to the point of wanting it to share his own life and bliss?

Of course, all this is true. But the question is *how* did God want the world to survive and share his own life? And, theologically speaking, the problem is how to state all this in a way that will not involve logical contradictions or stumble over fundamental scientific facts, which would exclude theology from normal scientific or philosophical discourse. For it is easy for theology to speak its own language to its own people and thus form an esoteric ghetto of its own. But we have started here with the assumption that theology can offer something to man in his attempt to face a crisis created by culture, including science and philosophy. And we intend to stick to this assumption in spite of our limitations in dealing adequately with such a vast and difficult problem. We therefore wish to articulate Christian theology in a way that will be *faithful to the logical consequences its own assumptions* and not contradict them.

Thus it is our assumption — and a doctrine of the Church — that the world was created out of nothing in the absolute sense of the term, a view that distinguished Christianity from ancient pagan religions and philosophies. The fact that in our time natural science does not find it inconceivable that the world was created out of absolute nothing can be a positive factor in enabling theology to enter into constructive discourse with the scientist. But even if the scientist were to disagree about this doctrine, the Christian theologian, having accepted it in the first instance, would have to be logically consistent with it. And this consistency will have to be observed also in trying to answer the question: How did God envisage the survival of the world, given the fact that he created it out of nothing?

We have already noted that it would be inconsistent to assume that God endowed the world with a natural capacity for survival. For such an assumption would imply that between God and the world there is a natural affinity (a *syggeneia*, as the ancient Greeks would say). Anything *naturally* common between God and creation would make the two realities one in a substantial way. This is why the Fathers had to reject the Neoplatonic idea of emanations, the Platonic and Origenist idea of the eternity of the souls, the Aristotelian view of the eternity of matter, etc., etc. It is a matter of logical consistency to seek the survival of creation in ways other than these.

But if we exclude the assumption that the world possesses in its nature some factor securing its survival and still want to secure this survival we are left only with one solution: we must find a way of uniting the world with God, the only eternal and immortal being, other than by *natural* affinity. We must find a link between the two which will secure the communication of link between them without abolishing the natural 'otherness' of God and creation. Can such a link be found? And can such a link make any sense?

III. Part Three

Christian doctrine offers as a solution to this problem the place of humanity in creation. It is in the human being that we must seek the link between God and the world and it is precisely this that makes man responsible, the only being, in a sense, responsible for the fate of creation. What an awful responsibility and what a glorious mission at the same time! 'Man is the glory of God,' declares Saint Irenaeus,[5] and with good reason. But why and how can man be the solution to the problem of the survival of creation? What qualities does he possess enabling him to achieve this? And why has he failed in this mission? These are questions we shall attempt to discuss in the next sections.

1. A Theological *Anthropology?*

In the previous sections we saw how the Christian Church, through her main theological representatives in the early centuries, viewed the world as God's creation. Against Gnosticism she stressed the view that God the Father himself directly — through his own two hands, the Son and the Spirit, as Saint Irenaeus put it — created the material universe freely and out of love.[6] Against the Platonists and pagan Greek thought in general she emphasized that the world was created out of 'nothing' in the absolute sense of the word, thus ruling out any natural affinity

5   *Ad. Haer.* 4.20.7.
6   *Ibid.*, 5.6.1.

between God and creation and at the same time any view of the world as eternal, co-existing with the eternal and immortal being which is God. This is only another way of saying that the world is contingent, that it may not have existed at all, and that its existence is a *free gift* not a necessity.

But the view that the world came out of nothing in this absolute sense and has no natural affinity with the eternal and ever-lasting God has its logical and existential consequences. It means that creation is under the constant threat of a return to nothingness, a threat which all particular beings which make it up experience as decay and death. The fear of death, so widespread in creation, implicit in every creature's attempt to survive at all costs, is not a fear of the suffering death can cause, but of the return to nothingness that it involves. Creation as a whole, taken in itself, is also subject to extinction. Natural scientists today seem to say this, as they also seem to endorse the view — or at least do not exclude it — that the universe came out of nothing. Both logically and existentially the doctrine of the creation of the world out of nothing implies that the world can be extinguished, for it has no natural capacity for survival.

But Christian faith goes hand in hand with hope and love. If God created the world out of love — for what other motive can we attribute to him, knowing what he has done for the world — there must be hope for the world's survival. But how? A simple, perhaps simplistic, answer to this might be that God is almighty he can simply order things to happen so that the world may survive in spite of its contingency. In other words, miracle working could save the world. Perhaps this is the answer given by most people in the face of apocalypse. But Christian faith does not believe in *deus ex machina* solutions. We cannot, like the ancient Greeks, introduce divine intervention at the end of a tragedy in which everything moves with mathematical accuracy to destruction. In creating the world, God did not leave it without the means for survival. In creating it he provided for its survival as well. What does this mean?

We insisted earlier that we cannot introduce solutions to the problem of the survival of creation which are logically inconsistent with the doctrine of *creatio ex nihilo* and all that it involves. Above all we cannot introduce into the world natural capacities for survival. And we said before concluding that the solution of the problem lies in the creation of man. Now we shall try to see how and why the human being is understood by the Christian faith to be capable of performing such a role. We shall thus arrive at some idea of what we intended to mean when in the sections above we called man the 'priest of creation'. On the basis of this we shall then try to draw some final conclusions concerning the relation between theology and the ecological problem.

2. What is Man?

In section I.3 above, we referred to Darwinism as a healthy and helpful reaction against the view, widespread since the Middle Ages in particular and also long before that, that the human being is superior to the rest of creation because of the intellect it possesses. This has had several consequences. On the one hand it implies that in the scale of beings the highest beings after God — in a sense the link between God and creation — are the *angels*, owing to their spiritual and non-corporeal nature. On the other hand this view also implies that it is in and through human *reason* that the world can be joined to God and thus survives. Even today the idea of man as the 'priest of creation' is understood by some in terms of rationality. Man's task is understood as being 'to interpret the books of nature, to understand the universe in its wonderful structures and harmonies and to bring it all into orderly articulation... Theological and natural science each has its proper objective to pursue but their work inevitably overlaps, for both operate through *the rational structures* of space and time'.[7]

Such a view of Man's distinctive identity and role in creation in terms of rationality has contributed a great deal to the creation of the ecological problem, as we have noted in our first lecture. For rationality can be used in both directions: it can be used as a means of referring creation to the Creator in a doxological attitude — and it is apparently this that the above mentioned view of 'priest of creation' intends — but it can also be used as an argument for turning creation towards man, which is the source of the ecological problem. In fact, in this culture of ours in which the rules of the game are set by the Enlightenment, the discussion of whether it is more 'rational' to refer creation to God or to man can only tend to reinforce the presupposition laid down by the Enlightenment that reason is all that matters. In any case, Darwinism has dealt a blow to this presupposition with regard to the distinctive characteristic of the human being. Man's particular identity in relation to the rest of the animals does not lie in reason, since lower animals also possess reason and consciousness to a lower degree. If we wish to establish the specific characteristic of the human being which no animal possesses, we should look for it elsewhere, not in rationality.

Before we discuss what the Christian tradition has to say on this matter let us have a quick look at what the non-theological world seems to us to be saying today on the question of man's particular identity. Very briefly, a consensus seems to emerge among philosophers

---

7   T.F. Torrance, *Transformation and Convergence in the Frame of Knowledge: Explorations in the Interrelations of Scientific and Theological Enterprise*, 1984, p. 263.

today that the human being differs fundamentally from the animals in this particular respect: whereas the animal, facing the world in which it finds itself, develops all its — why not call them so? — 'rational' capacities to *adjust* to this world, the human being wishes to create its *own* world. The animal also discovers the laws of nature — sometimes even more successfully than a human being. It can also invent ways of tackling the problems raised for it by its environment, and can amaze us by its cleverness. All this man can do as well, sometimes even to a higher degree, as our modern technology demonstrates. But man, and only man, can create a world of his own through culture, history, etc. Man can reproduce a tree as his own personal creation by painting. Man can create events, institutions, etc., not simply as means for his survival or welfare, but as landmarks and points of reference for his own identity. Man can say, for example, 'I am English' and not mean by that simply that he lives in a certain geographical area, but a great deal more that has to do with things of his own creation, things quite other than what is given to him by his environment.

Now all this can be perhaps explained by rationality. In this case Man, in his higher degree of rationality as compared with that of the animals, would create culture, history and civilization. Much can be said against this assumption, however, for the creation of culture involves a far more radical kind of difference between man and animal than degrees of rationality would imply. There is something in man's creativity that we can hardly attribute to rationality, since in fact it is its opposite. Man, and only man, in creating his own world very often goes against the inherent rationality of nature, of the world given to him: he can even destroy the given world. This is precisely because man seems to be challenged and provoked by the *given*. In wishing to create his own world or simply to assert his own will he is disturbed by the already existing world. All great artists have experienced this. Michelangelo used to exclaim: 'When shall I finish with this marble to start doing my own work?' And Picasso is reported to have said similar things about forms, shapes and colours. Plato's creator, too, being conceived by the philosopher as an artist in the *Timaeus*, suffers because he has to create out of pre-existing matter and space which impose on him their conditions. No creator can be content with the given. If he succumbs to it, he is frustrated and uneasy, as all creative artists in all ages seem to be. If he does not succumb to it, he has to destroy it and create out of nothing. But as creating *ex nihilo* can only be the privilege of the uncreated Creator, all attempts by man to create his own world, whether in art, history and other areas of civilization, are bound to lead to frustration. There have, of course, been forms of human 'creativity' in history which have involved a copying of the world as it is. However, hardly anyone would call such things true art. Whatever involves a succumbing to the given, this man has in common with the animals. Whatever is *free* from it constitutes a sign of the presence of the human. This can lead as far as the destruction of the given by man. At this point the human phenomenon emerges even more clearly. For no animal would go against the inherent rationality of nature. Man *can* do this, and in so doing he shows that his specific characteristic is not rationality but something else: it is *freedom*.

What is freedom? We normally use this word in order to indicate the capacity to choose between two or more possibilities. We are free to read or not to read this chapter; we are free to vote for this or that party, etc. But this is a relative, not an absolute freedom. It is limited by the possibilities given to us. And it is this *givenness* that constitutes the greatest provocation to freedom. Why choose between what is given to me and not be free to create my own possibilities? You can see how the question of freedom and that of the creation out of nothing are interdependent: if one creates out of something, one is presented by something given; if one creates out of nothing, one is free in the absolute sense of the word.

Now we have seen in the previous section that the Church insisted on the idea that God created out of absolute nothing. We can appreciate this fully only if we attach to our notion of God the absolute sense of freedom: to be God means to be absolutely free in the sense of not being bound or confronted by any situation or reality *given* to you. For if something, even in the form of a possibility, is *given* to you, this implies that someone or something else exists *besides* you. This would rule out any absolutely monotheistic view of God such as the one proclaimed by the Bible.

But what about the human being? Man is by definition a created being. This means that he is presented with a *given*. The fact that in the biblical account of man's creation he emerges at the end of the creative process makes the human being doubly restricted: the world is given to him, and God the creator is given to him, too. He can choose what he likes but he cannot avoid the fact of givenness. Is he, therefore, free in an absolute sense?

It is at this point that the idea of the *imago Dei* emerges. Christian anthropology since its earliest days has insisted that man was created 'in the image and likeness of God'. This idea — or, rather, this expression — appears for the first time in Old Testament, in the Genesis account of the creation. And it is taken up by the Fathers and Christian theology throughout history. Various meanings have been given to this expression, including the one we mentioned earlier which identifies the image of God in man with his reason. Whatever the case may be, one thing is certain: if we speak of an 'image and likeness of God', we must refer inevitably to something which characterizes God in an exclusive way. If the *imago Dei* consists in something to be found outside God, then it is not an image of *God*. We are talking, therefore, about a quality pertaining to God and not to creation.

This forces us to seek the *imago Dei* in freedom. Gregory of Nyssa in the 4th century had already defined this idea as the *autexousion* (man's freedom to be the master of himself). And if this freedom is taken in the way in which it is applied to God — which is what it ought to be if we are talking about an image of *God* — then, we are talking about absolute freedom in the sense of not being confronted with anything given. But this would be absurd. For man is a creature, and cannot but be confronted with a given.

It is at this point that another category, pertaining exclusively to the definition of the human, emerges: it is *tragedy*, the tragic. Tragedy is the impasse created by a freedom driving towards its fulfilment and being unable to reach it. The tragic applies only to the human condition, it is not applicable either to God or to the rest of creation. It is impossible to have a complete definition of Man without reference to the tragic element. And this is related directly to the subject of freedom.

Dostoevsky, that great Christian prophet of modern times, put his finger on this crucial issue when he placed the following words in the mouth of Kirillov, a character in *The Possessed*:

> Every one who wants to attain complete freedom must be daring enough to kill himself... This is the final limit of freedom, that is all, there is nothing beyond it. Who dares to kill himself becomes God. Everyone can do this and thus cause God to cease to exist, and then nothing will exist at all.[8]

If man wishes to be God, he has to cope with the givenness of his own being. As long as he is faced with the fact that he is 'created', which means that his being is given to him, he cannot be said to be free in the absolute sense.

And yet man in so many ways manifests his desire to attain to such an absolute freedom, it is in fact precisely this that distinguishes him from the animals. Why did God give him such an unfulfillable drive? In fact many people would have wished for themselves — as well as for others — that they were not free in this absolute sense. The Christian Church herself has produced throughout the centuries devices by the

---

8   Editor's note: This appears to be Zizioulas's own translation from Russian or French into English, cf. Foyodor Dostoevsky, *The Possessed*, 1954, p. 106.

help of which man, particularly the Christian, would be so tamed and so domesticated that he would give up all claims to absolute freedom, leaving such claims only to God. But certainly, if God gave such a drive to man, if he made him in his own image, he must have had a purpose. We suggest that this purpose has to do precisely with the survival of creation, with man's call to be the 'priest of creation'. But before we come to see how this could be envisaged let us see how in fact man has applied this drive and how creation has been affected by that.

3. Man's Failure

Christian anthropology speaks of the first man, Adam, as having been placed in paradise with the order to exercise dominion over creation. That he was supposed to do this in and through his freedom is implied in the fact that he was presented with the opportunity to obey or disobey a certain commandment by God (not to eat from a certain tree, etc.). This commandment involved the invitation to exercise the freedom implied in the *imago Dei*, i.e. to act as if man were God. This Adam did, and the result is well-known. We call it in theological language: the *Fall* of man.

At this point the question arises: why did man fall by exercising what God himself had given him, namely freedom? Would it have been better for him and for creation had he not exercised, but sacrificed and abolished this absolute kind of freedom? Would it not perhaps been better for all of us if Adam had been content with relative freedom as befits a creature? Did the tragedy of the Fall consist in the *exceeding* of the limits of human freedom?

The answer commonly given to these questions is a positive one: Yes, Adam exceeded the limits of his freedom, and this is why he fell. It is for this reason that Adam's Fall is commonly associated with Adam's *fault*, a fault understood therefore forensically: Man should not exceed his limits, if he wishes to avoid punishment.

Now, this sort of attitude to the Fall of Man provokes immediately two reactions. The first is that it reminds one immediately of ancient Greek thought. We all know, I suppose, the Greek word *hybris*, by which the ancient Greeks indicated that the human being 'falls', that is, sins and is punished, every time he exceeds his limits and tries to be God. This of course does not prove in itself that the Christian view of things ought to be different from that ancient Greeks. It simply warns us that something may be wrong with the above interpretation of the Fall. The real difficulty comes with did question: If Adam ought not to exercise an absolute freedom, why did God give the drive towards it?

We must seek ways of interpreting the Fall other than by placing the blame on Man for having exceeded the limits of his freedom. We shall have, perhaps, to abandon forensic categories of guilt. It may be more logical, more consistent with our view of the *imago Dei*, if we followed not Saint Augustine but Saint Irenaeus in this respect.

Saint Irenaeus took a very 'philanthropic' and compassionate view of Adam's Fall. He thought of him as a child placed in paradise in order to grow to adulthood by exercising his freedom. But he was deceived and did the wrong thing. What does this mean? It means that it was not a question of exceeding the limits of freedom. It was rather a question of applying absolute freedom in the wrong way. Now this is very different from saying that Adam should have adjusted his drive for freedom to his creaturely limitations. For had he adjusted his freedom in this way, he would have lost the drive to absolute freedom, whereas now he can still possess it, though he needs to re-adjust and re-orient his freedom.

The implications of what we are saying here are far reaching and cannot be discussed in the space available. They include all sorts of consequences for legalistic views of sin (which, not by accident, go hand in hand with cries for relativized freedom). But we shall limit ourselves to the implications that have to do directly with our subject, which is the survival of creation through man. Man was given the drive to absolute freedom, the *imago Dei*, not just for himself but for creation. How are we to understand this?

We have already noted that creation does not possess any natural means of survival. This means that if left to itself, it would die. The only way to avoid this would be communion with the eternal God. This, however, would require a movement of *transcendence* beyond the boundaries of creation. It would require, in other words, *freedom* in the absolute sense. If creation were to attempt to achieve its survival only by obedience to God, in the sense of its realizing its own limitations and not attempting to transcend them, its survival would require the miracle or *Deus ex machina* intervention of which we spoke earlier. This would result in a claim which would bear no logical relation to the rest of Christian doctrine, as is the case with all *Deus ex machina* solutions. If we accept the view that the world needs to transcend itself in order to survive (which is the logical consequence of accepting that the world has had a beginning), we need to find a way of achieving this transcendence. And this is what the *imago Dei* was given to man for.

The transcendence of the limits of creation — which is, I repeat, the condition for its survival — requires on the part of creation a drive to absolute freedom. The fact that this drive was given to man made the whole of creation rejoice. In the words of Saint Paul, 'creation awaits with eager expectation the revelation of the glory of the children of

God', that is, of man. Because man, unlike the angels (who are also regarded as endowed with freedom) forms an organic part of the material world, being the highest point in its evolution, he is able to carry with him the whole of creation into transcendence. The fact that the human being is *also* an animal, as Darwin has reminded us, far from being an insult to the human race, constitutes the *sine qua non* for his glorious mission in creation. If man gave up his claim to absolute freedom, the whole creation would automatically lose its hope for survival. And this allows us to say that it is better that Adam fall because of his claim to absolute freedom, than that he should give up this claim, for this would reduce him to an animal. In this understanding of the Fall it is not right to speak of a 'total depravity' of the image of God in man. Man in his negative attitude to God still possesses and exercises his claim to absolute freedom, albeit using against his own good and against that of creation. For only his claim to absolute freedom can lead to a revolt against God.

But how can man liberate creation from its boundaries and lead it to survival through his freedom? At this point Christian theology will have to rely on its doctrinal resources rather heavily, yet we shall try to do it in such way as not to make it a matter of 'esoteric' language, which would exclude from our discourse the non-specialist.

We have already referred to man's tendency to create a new world. This tendency is a specific characteristic distinguishing him from the animals and in this sense is an essential expression of the image of God in him, analysed deeply this means that man wishes to pass through his own hands everything that exists and 'make it his own'. This can result in one of the following possibilities:

(a) 'Making it his own' may mean that man *uses* creation for his own benefit, in which case by being placed in man's hands creation is not truly lifted to the level of the human, but subjected to it. This is one of the ways in which man can understand God's commandment to have dominion over the earth: it could be called the *utilitarian* way.

Now, an analysis of this situation would involve that (i) theologically speaking Man would become the ultimate point of reference in existence, i.e. become God; and (ii) anthropologically speaking man would cut himself off from nature as if he did not belong to it himself. The utilitarian attitude to creation would then go hand in hand with the view that man differs from the rest of creation by way of his capacity to *dissociate* himself from it rather than to *associate* himself with it. It would also go together with the possibility of denying God and divinizing man. Atheism and man's dissociation from nature would thus be shown to be interconnected. They both spring from the *imago Dei* and confirm the view that the difference between man and creation relates to the question of freedom.

Needless to say, the ecological problem is rooted deeply in this kind of anthropology. In this case taking the world in man's hands means the world as man's *possession*, as a means of self-satisfaction and pleasure. Science and technology would in this case signify the use of man's intellectual superiority for the purpose of discovering ways by which man can draw the biggest possible profit from creation for his own purposes. A theology based on the assumption that the essence of man lies in his intellect would in this case be co-responsible with science and technology for the ecological problem.

(b) Making the world pass through the hands of man may, on the other hand mean something entirely different from what we have just described. In this second case the utilitarian element would not arise. Of course man would still use creation as a source from which to draw the basic elements necessary for his life, such as food, clothing, building materials, etc. But to all this he would give a dimension which we could call *personal*. What would this personal dimension involve? The person as distinct from the individual is marked by the following characteristics:

(i)   The person cannot be understood in isolation, but only in relation to something or someone else. A personal approach to creation as distinct from an individualistic one would regard the human being as something whose particular identity arises from its relation with what is *not* human. This could be God, creation, or both. (We shall see in a minute what is involved in each of these possibilities.) It is not, therefore, in juxtaposition to nature but in association with it that man would find his specific identity. Man would be other than nature not by separating himself from it but by relating himself to it. This will become immediately evident in culture: the way someone eats or is dressed or builds his house would involve a close relationship with what is not human, with what is significantly called 'the environment'. A personal approach to creation would thus elevate the material world to the level of man's own existence. The material creation would be in this way liberated from its own limitations and by being placed in the hands of man it would acquire a personal dimension itself; it would be *humanized*.

(ii)   The personal dimension, as distinct from the individual one, would involve what we may call *hypostasization* and *catholicity*. These terms are technical in theology, but they can be easily transferred to non-theological language. A hypostasis is an identity which embodies and expresses in itself the totality of a nature. To take an example, killing someone could be regarded as a crime against the totality of human nature, whereas in fact it is only a crime against a particular individual. It could be argued that murder would be more 'rationally' and perhaps more effectively prevented in a society which does not appeal to the rationality of the 'rights of the individual', but has a view of each human being as the hypostasis of the totality of human nature (cf. the doctrine of the Trinity). The personal approach makes every being unique and irreplaceable, whereas the individual approach makes it a number in statistics (cf. the casualties in a war). If man acts as a person rather than as an individual in treating creation, he not only lifts it up to the level of the human, but he sees it as a totality, a catholicity of interrelated entities. Creation is thus able to fulfil its unity which, as natural science observes today, is inherent in its very structure.

Now, all this the human being can do without needing God, and without any reference to him. Certainly in the utilitarian approach God is not needed except, in the best of cases, in order to be thanked for what he has given us to have dominion over and enjoy — a verbal and rationalistic or sentimental thanksgiving, like the one we find in so much of Christian tradition. But in the personal approach things cannot stop with man. They cry loud for a reference to God. Why?

If we look at what the story of Adam's Fall implies for creation, we notice that the most serious consequence of this Fall was death. This has normally — ever since Saint Augustine influenced our thinking — been taken to mean that death came to creation as a punishment for Adam's disobedience. This, however, would imply a great deal of unacceptable things. It would mean that God himself introduced this horrible evil which he then tried through his Son to remove. It would also seem to imply that before the arrival of man in creation, there was no death at all. This latter assumption would contradict the entire theory of evolution in creation, and would also make it cruel and absurd on the part of the Creator to punish all creatures for what one of them did.

These difficulties lead us to the conclusion that the view of Irenaeus, Maximus, *et al.* is more reasonable on all counts, including the theory of evolution. Their view sees creation as being from the beginning in a state of mortality — owing to its having had a beginning — and awaiting the arrival of man in order to overcome this predicament. Adam's Fall brought about death not as something new in creation, but as an inability to overcome its inherent mortality.

If we take Adam's Fall to consist in his making man the ultimate point of reference in creation, we can easily see why death entered creation through his Fall: it was simply because Adam himself was a creature and creation could not overcome its limitations, including that of mortality. This could have been avoided, but to do so means making man the priest of creation.

Personhood in man demands that he should at all times embody in himself the totality of creation. The drive towards freedom, as we described it earlier, implies that in everything man does the whole world should be involved. But if all that he seeks to embody in himself is to *survive*, to truly be, then it must also be related to what is not creation. Otherwise man's personhood will remain tragic and unfulfilled, and in the end creation will be subject to its natural mortality.

Conclusion

In conclusion, let me say that I have deliberately avoided doctrinal language as much as I could. Perhaps it is time that I translate some of what I have said into such language before bringing this chapter to a close. We Christians believe that what Adam failed to do Christ did. We regard Christ as the embodiment of the *anakephaleōsis* of all creation and, therefore, as the man *par excellence* and the Saviour or the whole world. We regard him, because of this, as the true 'image of God' and we associate him with the final fate of the world. And we believe, therefore, that in spite of everything the world will survive, for the true man now is a reality. In Christ he exists.

On the basis of this belief we form a community which in a symbolic way takes from this creation certain elements — bread and wine — which we offer God as the body of Christ, thus referring creation to the Creator and to God it from its natural limitations. We believe that in so doing we, like Christ, act as priests of creation. When we receive these elements back after having referred them to God we believe that because of this reference to God we can take them back and consume them no longer as death but as life.

All this is a belief and a practice which cannot be imposed on anyone else. This we are unwilling to do. Nevertheless we do believe that all this involves an ethos that the world needs badly in our time. Not an ethic, but an ethos. Not a programme, but an attitude and a mentality. Not a legislation, but a culture.

It seems to me that the ecological crisis is a crisis of culture. It is a crisis that has to do with the loss of the *sacrality* of nature in our culture. And I can see only two ways of overcoming this. One would be the way of *paganism*. The pagan regards the world as sacred because it is penetrated by divine presence; he therefore respects it to the point of worshipping it explicitly or implicitly. He never worries about its fate, however, for he believes in its eternity. The other way is that which we have tried to describe here. It is the Christian way, for the Christian regards the world as sacred because it stands in dialectical relationship with God; thus he respects it (without worshipping it, since it has no divine presence in its nature), but he always worries about its fate: a breach of communion with God will amount to its extinction.

Of these two ways it is the second one that gives to man responsibility for the fate of creation. The first sees man as *part* of the world; the second sees him as the crucial link between the world and God, as the only *person* in creation that can lead it to survival. Unless we are to return to paganism, this second way would appear to be the only way to face the ecological crisis and respect again the sacrality of nature.

SOURCES

Chapter 1 appeared first in French as "'L'eucharistie: quelques aspects bibliques." Pages 13–74 in L'Eucharistie, John D. Zizioulas, Jean M. R. Tillard, and Jean-Jacques von Allmen. Tours, France: Mame, 1970. The present text is a translation by Luke Ben Tallon.

Chapter 2 was published originally as a three-part article in *Sourozh* 58 (1995): 1–12 and 59 (1995): 1–12; 22–38.

Chapter 3 was published originally in *Sourozh* 79 (2000): 2–17.

Chapter 4 was published originally in *Nicolaus* 10 (1982): 333–49.

Chapter 5 was published originally in *Sobornost* 5 (1969): 644–62.

Chapter 6 appeared first in French as "La Vision Eucharistique du Monde et L'Homme Contemporain." *Contacts, Revue Française de L'orthodoxie* 57 (1967): 83–92. The present text is a translation by Luke Ben Tallon.

Chapter 7 was given first as the keynote address of the first plenary session of the *Baltic Sea Symposium on Religion, Science and the Environment*, 2003, www.rsesymposia.org.

Chapter 8 was published originally as a three-part article in *Sourozh* 39 (1990): 1–11; 40 (1990): 31–40; and 41 (1990): 28–39.

INDEX OF SCRIPTURE

INDEX OF NAMES